The Latest
Dan and Rivka Sherman Mystery

Death Steals
A Holy Book

by Rosemary and Larry
Mild

Magic Island Literary Works • Honolulu, Hawaii • 2016

Interior book design by **Larry Mild.**
Cover design by **Marilyn Drea,** Mac-In-Town, Annapolis, MD.

Selected quotes from *Menoras Hamaor,* translated by
Rabbi Yaakov Yosef Reinman, 1982, C.I.S. Publishers.
Reprinted by permission.

Library of Congress Cataloging-in-Publication Data
Mild, Rosemary P. ; Mild, Larry M.
Death Steals A Holy Book
Mild, Rosemary P. ; Mild, Larry M.
ISBN 978-0-9905472-0-4 First Edition 2016

10 9 8 7 6 5 4 3 2 1

Dedication

For our beloved grandchildren—
Alena, Craig, Ben, Leah, and Emily

For our wonderful daughters—
Jackie and Myrna

For our marriage—soul mates, partners, lovers

Acknowledgments

Our special thanks for all their advice, expertise, and assistance to:

David J. Gilner, Ph.D., Director of Libraries, Hebrew Union College-Jewish Institute of Religion; notably, as Director of the Klau Library, Hebrew Union College, Cincinnati, Ohio, where Larry's donation resides. We would have been lost without Dr. Gilner's guidance and infinite patience.

Rabbi Yaakov Yosef Reinman. We are profoundly grateful for his English translation of *Menorat ha-mor* (*Menoras Hamaor, The Light of Contentment*) and for his permission to include quotes from it.

Robert J. Littman, M.Litt., Ph.D., Professor and Chair of Classics, University of Hawaii. Dr. Littman provided us with the on-line link that enabled us to buy a copy of the *Menoras Hamaor* in English—thus rescuing us from a months-long fruitless search.

Rabbi Ken Aronowitz at Temple Emanu-El in Honolulu. Rabbi Ken is always there for us: as our spiritual leader, teacher, and scholar.

Daniel Bender, Ph.D. Hon., a valued fellow member of Rabbi Ken's "In Search of Wisdom" Group, for reading our manuscript.

Diane Farkas, for her outstanding copy-editing.

Larry Steinberg, archivist at Temple Emanu-El, Honolulu, for his research assistance.

Rabbi Ari Goldstein, Temple Beth Shalom, Arnold, MD, who was so instrumental in our gifting of *Menorat ha-maor* to the Klau Library.

Creative International Services (C.I.S.), publisher of *Menoras Hamaor*.

Sisters in Crime/Hawaii Chapter and **Hawaii Fiction Writers**. Our two writers' groups reward us with excellent advice, literary adventures, and camaraderie.

Disclaimer

Death Steals A Holy Book is entirely a work of fiction. The entities, plots, and events depicted herein are of the authors' imagination and invention. All characters are fictitious and any resemblance to living persons or persons having lived in this century or the past few centuries is purely coincidental.

Special Credits

othic Leaf font was chosen by the authors of *Death Goes Postal* to represent what Gerheardt Koenig's floral font might have looked like, as in the illuminated first character in each chapter. The authors have chosen to continue the practice in *Death Takes A Mistress* and *Death Steals A Holy Book*. Many thanks to Rob Anderson and the Flight of the Dragon organization.

"This font was created by Rob Anderson of Flight of the Dragon, using CorelDRAW version 5 and 6. This font is freely available, and may be distributed in any way as long as this message is included:

"The author of the font makes no guarantee about the viability and usability of this font and is not responsible for any damages related to the use."

"© All rights reserved. Copyright 1997, Flight of the Dragon."

Table of Contents

Table of Contents (Continued)

Other Books by the Milds

Coauthors of the Dan and Rivka Sherman Mysteries

- *Death Goes Postal*
- *Death Takes A Mistress*

Coauthors of the Paco and Molly Mysteries

- *Locks and Cream Cheese*
- *Hot Grudge Sunday*
- *Boston Scream Pie*

Coauthors of the Adventure/Thriller
Cry Ohana

Coauthors of Two Short Story Collections

- *Murder, Fantasy, and Weird Tales*
- *The Misadventures of Slim O. Wittz*

✶ ✶ ✶

Books by Rosemary

- *Miriam's World—and Mine*
- *Love! Laugh! Panic! Life with My Mother*

"Don't let me struggle alone; help me to understand, to be wise, to listen, to know....Lead me into the mystery."

Mishkan T'filah, A Reform Siddur, p. 151, Central Conference of American Rabbis

Preface

My Sacred White Elephant

Many of us possess something out of the past for which we have never found a practical or decorative place. Maybe it's a gilt-framed picture of a great-great uncle, a bewildering trinket, an ugly vase, or a haphazard stamp collection. Or it may be a trunk stuffed with such items—all deteriorating, occupying space, but guarded by the concept that this item is precious and should be kept in the family, even though no family member recalls exactly why.

My own white elephant is a rare holy book passed down from my maternal grandfather to my mother and then to me. *Sefer Menorat ha-maor* arrived at our house in a flimsy, white department store gift box nestled in tissue paper. This edition is written in Yiddish, the language that predominated among European Jews at the end of the eighteenth century when it was printed. *Sefer* means book. The English translation of **Menorat ha-maor** is **The Candlestick of Light**. It was originally written in Hebrew in the fourteenth century as a moral and religious household guide for Jews in the Middle Ages. One of the most important books of its time, it is filled with biblical topics and rabbinical interpretations on righteous living; a compilation of sermons, anecdotes, and tales drawn from both written and oral Jewish law and ethical teachings.

ix

I cannot read Yiddish. The *Sefer Menorat ha-maor* sat in my house year after year deteriorating. In 2008 I opened the gift box, gently lifted the book out, and placed it on the table. Small brownish flecks of the heavy leather cover fell off. Carefully opening the cover, I found neat script on the flyleaf: dates ranging from 1803 through 1836, along with names I did not recognize—births, I presumed. The edges of the yellowed pages had turned brown as well. They were brittle, too brittle to continue in my care. The projected extent and cost of restoration were beyond anything I could manage. Sadly, in its condition, I could not display this fragile holy book in the place of honor it deserved. I sought professional help.

After consulting with a cantor and three rabbis, my *Sefer Menorat ha-maor* was carefully packaged and sent on its way to Cincinnati, Ohio, for curator evaluation at the venerated Klau Library of the Hebrew Union College-Jewish Institute of Religion. Following, on page xii, is a description by Dr. Dan Rettberg, of blessed memory, who attested to the book's authenticity. Its permanent home is in the Klau Library's Rare Books Collection. It was my honor to donate it.

Sefer Menorat ha-maor inspired me to create the basic plot for *Death Steals A Holy Book*. Forgive me for taking a few literary liberties with its condition, content, and monetary worth for the sake of the story.

—— Larry

In the long-standing Jewish tradition of seeking and passing on the wisdom of the ages, we have excerpted quotes from the holy text to include as chapter heads in our mystery text. The reader may notice that we give the source of the quotes as *Menoras* with an "s." Larry's donated Yiddish copy of the *Sefer Menorat ha-maor* spells *Menorat* with a "t": the Sephardic, or Spanish, spelling. The quotes we have chosen are from the recent English translation (1982), with *Menoras* ending in "s": the Ashkenazic, or Eastern European, spelling. (Capitalization and hyphenation also vary between the two titles.) Be assured it's the same book.

—— The Authors

The Klau Library
OF THE HEBREW UNION COLLEGE · JEWISH INSTITUTE OF RELIGION

We are grateful to you for your gift to the Library of the Hebrew Union College-Jewish Institute of Religion

David F. Gilner

Librarian

Description of Gift:

Sefer Menorat ha-maor, description attached.

Lawrence and Rosemary Mild
120 Kennedy Dr.
To: Severna Park, MD 21146

March
2009

CINCINNATI

No goods or services were provided for this donation.

xi

Description of Donation:

Author/compiler: Aboab, Isaac, 14th century
Title: Sefer Menorat ha-maor.
With Yiddish translation by Mosheh Frankfort.
Printed in Sulzbach in the house and the press of the partners
Aharon and his son Zekel in the year 5550 [1789 or 1790].

Text divided into seven separate sections after the seven branches of
the Temple menorah. Title within wood-engraved border depicting
the Temple menorah above, Moses to the viewer's right, Aaron to
the viewer's left, and the Akedah (attempted sacrifice of Isaac) and
Jacob's dream below. T.p. [Title page] partly damaged; lower left
hand corner of the engraving lacking. Initial words within borders
of black type ornaments. Includes index. Bound in contemporary
leather (calf?) over pasteboards; tooled in blind.

According to the "Encyclopedia Judaica", v. 2, col. 90, the Menorat
ha-maor ("Candlestick of Light") was "one of the most popular
works of religious edification among the Jews of the Middle Ages."
Written for all, "… the work has over 70 editions and printings (1st
ed. Constantinople 1514; Jerusalem, 1961), and has been translated into Spanish, Ladino, Yiddish, and German. It has been suggested that he [Aboab] wanted to provide a structured compilation
of aggadah, similar to that which Maimonides, in his Mishneh
Torah, had provided for the halakhah."

"Hark then you noble gentry
So ravenous for luxury
Turn away from the thunder
That tears mountaintops asunder
And illuminate your sight
By the seven gleaming lights."
Menoras, p. 230
("Ode to the Menorah")

Chapter 1
Loss of Innocence
Monday, January 8th, 2007

wooden sign over the door read "Fine Old Books Restored." The tiny shop at 59 Beuller Street reeked of fermenting leather, neatsfoot oil, and musk—exuding from rare tomes and the noble attempt to resurrect them. Could such an unusual stench follow the dreadful journey of two rare books?

The shop's small front room served to greet customers. Beyond it lay the inner sanctum, the artisan's hallowed workroom. A man in a yarmulke, a black knit skullcap, sat hunched over his large work table, deep into the project before him: a rare ancient book he had just restored. No longer any sign of mildew—the pages more pliable—their stains now barely perceptible—the cover and binding newly supple. With a tweezer-like tool, this fifty-two-year-old artisan carefully tugged at a frayed re-weave of the original stitching. His cotton-gloved hands and sinewy forearms moved with a deftness and assurance that only an experienced and loving craftsman might display. No ordinary shopkeeper or tradesman here. Nothing was bought or sold here. He simply provided a valuable, singular service.

A broad blue mask with thick binocular lenses hid the upper half of his angular face, while its strap disappeared behind his head into ridges of bristled, gray-black hair. The skullcap person-

1

ified his belief in the ever-presence of God above him. Beneath a generous coffee-stained mustache, his thin lips exposed a hint of protruding pink tongue, a boyish gesture suggesting the deep intensity required by the task at hand. *There, almost finished*, he thought.

The tiny bell above the street door jingled, startling him. He'd flipped the OPEN sign to CLOSED several hours earlier at 5:30. He wasn't expecting any customers this late. *Ah, it's probably my lovely Peggy schlepping my supper.* He had left the shop's door unlocked for her. *She's such a good woman, a friend like I've never had before. A little meshugge with all that Goth makeup and jewelry, but I'm in love with her anyway—God forgive me.*

He heard footsteps in the front room, and wondered why she wasn't calling to him. Pushing his chair back, he stood up, eager to receive her. But actually seeing who had entered was impossible with the magnifying aid in place. As he slipped the mask up his forehead, a gold-monogrammed briefcase caught his attention. It dropped to the floor near the table. Without warning, the business end of a Saturday Night Special loomed into his view from out of the darkness. Before he knew who or why, Israel Finestein heard a shot and looked down to see blood pouring out of his own chest. He never heard the second shot, nor the abandoned .38 caliber revolver falling with a thud on the vinyl floor. Israel slumped first into an awkward heap. Then gravity slowly leveled him out flat.

The killer picked up the tan leather briefcase, set it upright on a corner of the table, and undid the buckles on the two straps. Black-gloved hands removed a chamois cloth and spread it out on the table. The dark-clad figure gently closed the rare old text and laid it in the middle of the cloth, wrapping it securely before tucking it into the briefcase. After buckling the straps, the killer turned off the lone lamp and exited quickly to the faint sound of the door-bell jingle.

* * * *

Peggy Fraume was on a happy mission: to bring her lover

2

his supper. In her left arm she cradled a tuna-noodle casserole inside an insulated bag. Under the streetlights, she began walking to his shop only a few blocks away. Izzy had entrusted her with the keys to his apartment. It was *his* supper she carried—in *his* yellow crockery bowl, prepared by *him* in *his* kosher kitchen, and merely reheated by Peggy in *his* oven.

Peggy worried about him. He often skipped meals or ate them unheated, so a few times each week she took his own hot food to him at his shop, enough for a couple of days, knowing that he sometimes slept in that old shabby recliner in a corner of his workroom. This woman with short, punk, black hair and wild gypsy eyes felt far more than compassion for her friend. Peggy and Izzy lived in adjacent apartments on the eighth floor of a quiet Baltimore City neighborhood. They had immediately connected when they discovered they both played chess. After several months of casual dating and hours-long chess games, fondness had bloomed into passion to the point where they were planning a most unlikely marriage. They had even sent out save-the-date notices without considering all the contrasting consequences. They were blindly in love.

As Peggy approached the first-floor shop, she hesitated. *Why is it so dark inside? Could he have left early without letting me know?* She looked at the illuminated dials of her watch: eleven minutes past eight. The hairs at the nape of her neck bristled. She tried the door. Surprisingly, it wasn't locked. She stepped inside and flipped on the front room light switch next to the door. Without looking about, she lifted the yellow crockery bowl out of its insulated bag and set it, along with her purse, atop the nearest display case. Only then did she venture into the darkness of the workroom.

Peggy moved cautiously. *This is so strange. Where's Izzy? Is he okay?* She fumbled for the overhead light switch on the wall to her right, and while she adjusted to the glare, she heard a muffled moan. It came from behind the massive work table. She followed the source of the faint uttering. Izzy was sprawled out on his stomach, with the left side of his head on the floor and his face turned toward her. She knelt beside him. He wasn't moving, but his mouth whispered what sounded like the *Shma*, the prayer at the heart of Judaism, a pronouncement of the Oneness and Greatness of God. Then he mumbled something she couldn't quite discern. *The letters M-P-S or N-T-S maybe.* Peggy knelt closer. *Did he say "briefcase"?* Then she thought he was asking for the police. As soon as these pitiful mumblings ended, her Izzy died.

As the pool of blood rapidly expanded, Peggy, still on her knees, backed away until she encountered something hard under her left shin. Reaching down, she grabbed the cold irritating object—and screamed. She had retrieved the murder weapon. Realizing she'd left her fingerprints all over the grip, she gathered up the hem of her long skirt with the intention of wiping away those prints.

"I wouldn't do that if I were you," said a booming voice behind her. "Just lay the damn gun on the floor and get up. Slowly now, woman! Keep your hands where I can see them. It's murder all right, and I've caught you red-handed." A stocky, pug-nosed, uniformed police officer stood over Peggy with his service weapon pointed directly at her.

"But...But I found him this way!" Peggy screeched. "Izzy was already dying."

"His name was Izzy?"

"Israel. Israel Finestein, but I called him Izzy. Officer, I didn't do anything. I didn't kill him. He was my fiancé! I loved him. Why would I kill him?"

"Put both your hands on the arms of that recliner," the officer commanded. "You have the right to remain silent...," he recited while frisking her one-handed, clumsily, near her breasts and down her hips and legs. Satisfied with the search, finding no additional weapons, and having finished reciting her Miranda rights, he seized and cuffed her wrists behind her back and pushed her into the front room. The officer followed so closely she could smell his cheap aftershave.

Nodding toward the yellow crock on the display case, she

decried her innocence once more. "I was just bringing my fiancé his supper. See there on the counter? It's a tuna-noodle casserole. I just heated it up for him. Doesn't that make sense to you?"

But Officer James Francis O'Mera wasn't listening. He was busy reporting a crime, speaking into his shoulder microphone. "Yes, sir! A woman yelled out a second-floor window at me. Said she heard shots in the shop downstairs, and I responded....No, sir! I didn't get any names yet. Found a woman perp hovering over the male victim with a recently fired gun in her hand. Yeah, she's in custody. Got 'er cuffed. Sure I read 'er her rights....No, I didn't touch anything....Okay. I'll wait for the detectives and transportation."

Letting go of the transmitting button, Officer O'Mera turned to his prisoner. "What's your name, lady?"

"Fraume, F-R-A-U-M-E, Margaret Fraume. But I tell you I'm innocent. You're letting the real killer get away."

"Sure, sure, I got it all wrong. That's what they all say. I got you dead to rights, ma'am. You got any ID, Fraume?"

"My purse," she said, tilting her head toward the display case and the black cloth shoulder bag sitting there. She watched him upend the purse contents onto the countertop: lipstick, compact, cell phone, keys, handkerchief, a Kleenex mini-pack, and a vinyl wallet. He flipped open the snap and spread the wallet until he saw her driver's license in its compartment window.

"Ah, Margaret Fraume it is. Age forty-eight. You don't look it, lady."

"Thanks, but I—"

"So who's the poor slob on the floor in the other room?" Officer O'Mera began to write in a small notebook he'd taken from his breast pocket.

"His real name is Israel Finestein, but everybody calls him Izzy. And don't you dare call him a poor slob. I love him. He's a wonderful, hard-working mensch, and the proprietor of this shop."

"Does he own the joint?"

5

"He rents from some lady upstairs. I don't know her name." Peggy shuddered. She suddenly realized she was talking about her beloved as if he were still alive.

Vehicles screeched to a halt out front and car doors slammed shut. "Homicide!" the first man through the door said. "Officer, I'm Detective Sergeant Shap and this here is Detective Sullivan. He's assisting me in this investigation. Anything appear to be missing from the shop? Cash or something else valuable?"

"Nothing obvious, sir. I haven't had much of a chance to look around yet."

"Good thing," said Shap. "Wouldn't want you lousing up my crime scene now, would I?"

"Yes, sir. I mean no, sir. Didn't touch a thing."

The two detectives perused the crime scene room for about fifteen minutes before calling in the lab people. Then Shap called Peggy into the workroom and sat her down in the recliner. He stood before her in a leather jacket and black pants, almost six feet tall, with a clean-shaven, handsome face and wavy walnut-brown hair brushed back with no part.

"Ma'am, I'm Detective Sergeant Shap. Did you know Mr. Finestein well?"

"Very well. We are—I mean, we *were*—neighbors and best friends. More than that. He was my fiancé, for heaven's sake." A sob caught in her throat. "The only reason I'm here is that I brought Izzy his supper, in that yellow crock in the front room. I didn't kill him. I couldn't do anything to harm that lovable man. Did you know we were engaged?"

"No, I didn't know," he responded sarcastically. "How could I?" Shap circled behind her, and examined her cuffed hands. He saw two rings on her right hand, one a carved silver rose, the other a black onyx stone. "So where's the diamond ring if you're engaged?"

"We hadn't gotten around to that yet."

"I see," said Shap. "And if you were engaged, why would Officer O'Mera believe you murdered your lover? Was it a lover's

6

quarrel?"

"No, no, no!" Peggy, near tears now, said, "I'll explain everything, but can't you take off these horrible cuffs? They're cutting into my wrists and my shoulders are getting sore."

"No way."

It occurred to her that the detective was enjoying her misery. She had no choice but to relate her whole story, beginning with finding the shop dark and ending with the attempt to wipe her fingerprints from the murder weapon. At several junctures she proclaimed her innocence. She was so despairing, so distraught that Izzy's final utterings had completely slipped her mind. She offered them now.

Shap said, "You say you found the room dark. Why would Finestein be working late in the dark?"

"That's just it," she replied. "He wouldn't be in the dark. He'd be working late to finish the rare holy book for Rivka and Dan Sherman. They're supposed to pick it up the day after tomorrow. The book is gone! It should have been on the work table with the light over it. That's why I became so concerned."

"Who are these people, the Shermans?"

"They own The Olde Victorian Bookstore in Annapolis and they're good friends of mine as well."

"So where's this so-called holy book now?" asked Shap.

"I just told you—it should have been on the work table. Otherwise, it would be stored in the locked cabinet for safekeeping."

"In there?" he pointed. The steel cabinet's door was slightly ajar, indicating that it had been left unlocked. Shap swung both doors open wide and saw two books and a rolled papyrus parchment. "One of these?" He gestured with his open hand.

"No!" Peggy said. "The Shermans' rare book was at least twice the size of either one of those. And much older."

"Just how holy was this book?" Shap pressed on. "It's obviously not the Bible or the Torah or Haftarah."

Peggy eyed him with curiosity. "How would you know? Are you Jewish?"

"Yeah," he said. "Shap was once Shapiro. My father's idea entirely."

She'd never met a Jewish cop before. "Well, Detective, it's the *Sefer Menorat ha-maor*."

"Never heard of it."

"*Sefer* means book. *Menorat ha-maor* means *The Candlestick of Light*. The way Izzy explained it to me, it's a precious book of religious truths and ethics. This copy is in Yiddish and there are other translations, too. It was the most popular book in Jewish households in the Middle Ages. How the righteous should live their lives." She steadied her voice, praying that she was appealing to his more rational side. "So you see, robbery is the real motive here, and I don't have the book. Ergo I am innocent."

"Not so fast, lady. You could have had an accomplice. Mrs. Fraume, I—"

"It's Ms. now since my divorce and I don't have any accomplice."

"Ms. Fraume, while your version of what transpired here may well be plausible, there are circumstantial facts sufficient to cast doubt on your explanation. Enough for you to remain in custody, at least for the time being. The question of your guilt or innocence may well rest with the courts. You may be able to get bail fixed at your arraignment."

In the front room, Officer O'Mera shifted from foot to foot. He was alone and had nothing to do. He'd worked with Detective Shap before, *arrogant SOB*, and right now O'Mera's stomach grumbled, reminding him that he hadn't eaten anything since two doughnuts on his morning coffee break. He lifted the lid of the yellow crock, plus a corner of the Saran Wrap, and sniffed. *Mmm! Smells good and it's still warm. It'll go to waste if it just sits there. Besides, it can't be evidence. Who's gonna miss a coupla mouthfuls anyway?* He took another sniff and checked to be sure nobody could see him. Using three fingers, he scooped up a small portion of tuna and noodles covered with cream of mushroom soup, and popped it into his wide-open mouth. *Delicious.* He faced the door so no one would see him chew and swallow. With nobody watching, he repeated the procedure until only a quarter of the casserole remained.

Just as Peggy and the two detectives emerged from the workroom, the crime scene investigators arrived in a long white van. At the door, gloves and cloth footies were distributed to the team. Soon both rooms were taped off, leaving only a narrow passage from the entrance to the workroom. They even covered that with heavy brown paper. A crime-scene announcement prohibiting entry to unauthorized persons was posted on the window next to the shop's front door.

No one noticed Shap lifting the cover off the yellow crock. He peeked under the Saran Wrap, smiled, and nodded. *Just as I thought.* "Let's get out of their way so they can dig up some more juicy evidence," he said to Sullivan. His sidekick shrugged. Blue-eyed, with a crew cut, he tended to be an obliging sort.

"What about my purse?" Peggy blurted out as Shap guided her toward the black unmarked cruiser.

"Your purse is now inventoried evidence. It will be returned to you as soon as the lab people have cleared it."

"But it's my whole identity," she protested.

"Sorry, miss," replied Shap, his voice hard and not at all sorry. He pushed down on her head as she reluctantly entered the rear seat of the unmarked police car.

> "The only desires that should be nur-
> tured are the desires for wisdom and
> knowledge."
>
> *Menoras*, p. 22

Chapter 2
Bernie's Legacy
One Month Earlier—Sunday, December 10th, 2006

Daniel and Rivka Sherman lived on the third level of The Olde Victorian Bookstore at 123 East Franklyn Lane in Annapolis, Maryland.

The Shermans had no intention of becoming entrepreneurs. What did they know about bookselling or running any business? In their mid-fifties who would think of making a life change like this? But they mustered the necessary chutzpah—and why not? Dan, an electronics engineer, and Rivka, a newspaper editor, abandoned their careers to embrace four floors of erudition and precarious adventures.

Edythe Fraume Bender and her husband, Bernard, had been the bookstore's successful owners. But almost overnight, or so it seemed, Alzheimer's disease took hold of Bernie's brain, leaving his wife with a grim choice. She could dismantle and sell off the entire store piecemeal to pay for Bernie's permanent residency at a nearby nursing home. Or she could enter a beneficial partnership with her friends the Shermans. In return for receiving ownership of the store, Dan and Rivka agreed to finance Bernie's care for as long as he lived. Unexpectedly, cancer took Edythe. The Benders had no heirs, so The Olde Victorian Bookstore now belonged to the surviving partners, the Shermans.

In the brief period they knew each other, Rivka and Edythe had become fast friends—closer even than family. Because of that exceptional friendship, Rivka paid Bernie a visit two or three times a month, usually with a batch of oatmeal-raisin cookies for him and his caregivers. Bernie rarely recognized her, but somehow he knew this was the face of someone caring. A broad smile always awaited her, although he sometimes mistook her for his beloved Edythe and repeated a version of her name several times over.

Often, early in the day, the eighty-six-year-old Bernie would become completely lucid for brief intervals. In his better days he had been a poetry aficionado, and that great storehouse still lay somewhere in the nether of his brain. Rivka knew that a line or two of poetry might educe one of these interludes, so she always came prepared. What she didn't know was that he had been started on a new medication to enhance lucidity.

Rivka found the nursing home clean and cheerful in décor, yet burdened with long rows of nearly zombied patients in recliners. Today Bernie was sitting alone in his room in a chair by the window. The fine-featured, white-haired old man wore his favorite blue cardigan with the small hole by its pocket and a missing middle button. He greeted her with a token smile.

"Refreshments for the body," Rivka said, setting the bag of cookies on the nightstand. She sat down on the edge of his bed and offered him the following verse, refreshments for his soul:

> Drink to me only with thine eyes,
>   And I will pledge with mine;
> Or leave a kiss but in the cup
>   And I'll not look for the wine.

Immediately, the dullness in his eyes ignited, his sluggish posture turned erect. "It's Ben Jonson's poem 'To Celia,'" declared Bernie, and he began to recite back, with full feeling, the entire romantic poem:

11

> Drink to me only with thine eyes,
>   And I will pledge with mine;
> Or leave a kiss but in the cup
>   And I'll not look for the wine.
> The thirst that from the soul doth rise
>   Doth ask a drink divine;
> But might I of Jove's nectar sup,
>   I would not change for thine.
>
> I sent thee late a rosy wreath,
>   Not so much honouring thee
> As giving it a hope that there
>   It could not wither'd be;
> But thou thereon didst only breathe
>   And sent'st it back to me;
> Since when it grows, and smells, I swear,
>   Not of itself but thee!

Although the poem was finished, Bernie was not. A glimmer of excitement still remained. His body stiffened, his mind willed itself to stay.

"Riv-a, Riv-a, I want to give you a book. It belonged to Edythe and me in London. This book I give to you is old and rare and very valuable. It is hidden in the store, the poetry stacks, but I'll make a game of it with these lines, though they have naught to do with the book—only its clothing:

> So, we'll go no more a-roving
>   So late into the night,
> Though the heart be still as loving,
>   And the moon…The moon…The…

Bernie's voice faded like an echo in an empty barrel, and stumbled, unable to finish the last line. He slumped in his chair, and a once-bright mind slipped behind its shutters. Bernie was again unreachable. Rivka read to him from a book of Shelley's poems for another twenty minutes, never sure he understood a word.

Before leaving the nursing home, she sat down in the lobby and made careful notes of Bernie's declaration. Driving home, she couldn't wait to tell Dan. She didn't know whether her excitement came from Bernie's lucid moments or the fact that he intended them to have his special book. Dan and Rivka knew the Benders' history. They had financed the bookstore—and a fresh start in America—by selling their vast collection of books after their London bookshop was nearly destroyed by the German blitz. Rivka wondered, *Is there really a valuable edition hidden in our stacks? If there is, is it in good enough condition for the collector or museum markets? Or was this another delusion of an old man's disease?*

Rivka returned home just before noon, in time to share grilled cheese sandwiches at the kitchen table with Dan. He usually took a shift at the register at one o'clock, relieving their clerk, Ivy Cohen, to circulate and assist the patrons and customers. Still more than enough time to tell Dan everything about her visit and the lines of poetry. She had majored in journalism and minored in English literature at the University of Maryland; she had immediately recognized "So, we'll go no more a-roving" as a passage from Lord Byron.

To her delight, Dan knew the poem well enough to finish the last line of the first stanza: "And the moon be still as bright." Together they recited the remaining two stanzas.

> For the sword outwears its sheath,
>   And the soul wears out the breast,
> And the heart must pause to breathe,
>   And love itself have rest.
>
> Though the night was made for loving,
>   And the day returns too soon,
> Yet we'll go no more a-roving
>   By the light of the moon.

Husband and wife had both been required to memorize it at some point in their grade-school classes. "We must have several dozen books containing that verse, some new and some used," declared Rivka. "George Gordon Byron lived around the turn of the nineteenth century, so the book can't be too ancient. Both Byron and the piece are extremely popular, so there must be copies galore in existence. It has to be something unique about the edition or writing in the flyleaf that would make it important. How would we recognize it?"

After lunch Dan went to the checkout register, and Rivka stayed behind to do up the few dishes. Later, she came downstairs in jeans and turtleneck sweater and plopped down on the floor cross-legged in front of the poetry stacks. Atop this stack was a kitty basket lined with a Strathclyde tartan plaid in blue and purple. From his high perch, a reincarnated Lord Byron looked quizzically over the edge at her, but not for long. Three graceful bounds brought the full-grown feline to the floor, landing smack in the middle of Rivka's lap. She tickled the black fur behind his kitty ears and whispered to him, "I'll bet you know all about a-roving by the light of the moon, don't you, m'lord? Maybe you'll tell me where to find this book." His amber eyes looked up at her as if to say "I'm busy now," then closed them and curled up for his fourth nap of the day.

Rivka started her search with some of the older, more worn volumes. One by one, she removed each book she was certain contained the passage and carefully examined it. Some of the books were Byron's collections alone; others just included a sampling of his signature works. There were multi-volume sets and mere pamphlets. She ran her hands sensually over several collectors' editions, gently fingered their embossed leather bindings, then slowly turned each leaf, never abusing the fold. She checked the fly-leaf, the title page, and the particular passage itself for a possible inscription and found a few original-owner signatures, but none so famous nor dated as to make them significant. By 3:30 her legs began to cramp. "What will we do now, m'lord? Your namesake is giving us the ruddy slip." She gently heaved Lord Byron the cat from her lap and tried to stand on legs that were still asleep. Slowly, her walking legs gave up their pins and needles.

Chapter 3
The Light of Day
Thursday, December 13th, 2006

ach time Rivka traversed the poetry aisle, her brain zeroed in on Bernie Bender's promise. She kept asking herself, *Was this the addled nonsense of an Alzheimer's mind, or was it an exacting game of a brilliant, though temporary, wit to deliver a valuable book into our keeping? Or was this a game conceived and executed during a period of genuine lucidity or a mix of the two minds?* There was no way for her to tell, but she knew it would be foolhardy not to keep looking. Bernie was known for his good nature, not as a mean-spirited trickster.

Rivka stopped this time because she felt she hadn't used all the clues Bernie had given her. She tried to remember his exact words, but couldn't. Then she remembered the slip of paper in her jeans pocket, unfolded it, and read: "It is hidden in the poetry stacks, but I'll make a game of it with these lines, though they have naught to do with the book—only its clothing."

As she scanned the poem again, the lines didn't appear to take on any additional meaning. They portrayed a rascal lover now renouncing his roving ways and swearing faith to only one love. Beginning to revel in the hunt, she challenged the rules of the game. *There's no doubt that the book is here in the poetry stacks. But why did Bernie use the Byron lines if it isn't among the Byron books?*

16

And if it is among them, what was to prevent a random patron from removing it from its resting place and claiming it as a purchase? The word "clothing" must have something to do with its seclusion. What is a book's clothing if not its cover?

Assuming that the person who hid the book wouldn't deface a brand-new volume, Rivka took one of the used books in poorer condition from the shelf and checked to see if the cover data matched that of the title page and contents. There were no discrepancies. Starting with the right-hand side and top-to-bottom, she repeated the orderly process through the entire stack until she reach three new collections of Byron, Keats, and Shelley in brightly colored jackets, which also qualified as clothing, she thought, but the result was the same.

Rivka repositioned her legs and prepared to replace the three jacketed editions on the bottom left shelf when she noticed something odd. In addition to the much larger screws that fastened this partition to the next, there were six tiny screw heads embedded in the left partition. She called to Dan for help.

"What are you doing down there on the floor, hon?" he asked, sauntering down the aisle.

"I'm tunneling down to China. Want to come along? Actually," she said, "I think I've found something—maybe where Bernie hid his book. Look here at these six screws."

Dan knelt down to study them, his hazel eyes peering out from horn-rimmed glasses. "They don't seem to have any structural purpose." He ran a practiced hand over the wood surface and found grooves outlining an access panel. He guessed it to be approximately nine inches wide by twelve inches tall, cut into a partition wall space ten inches deep by thirteen inches tall. "I do believe it's a removable panel in the one-by-twelve board partition."

"I'm impressed, dear," Rivka said. "Your 'approximately' is usually more precise than most people's measurements."

He grinned and backed away, still on his haunches, his lanky frame making him look like a daddy-longlegs. He checked where the partition of this stack met the partition of the next one.

There were three additional thicknesses of wood between the stacks and sufficient space behind it for the perfect cache. Bounding up to his full five-foot-eleven height, he went for his tool box and returned with a Phillips-head screwdriver—and a spectator. Lord Byron had come to investigate what was going on in his neighborhood. Rivka sat cross-legged on the floor a few feet away and Lord Byron took advantage of her comfortable lap while Dan undid the six tiny screws and pulled out the panel.

Inside they found a package wrapped in a brown cloth pouch. Rivka gently bounced the cat off her lap. Both Shermans quickly stood. Dan carried the package to the nearest reading room and laid it out on the table. Carefully undoing the pouch, they came across a layer of calfskin in the form of a protective sheath. A gold elastic cord tied in a bow held the sheath together.

Rivka murmured, "I'm not sure I should even be handling something so old and delicate. But I have no intention of waiting around for weeks until some expensive expert opens it in the same way."

"Do it, babe."

Rivka slipped the cord off without undoing the bow. The four corners of the sheath flopped open. A hodgepodge of Latin and Germanic writing filled the outer cover. Rivka was able to pick out isolated words such as Dissertationem, Flora, Fauna, Germanica.

"A Handbook of Flowers and Animals of Germany," declared Rivka. "That's as near as I can translate."

The cover itself looked like a laminate of well-seasoned animal leather. The binding had thin calfskin laces and sewn pages with long-since-disintegrated glues. The first author's name, in the largest font, was Dn. Wilhelm von Bräuer. The second largest name was Brege Weifen, the illustrator. At the bottom of the page, Rivka pointed to two lines, Typis: Joachimi Goethe and Ilustri Typis: Gerheardt Koenig.

"Now there's a name I recognize," said Dan. "Gerheardt Koenig produced those historic printing relics that Abner Fraume,

Peggy's father, was murdered for two years ago."

"How well I know," said Rivka. "Let's do this." The two of them turned the cover over and set it gently on another book of the same height, so as not to stress the binding. This effort exposed the title page and a folded piece of modern stationery, which Rivka set aside. They saw that the title page was an exact reproduction of the cover on lighter-weight paper resembling modern pulp and rag-fiber paper. "Hey, Dan, this book is no more than a pamphlet on flora and fauna. It doesn't even have a back cover. And the pages are loose."

Dan spied something else. "I think there's another book underneath this one."

"You're right!" Rivka said. They eased the pamphlet to another part of the table and peered down at their new discovery.

"Wow! This is a big tome," said Dan. "Look at the title page, babe. Is it in Hebrew? You're the Hebrew expert in the family. What's it say?"

"It looks like Hebrew characters all right—even if it had the vowels to go with them, I wouldn't recognize any of the words at all. It must be Aramaic, one of the truly old languages. Although it could even be Yiddish. In any case I don't recognize it."

"Maybe the note on that piece of stationery can tell us something about it," Dan said, picking up the single sheet. "The letterhead shows that the stationery belonged to Edythe. The letter is dated two years after the Benders opened our bookstore."

Rivka leaned against her husband and rested her chin on his shoulder to follow along as he read aloud.

April 18, 1959

To Whom It May Concern,

These are the last two of six rare books given to us by my brother-in-law, Abner Fraume. Bless his soul, for without the sale of the first four books, Edythe and myself could not have afforded a fresh start here in Annapolis. We lost everything else in London during the Jerry blitz. Through Abner's kindness and Edythe's vision, The Olde Victorian Bookstore became a reality.

The sale of the first four books gave us sufficient funds, so I have secreted the last two as an emergency stake should we ever need one again. I don't believe the flower and fauna book will bring much because it is incomplete, but what's here is certainly of museum quality.

Even Edythe does not know of this cache, and we both may go to our graves without finding it necessary to retrieve these last books.

Congratulations on your good fortune. Best wishes,
Bernie B. Bender
Bernard B. Bender, Bookseller

"So Bernie knew what he was talking about after all," said Dan. "Now what do we do?"

Rivka's plump cheeks flushed and her eyes, the color of coffee brewing, sparkled. "Dan, this is so thrilling. First, we get an appraiser in and find out its financial and esoteric worth. Then I suggest we look for a buyer. The proceeds would make an excellent beginning to a trust for our grandchildren."

"I agree," said Dan. "But where do we keep it safe in the meantime?"

"We could put it back in its cache. It's been safe in there up 'til now."

"Or we could get a larger safety deposit box at the bank," said Dan. "Better temperature control. And we won't have to worry about it getting stolen. And it might be easier to access for appraisal, showing, and selling."

"You're right." Rivka fell into his arms. "I'm so excited."

* * * *

"Hi, Miz Irma," said the cabbie holding the passenger door open for her. "Ya wanna sit up front with me?" The olive-skinned man with thick black eyebrows and matching mustache doffed his cap.

"Yes, Gino. You know I get real dizzy when I sit in the back seat." At eighty-six and more frail than she let on, she loved his—or anyone's—attention.

"Sure, Miz Irma. I cleared everything off the front seat when the dispatcher said you called for me."

"I always ask for you, young man. You're always so obliging."

"So where to this morning, Miz Irma?"

"I've got some legal hogwash to attend to, so I need to go to State Circle. Mr. Wise's office at number 129."

The independent cabbie closed the passenger door, walked around, and slid into the driver's side. They'd been friends for years, so he didn't mind that the ride was only a mile and a half. The spunky old lady always tipped nicely. He pulled up in front of a fire hydrant to let her off. The brownstone sat opposite the majestic statehouse of Maryland, the oldest statehouse in the United States still in use. Gino left his cab to assist Irma up the stairs, then ran back down and jumped into his vehicle before he got ticketed for illegal parking.

Joel Wise's secretary ushered her in.

"Ah, Mrs. Riley, how nice to see you again," said the short, balding lawyer standing behind his teak desk. He held out his hand and she shook it briefly. "Have a seat," he said, gesturing to a red leather armchair.

Irma eyed it critically and bullied it closer to the desk before sitting down. "Thank you, Mr. Wise. And call me Irma, because I intend to call you Joel. Now then, Joel, I want to change my will. I've been doing a great deal of thinking about it lately and now I want to do something about it."

"I'm sure we can help you there. What prompted this sudden change of mind?" he asked.

"Quite a number of things." Irma pressed her thin lips together, setting determination on her creased face.

"Wait!" said Joel. "Before I start, may I turn on my digital recorder? Then I won't miss anything you specifically want when I sit down to draw up the documents."

"Of course," she said. "That sounds like a good plan, even

though I don't hold much with those new-fangled electronic gadgets." She waited while he removed the small recorder from his top drawer, placed it on his desk, and pressed RECORD.

"So here's the problem, Joel. My sister, Agnes Winnen, passed on six months ago. We were close, so she was my only heir up to now. I haven't any other living relatives." Irma's face screwed into a frown. "And I don't want anything of mine going to that horrible, despicable stepdaughter of hers, Mae Winnen." Irma punctuated her meaning in a deep, rasping voice.

"And just how would you like your estate to be executed?"

Irma's face softened slowly and a smile emerged. I would like my home, my savings, and all my possessions to go to Ivy Cohen."

"I thought Ivy was just renting a room from you. Besides, you've only known her a short time."

"Not true, sir," Irma retorted. "She's been renting from me for over a year, fourteen months to be exact. Sure, Ivy's my tenant, but she means so much more to me than that. Having her in the house has made a new woman of me. She's become like a daughter to me, and the reverse is true, too. She mothered me when I broke my leg. She cooks for me, helps me up and down stairs, and even does my laundry. I couldn't ask for a better companion. We talk for hours on end. She's so literate; she was an English major at her university in London, but she's not show-offy about it. I love her and I believe she feels the same way about me. She has no mother of her own."

"Okay, Irma. If you're that sure, I'll draw up the necessary papers. Did you have any additional bequests or instructions?"

"Yes, I've written them all out in longhand." Irma handed him several sheets torn from a lined steno pad. "One thing I must insist on is that no one know of this will until after my death. Your fee and the funeral and burial costs are also covered in these notes. As for my so-called stepniece, that wicked girl, I want it made clear that her inheritance consists of only two things: my most prized antique vase and exactly one dollar in cash. Nothing else." Irma continued in impassioned detail about her strained relationship with Mae Winnen.

"Of course, my dear. I'll have everything ready for your signature sometime next week."

"Because this work will shed much light
For all that seek to find the light
To separate the dark from light
I've called it Menorah of Light."
Menoras, p. 225
("Ode to the Menorah")

Chapter 4
New Literary Interests
Monday, December 18th, 2006

vy sang out, "Morning, Rivka," as she let herself into the store with her own key. "Shall I take the first shift at the register?"

"Please do, Ivy," Rivka said. "I've got stuff to do, and Dan has to take the two books to the vault at Annapolis Bank and Trust. I'm so nervous about them sitting around here. Especially after our burglary last year."

"Do you plan to sell them right away?" asked Ivy.

"We're booksellers, aren't we? But we need to get them appraised first. Perhaps the appraiser can locate a buyer for us."

"How much do you think they'll bring?"

Rivka shrugged. "Hard to say. We Googled several sites. With luck, we might be able to get around twenty thousand for them."

Ivy made a whistling sound. "Any plans for your windfall yet?"

"Dan wants to talk with Joel about starting a trust fund for the grandkids. And then we'll want to have our broker invest it conservatively for at least the next twenty years. But it's too early to talk about that. I don't want to jinx us."

"I don't know what I'd do if I suddenly came into a bundle

of cash like that," Ivy said.

Rivka picked up the pile of morning mail from the wicker basket on the desk and flipped through it. Bills she expected. But the charities—*oy*. Her dark brown curls flopped about, unruly bangs nearly hiding her eyebrows as she shook her head in exasperation. She gave once a year to a couple dozen charities, but the deluge of requests never stopped. Four, five, even six times a year. *Don't they realize how many trees they're killing? Or don't they care? And how many zillion address labels can I use?*

At the computer, Ivy announced: "Well, this is fun. An email for all of us. I'm printing it out."

Rivka took the printed page and read aloud:

"Please save the date: February Eleventh, Two Thousand and Seven for the upcoming marriage of Mr. Israel G. Finestein to Miss Margaret (Peggy) Fraume at two p.m. Details to follow soon." Rivka smiled. "How lovely. Peggy's found herself a nice young man."

"That's going to be some marriage."

"What a strange thing to say, Ivy. What do you mean?"

"Maybe I shouldn't be gossiping, but—"

Rivka interrupted. "No, you shouldn't, but tell me anyway."

Ivy folded her arms over her cable-knit sweater. She liked being on stage. "The other night when Mark and I were at the Double T Diner, Frieda Fraume was our waitress. She was having a slow night, so she told us that Peggy was going steady with an Orthodox Jew. She called him Izzy, and—well, you know Peggy, with her far-out way of dressing. All her Goth clothes and makeup and everything. How's that going to work out?"

Rivka had no time to digest this news. The entrance bell tinkled and a short, heavyset woman with glasses came into the store clutching her hobo purse. Ivy recognized Mrs. Tate-Williams, a frequent visitor to the bookstore. She headed straight for the magazines and newspapers. Free reading.

Fifteen minutes later, the bell tinkled again and a large,

muscular man with a shiny face came through the door.

"Good morning, sir," said Ivy. "Beautiful day, isn't it?"

"Yes it is." He hesitated for a moment. "Is Mr. Sherman on the premises?"

"Hi. I'm his wife, Rivka. Mr. Sherman is about to leave the store on an errand. Is there something I can help you with?"

"My name is Anton Gleuck. Your husband called me yesterday about some antique books he's acquired. He asked me to come here to have a look at them."

Rivka hid her surprise. Dan hadn't said anything to her.

"That's fine. Here he is now." Dan came clumping down the stairs in his ski jacket.

"Hi, Mr. Sherman. Sorry to just pop in like this. You wanted my opinion on some books you've recently acquired?"

"Yes, sir, Mr. Gleuck. You've come just in time." They exchanged a hearty handshake. "They're in here waiting for me to take to the bank for safekeeping." Dan indicated the first floor reading room. As he entered, a look of alarm, then annoyance, crossed his face as he scanned the room. Mrs. Tate-Williams was sitting at the far end of the table, reading a magazine. *How could I have been so careless?* he asked himself. He had left the box containing the two books on the long table, unattended and unprotected. On seeing Dan, she hastily moved to a small table in the corner.

Anton's eyes lit up when Dan lifted the lid off the white department store gift box, revealing the book's bare frayed cover. He gingerly opened to the title page. "It is not Aramaic as you originally thought," he said, "but actually a Yiddish translation by Mosheh Frankfort. *Sefer* means book, and this one is a classic commonly owned by medieval Jews. I am quite familiar with the work." He kissed the tips of his fingers and gestured a thrown kiss in the direction of the book.

"Is it a Bible?" asked Rivka.

"No, no, no, nothing like that," said Anton. "It's called *Sefer Menorat ha-maor*. In English: *The Candlestick of Light*. The author was Isaac Aboab, who lived in the fourteenth century. The title refers to the description of the original seven-branched meno-rah (candlestick) of the Tabernacle found in Numbers. Each of the seven sections of the book is titled with the prefix "Ner," meaning Lamp. You might call the book a code to live by. It embraces many of life's most trying questions and situations and evokes discussions, even debates, over the ethical and Godly way to deal with them.

"My wife found the number 5550 on the title page," said Dan. "I find that confusing."

Anton slipped on a pair of cotton gloves, lifted the precious book out of its box, and re-opened the cover, resting it gently on the box lid. He pointed to the Yiddish numerals on the title page.

"It was published, distributed, and sold by Aharon and his son, Zekel, of Sulzbach, Germany in the Hebrew year 5550. That's 1789 in our secular calendar."

"Earlier you mentioned medieval Jews," said Dan. "But 1789 is hardly medieval."

"Remember, Dan, this is a translation," replied Anton. "The original was written by a Talmudic scholar, Isaac Aboab the First, a Spanish Jew near the end of the fourteenth century."

"Would that make it as valuable as I think it does?" asked Rivka.

"It should have considerable commercial value."

"How much do you think it will bring, Anton?" she asked, sounding a bit over-anxious even to herself.

"I can't answer that. It will depend on page clarity, staining, moisture and mildew content, structural soundness of the spine, cover damage, and market expectation. I'm only an educated and bonded agent in a highly specialized field. I buy and sell on consignment, but I already have noted a few flaws, which must be attended to before we can think of selling. I work closely with a small number of people who are artisans at restoration and experts on book appraisal. They're all honest and exceptionally good, almost magical, but they do not get involved with selling. I do. I can put you in touch with them or you can hire me as your agent and go-between." As he spoke, he wrote down the names and addresses of three artisans in the Baltimore area. He tore off a page from his little pad and handed it to Rivka. "Wasn't there a second book?"

"Yes, a Latin book. You might as well have a look at that one, too, while we're at it," said Dan.

For the next twenty minutes Anton pored over the second book. When he looked up he said, "The fact that it is older and in such good condition would have brought an even greater price in the collectors' market. Except for one thing: one-third of the book is missing. However, there are always museums that will pay, although marginally, to display incomplete books."

"Just what is your fee, Anton?" asked Dan.

"If it results in a sale, I get 15 percent of the gross; 5 percent of the assessed value otherwise. You don't have to let me know right away. Just give me a call when you're ready."

"Thank you, Anton. We'll give you a call in a few days," said Rivka. "We'd like to think everything over. After all, there's a good deal of money at stake here. And especially if we have to lay out money in advance for the restoration."

After Anton shook hands with both of them and left the shop, Rivka studied the three names he had given her. One of them looked familiar. "Finestein. Finestein. Israel Finestein. Where have I heard that name before? Only recently, too."

"The wedding announcement, Rivka," said Ivy, from her chair at the computer. She'd become quite expert at eavesdropping. "The save-the-date email from Peggy." She pointed up to the bulletin board. "Here it is. It's the same man Peggy intends to marry."

"Couldn't it be someone else with the same name?" challenged Dan. "What's wrong, babe? Why the dirty look? I'm only playing devil's advocate."

"Rivka's right," said Ivy.

Dan cut in. "Taking sides, are we?"

Ivy tossed her head in mock indignation, letting her glossy black hair flop over one eye. "Not really. Here it is in the Baltimore yellow pages—Israel Finestein, Rare Book Restoration, address and all." She spun the thick phone book around for them to see.

"I fail to see any genuine logic here," Dan said. "If all three of these restorers come so highly recommended by Anton, I would think one's as good as another."

"This is a little different, Dan," said Rivka. "Mr. Finestein is Peggy's fiancé. I think that gives him a bit of an edge. He's almost like family. I guess we can trust the man—at least, I hope so—to do a good job on the *Sefer Menorat ha-maor.*"

"Okay, babe. We could take both books up there tomorrow."

Rivka said, "I'll call Peggy and let her know we're coming. Maybe we can all have lunch."

* * * *

Marie Tate-Williams let herself into the second-floor walk-up apartment, flipped on the light, and hung her coat in the hall closet. The climb up the stairs was always hard for the stocky widow of fifty-three. The place was dark, except for a dim light in the kitchen. She shook her head with its gray, rarely washed bun. *That no-good son of mine. He's gone off and left the stove hood light on again. The only time he ever shows up is when he's hungry and wants money.* She turned on the overhead fluorescent light and discovered her adult son sleeping on his arm at the Formica table. He stirred with annoyance.

"Where ya been, Ma?" asked the grungy young man in the tank shirt. "There's nothin' in the fridge except for that yucky yogurt." He screwed up his stubbled, angular face to emphasize his disgust.

"Never mind where I've been. Did you apply for that selling job you circled in the paper yesterday?"

"Yeah, Ma, but the man said I ain't the sort of person he was lookin' for. I can't help that, can I, Ma?" He scratched the top of his head with one dirty fingernail.

"I've got the only twenty-three-year-old son that can't find a job. I see you didn't even shave for the interview."

"Jeez, Ma, it's the style now. All the guys have stubble. It shows the girls how manly you are."

"Baloney, Damon Williams, you need a haircut, too. With all that wild hair and face fuzz, I wouldn't hire you either."

"Aw shucks, don't nag me. It's hard enough bein' rejected everywhere I go. I don't need no naggin' from you, too. What ya got t' eat, Ma? I'm hungry."

"I've got three eggs left," she said. "I'll fry them up for you."

"Any meat to go with them eggs? We ain't never got any meat anymore."

"I'm afraid not, son. If you get a job, we might be able to live a little better, and I wouldn't have to read my newspaper at the bookstore every day."

"So that's where you been all morning. Is there any good news?"

"Not much, I spent most of the morning listening to some interesting conversations about a couple of very old books that are worth a fortune."

"How much of a fortune, Ma?"

"Plenty! Maybe twenty or thirty thousand dollars."

Damon whistled through his teeth. "That's a bundle, all right. What are they gonna do with those books?"

"The Shermans say they're going to sell them, but the other feller there said one of them needs some fixing first. I think restoration is what they call it. He must be some kind of book expert, but he talks like a lawyer."

"Did they say where they're gonna do this restoration?"

"I really don't know, Damon, but why do you want to know?"

"No reason, just curious."

"There was some discussion about an email on the bulletin board. A name that was the same as the restorer they were going to use. Someone from Baltimore."

"Way to go, Ma."

"Damon, honey, you're not thinking of doing anything foolish, are you? You promised me and your poor departed father that you'd stay out of trouble."

"Of course not, Ma. I wouldn't think of breaking that promise. It's just a mental exercise."

Chapter 5
Faint of Heart
Tuesday, December 19th, 2006

Irma Riley arose as usual at six a.m. She clicked in her
dentures, then reached high into the medicine cabinet
for her daily calcium pills. Just as her fingers wrapped
around the bottle, a sharp, stinging pain zinged like an arrow down
her extended right arm, crossing her chest and lodging there, taking her full breath away. The bottle flew out of her weakened grip,
bounced once on the sink ledge, and then onto the floor, rolling to
the opposite side of the bathroom. Irma pulled her arm down as
quickly as she could, staggered sideways, then backward, collapsing
onto the toilet seat. She sat there motionless until the stinging sen-
sation eased slightly, allowing her to take one deep breath. But the
pain returned, this time pressing on her breastbone with a crushing
force she had never known before. She called out to Ivy, but there
was no way her weak wail could carry to the third floor, especially
with her own bathroom door locked and Ivy's bedroom door shut
as well. *Oh God, not yet. I'm only eighty-six.* Minutes passed, seem-
ing more like hours, but Irma hadn't the strength to stand. It had
all been sapped out of her.

Thirty minutes later, Ivy's door opened, and she headed for
the stairs. As she reached the second floor landing, she hesitated,
thinking she'd heard Irma's voice way off in the distance—not talk-

ing, more like pitiful crying. *There it is again. I'd better check on her.* Turning away from the stairs, she opened the door to her landlady's bedroom. The room was empty, but the door to Irma's bathroom was shut. The wailing sounded barely louder there. Ivy tried the knob.

"Irma, are you hurt?"

Sobs and gasps.

"Irma, it's Ivy. Can you open the door? It's locked. I can't get in." This time there was no reply at all. Ivy rushed to the phone next to the bed and punched in 911. The operator promised that an ambulance was on its way.

A sense of helplessness hung on Ivy as she stared at the locked door. But then she noticed a small slot in the center of the knob and remembered a trick her adoptive mom had used when she had locked herself in the bathroom as a small child. Ivy scanned the bedroom for any tool that might help. *Ah, Irma's manicure set on the dresser.* Unzipping it, Ivy found a metal nail file and snatched it up. She ran to the door, inserted the file into the slot, and rotated. One of the rotated directions produced a click that freed the lock. She found Irma slumped on the toilet seat, propped in the corner between the tank and the adjacent wall. Just then, she heard a pounding on the front door, then the urgent ring of the doorbell.

Ivy scurried down the stairs and allowed the two EMTs to enter. They followed her back upstairs, where they took complete charge. While they administered to the patient, they exchanged vitals data and instructions with Anne Arundel Medical Center by radio. In the gaps between those messages, one of them barked out questions to Ivy covering what she knew about her landlady's name, age, and medical history. In less than ten minutes, Irma, strapped onto a gurney, was on her way downstairs to the ambulance. She was still alive, but in critical condition.

Ivy called a cab, and while she waited, she snacked on a few cookies, along with sips of cold coffee. *I'll call Rivka when I get to the hospital,* she thought. She ran outside when the cab tooted.

When she slid into the back seat, Gino Fachetti said, "I was expecting Miz Irma. I always try to be her personal driver."

"Irma has had a heart attack and is on her way to the hospital in an ambulance right now. That's where I want to go, Gino."

"I'm sorry to hear that. Hope she makes it. I'll bring you to the emergency room entrance." He pulled away from the curb.

* * * *

Assuming that Ivy, their trusted clerk, would open the bookstore as usual at 8 a.m., the Shermans left for Baltimore a few minutes beforehand. Rivka left a note on the counter, telling Ivy where they were and when they expected to return. In fact, when her call to the bookstore at 8:11 went unanswered, Rivka merely assumed that she was busy.

The Shermans arrived at the little shop at 59 Beuller Street in Baltimore at nine o'clock. Super-cautious Rivka—superstitious, Dan would say—insisted they drop off the books before meeting Peggy for lunch. "I know it's unlikely, but there's always the chance of damage or even theft while we're carting them around," she argued. They had packed the *Sefer Menorat ha-maor* carefully, wrapping it in its original protection, and padding both sides, before placing it in Dan's leather briefcase. He also had packed the flora and fauna handbook in its box and placed it on the other side of the briefcase divider.

"Such a tiny shop, Dan. Do you think we should entrust such valuable books to this place?"

"What did you expect, hon? It's probably no more than a one- or two-person operation. The man's an artisan in what I'm guessing is a dying field, or at least a highly specialized one."

They pushed open the oak door and heard the little bell above jingle. Two men were in the front room talking business. One was tall and bony, with a stained mustache and wearing a yarmulke. The other man had a beet-red face and wooly reddish-black hair. He snapped his head toward them and held up a finger, as if signaling for them to wait their turn. A few minutes later, business done, their conversation ceased.

Rivka turned first to the man in the yarmulke. "Mr. Israel Finestein?"

"Yes, ma'am. I'm Izzy Finestein. Mr. and Mrs. Sherman, I presume. You called earlier about some rare books in your possession?"

"Why, yes. Mr. Anton Gleuck gave us your name. He spoke highly of you," said Rivka, hoping to set a good tone. "He said you could appraise and restore our old copy of the *Sefer Menorat hamaor.*"

"You mean Anton the *gonif?* That thief is *still* parading around as a rare book expert?" Izzy chuckled and said, "This is my colleague Boris Nabakov. He also restores books—up in Towson. You know where Towson is? It's northwest Baltimore. But he doesn't do quite as good a job as I do." Both men laughed.

"We know where Towson is," said Dan. "Our daughter graduated from the university there."

"Ah so. Now let's have a look at your holy book. Come in back where I have special lighting." Without ceremony, Izzy took charge. He snatched the heavy briefcase out of Dan's hand and led the way into his workroom. Hefting the case onto his massive work table, he snapped open the clasps and began unpacking it. Once freed from its bonds, the book lay on the examination table like an anxious patient, while Izzy donned his magnifying lenses and white cotton gloves and started his perusal. He muttered a few "Hmms," "Ahs," and "Oohs" as the scrutiny continued. Izzy finally looked up at them.

Dan, grinning, asked: "Will the patient live?"

"Dan!" Rivka half-scolded, fearful of breaking the spell.

"Yes the patient will live," said Izzy. "In fact, it's in remarkable shape for its age and exposure. There's a good deal of excess moisture and a few tiny signs of mildew taking hold. I also see a number of stains that can be lightened or removed, and the spine needs a little work."

"Just how much is this going to cost us?" Dan asked. Both

Shermans held their breath.

"Somewhere between ninety-eight hundred and eleven thousand. I can't be any more exact until I consider every page. It should take me from ten to fifteen working days, and with all the tumult going on this time of year, let's just say I can have it after the New Year, say Monday, January 15th."

"Whew!" Dan whistled, his chest and hopes deflating. He looked over at Rivka, who was shaking her head. "That's way too much, Mr. Finestein. We hadn't counted on that much."

"It's slow and meticulous work, Mr. Sherman. It's not a production line. It's a fine art. Collectors and museums are willing to pay big dollars for something like this. You should turn a handsome profit when you find the right buyer."

"Call me Dan, Mr. Finestein, and I quite understand. It's just that we don't have that kind of money right now. We've only owned the bookstore for two years. It took all our savings."

"I hear you, Dan. And you may call me Izzy. Tell you what. Anton said you had an incomplete copy of the *Dissertationem, Flora, Fauna, Germanica, Das Hambuch, und Mienze 1567*. If it's museum quality, as Anton says, it should bring as much as eleven thousand on the market. Did you happen to bring it with you?"

As if joined at the hip, both Shermans grew animated. "Yes!" they said in unison. Dan lifted the second box out of his briefcase.

A fearful silence filled the room as Izzy bent over the volume. He examined the damaged spine and at least twenty-five pages before saying: "The condition is just as Anton said. I'm willing to offer you an even trade: my work and materials on the *Menorat ha-maor* for complete ownership of this dissertation. That way you will not have to lay out any cash at all. Do you consider that fair?"

"What do you think, hon?"

Rivka's cheeks flushed with excitement. "I love it, Dan. It's the only way we'll be able to afford the restoration. We won't get near enough money trying to sell it without restoring it first."

Dan turned back to Izzy, "Okay. We have a deal."

"Excellent! I'll draw up a bill of sale," replied Izzy. "Come in the front room, and I'll make us some coffee."

"By the way, Izzy, we're planning to have lunch with your fiancé at the Inner Harbor later today," declared Rivka.

"With Peggy? How do you know my Peggy?" asked Izzy.

"She's an important member of the literary critique group at our bookstore," said Dan.

"Small world, isn't it," responded Izzy, still writing and now smiling.

While Izzy and the Shermans concluded their business, Boris Nabakov remained unnoticed in the workroom. He had donned Izzy's magnifying lenses and pored long and hard over the *Menorat ha-maor.* He emerged from the workroom with a gleam in his eye.

* * * *

Ivy had been sitting for hours in the waiting room and had leafed through every magazine on the coffee table. In the emergency room she had answered a barrage of questions and gotten very few answers in return. Then she learned that Irma had been transferred to an operating room. It was almost noon when a doctor in blue scrubs entered. "Is your name Riley? Are you Mrs. Riley's daughter?"

Ivy jumped up. "No, no. Is she going to make it, for God's sake?"

"Are you a relative?"

"There are no living relatives that I know of," said Ivy. "My name is Ivy Cohen and I'm the closest thing to a relative that she has. So please tell me if she's going to live. Is she going to be all right?"

"Mrs. Riley will live, but she is not all right. We tried unsuccessfully to put in a stent to inflate one of her blocked arteries. We're now hopeful that, with the help of medication, nature will take over and replace the damaged artery. She's not out of the woods yet, Ms. Cohen. Does Mrs. Reilly live alone? Is there anyone to take care of her?"

"I live with her, but I go to work every weekday. She's alone during the day. I work nearby and can fix her lunch, if that's what you're asking."

"In that case, I think it best that she go to a nursing home, at least until she recovers fully. We'd like to keep her here for a few days for observation, though. I suggest you make the necessary arrangements as soon as possible."

"Thank you, Doctor, I'll see to it. Oh—when can I see her?"

"I think it would be wise to wait until morning. She's resting comfortably now."

To the doctor, Ivy appeared almost childlike and innocent, but appearances can lie. At twenty-four, she was a persevering, resilient Englishwoman, who had resettled in Annapolis the year before—seeking justice. Justice for her mother's killer. More than two decades earlier, Ivy's mother was having an affair with a married man. She got pregnant. When she refused to get an abortion and revealed the baby, her lover beat her up and left her for dead. Three-month-old Ivy was raised to adulthood in a loving foster home. Scotland Yard had shelved the crime as a cold case. But Ivy knew better.

Chapter 6
Severed Relations
The Same Day

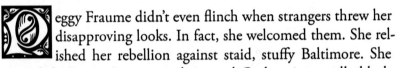eggy Fraume didn't even flinch when strangers threw her disapproving looks. In fact, she welcomed them. She relished her rebellion against staid, stuffy Baltimore. She entered the Rusty Scupper in her usual Goth attire: totally black. Skin-tight pants, a frilly top showing a bit too much of her generous breasts, and a rhinestone doggie collar encircling her neck. Not to break the effect: black lipstick, eye shadow, and painted nails.

Despite reveling in her dark appearance, Peggy was feeling upbeat, even joyous. She had shed the misery of her first marriage. Now she was on the brink of a new life—with Israel Finestein.

The glass-walled restaurant jutted out over the brisk waves of Baltimore's Inner Harbor. Stepping inside, she felt like she was on a boat, bobbing alongside the water taxis and sightseeing craft, surrounded by the towering skyline.

Rivka spied Peggy at the top of the stairs and waved her to their table, where she and Dan were mulling over poster-sized menus.

"Hi, guys," Peggy said. "Did your appointment with Izzy go well?"

"Sure did," Dan said. "He's a nice man. Congratulations on your engagement. You'll have to tell us all the details. Not that

39

we're overeager or anything." With his craggy face and lopsided grin, Dan felt wickedly entitled to learn more.

Rivka giggled at her irrepressible husband.

Peggy plopped into her chair. "I hardly know where to start. Give me a minute while I peruse the menu."

When the waiter had taken their orders, Rivka asked, "How in the world did you and Izzy meet?"

"First of all, we're neighbors," Peggy began. "I'm in 803 and he's in 805. We met in the hall and elevator a few times, but never exchanged more than a greeting or a smile. Then one day we met outside the entrance to our apartment building. Both his arms were full of groceries and I was getting my key out. I saw him trip on the one step up into the lobby. His grocery bags broke—all his purchases spread across the tile floor. Cabbage, tomatoes, a box of kasha, matzoh meal, everything. At that point I felt like Goody-Two-Shoes. I picked up as much as I could and helped him carry it all to his apartment.

"He was so appreciative, couldn't thank me enough, and invited me in. We started chatting and he made us tea while he put the groceries away. When he finally sat down and began conversing, I found the man fascinating. We talked for two hours."

"What could you two possibly find to talk about for so long?" Rivka asked.

Peggy smiled. "Strangely enough, we talked about our differences. He wanted to learn what Goth was all about, why I dressed the way I did; if it meant that I behaved any differently; were there any unusual cultural beliefs."

Getting antsy for their lunch, Rivka buttered her third roll and asked, "So what did you tell him?"

Peggy ran her fingers through her punk black hair, fetchingly streaked with white. She was loving her audience, especially the Shermans' kindly, unjudgmental curiosity. "I explained that I was tired of always being compared to someone else. I wanted to be my own unique person. Identifying with the Goth subculture was one way I could accomplish that aim. I could really stand out by dressing and behaving in the nineteenth-century Gothic horrific manner. People finally noticed who I was, and the Goth community readily accepted me. But let me get this straight. I believe in sexual freedom, but I don't hold with bizarre, satanic, or blatantly off-the-wall behavior. Nor do I have any wish to disrupt the norms of propriety. I guess you'd say I don't fit the Goth model perfectly."

"You don't have to tell us that, Peggy, we know you," Rivka said. "You're an upstanding citizen."

Dan couldn't resist. "Nobody's ever a downstanding citizen."

Rivka chuckled. Dan's quips and puns went on all day between them. She usually found herself in the role of complicit straight man. It was one of the things that kept their marriage solid.

The waiter arrived and set their plates in front of them. Broiled lake trout went to Rivka, salmon cakes to Dan, and grilled mahi-mahi for Peggy.

Munching on a mouthful of her succulent fish, Peggy said, "I've been reading Gothic novels since junior high. *The Turn of the Screw, The Fall of the House of Usher, Wuthering Heights, Flowers in the Attic, Rebecca*. All of them. And Anne Rice, of course."

"Ah," said Rivka. "I think we've sold you every vampire novel she's ever written."

"Absolutely. I like being surrounded by them in my apartment. They're my buddies, my inspiration. I especially love *The Picture of Dorian Grey.*"

"Apparently you were Goth enough to land that editor's job," offered Rivka.

"*Completely Dark* has been good to me and for me. I get to cover all the area events and write about them. And get paid a pretty decent salary, too."

"How did Izzy respond to all of this?" asked Dan.

"When we were just neighbors, he accepted who I was. No big deal. Besides, he claimed to be something of a dissident himself. He grew up as a Hasidic Jew, but about three years ago, he broke from the rigid, rigorous formalities and requirements of the Hasidic community. We both laughed over the fact that he also dresses in black. Now don't get me wrong. He's still a devout, observant Orthodox Jew. Later on, when he began to think of me as a possible date and even a love interest, he expected me to modify my lifestyle."

"And did you?" Dan asked.

"Some. I would say we both had to compromise if we wanted this relationship to survive. Love exerts that kind of force. And we're not youngsters just starting out in life."

Rivka persisted. "Does he still consider himself a Hasidic Jew?"

"No. Izzy's just as religious as he ever was, only he wanted a secular life as well. He still prays twice a day and with the *tefillin* in the morning." Peggy knew she didn't need to explain. The Shermans were Jewish. They both had learned from their own Orthodox grandparents about the *tefillin:* small boxes of prayer scrolls and their binding straps, a commandment from Deuteronomy, "Bind them for a sign upon your hand and let them serve as a symbol on your forehead"; a reminder that God brought the children of Israel out of the land of Egypt." Peggy eagerly continued, anxious that her fiancé be understood. "Izzy won't eat any food from my kitchen. He keeps a completely kosher home. The break from the Hasids was not easy. His parents totally freaked. He had to move out to pursue general knowledge, even if it meant less Torah study. He's definitely an intellectual. Cutting off his beard and *peyes* was a sacrifice to attain acceptance in the secular world. In a sense we're both seeking a sort of freedom. Maybe some would call us rebellious, but it is something we share."

"When did the relationship turn romantic, Peggy?" asked Rivka.

"That's hard to say. We saw a lot of each other over the past five months. He cooked meals for me and I reheated his suppers and carried them to him at work. We watched television in my apartment and played board games together—Scrabble and

Boggle, but mostly chess."

Peggy kept the rest of that story to herself. The romance started when they began touching each other. Not petting, simply holding hands. Then hugs and tender kisses. Israel had a tough time convincing himself that touching and kissing by unmarried couples were not damnable sins.

Rivka nibbled on an asparagus spear. "It seems that your Izzy has made a lot of concessions to accommodate your relationship. You must have conceded some things as well."

"It wasn't all that big a leap for me. After all, I *am* Jewish, even though I haven't been observant. I promised to keep a kosher home and attend *Shabbat* services with him. I also plan to bone up on my religious studies. Izzy reminded me that Judaism is not an isolating religion. We're a community. Which I knew, of course. When we're at *Shabbat* services, Jews all over the world are saying the same prayers in Hebrew together—accounting for the time differences, of course."

"What about your Goth style of dressing and makeup and all?" pried Dan, as he finished the last forkful of his salad.

"Izzy understands my need to carry on with my work. He also knows that my Goth appearance is essential to my job. I did promise him that I would dress more conservatively in the house and especially when we go to *shul* or go visiting. He does not expect me to shave my head and wear a wig in public."

"It sounds like you both have given this a lot of thought," said Rivka, laying her knife and fork across the top of her plate.

"That's just it, Rivka. Izzy is so easy to talk with and he's so reasonable. I admit—but only to the two of you—there's something comical about us as a couple: Peggy the Goth divorcee and the devout Orthodox Israel Finestein. Anyway, we're happy." She patted her lips one last time with her napkin and laid it on the table. "But now I have to get back to work." She stood and reached for her purse, opening it to pay her share when Dan signaled that it was his treat.

"Thank you so much." She blew each of them a kiss and

left.

* * * *

"Ah, good afternoon and *shalom*, Mendel," greeted Izzy, when his first cousin walked into his shop. "It's good to see you. How are Naomi and your two fine boys?"

"*Shalom*, yourself, Izzy," the man with a round face returned. They're all good. Naomi complains about her chronic arthritis, nothing new there, and both Youssel and Aaron are away at Yeshiva College. And you?" Mendel Levinson maintained a stone face as his knobby thumbs continually rubbed against his forefingers and his excessive weight seesawed from foot to foot.

"I have my health, important work to keep me busy, and a lovely woman I intend to marry soon. What more can a mere man ask of the Great One?" A broad smile grew across Israel's thin lips.

"That's good, Iz," said Mendel looking over toward the work table. "Work, eh? What's that you're working on. It looks quite old. And isn't that Yiddish?"

"Yes, it is all of that and more, a near-mint copy of the *Menorat ha-maor*. It's worth a great deal of money to a couple of booksellers in Annapolis, but it needs some of my expertise beforehand. But there's something else on your mind."

"There is something I've been meaning to talk to you about." Mendel raked a pensive hand over the bulk of his slate-gray beard.

"So talk already. What's with the *shpilkes*, the nerves, Mendel? If everything is okay with you and yours, what are you so distraught about?"

"It's Naomi. She wants to know if your young woman has ever been married before?"

"I'm sorry, Mendel, but it's none of her business."

"I know, Iz, but between you and me—"

"It's none of your business either. But between you and me, Peggy is legally divorced. It's no secret."

"Ah ha! Did she obtain a religious divorce, a *get*? Did her ex-husband make it a truly kosher *get*?"

"So that's where you're going. I really don't know, and what's more I don't give a hoot whether she got a *get* or not. As far as I'm concerned, her legal divorce is good enough for us to marry."

"But Izzy, you'll be ostracized. It's against God's way. No one will have anything to do with you. Your children will be called *momzers*. Is such a marriage worth all that?"

"I don't think it will come to that. What Peggy and I do is between God and the two of us. I pray at least twice a day. I'm an honest man and I give *tzedakah* to at least twenty charities. Peggy knows how to keep a proper *Shabbat*. She's a God-fearing, honest, and loving person who also gives to charity. All we want is to live our lives as we see fit. What's wrong with that?"

"She's already been a bad influence on you. You shaved off your beard for her, didn't you?"

"Not true, Mendel. My beard came off three years before we even met."

"And you know she won't be a stay-at-home wife and keep a kosher house for you. She's not even religious."

"How can you say that? You don't know her. You've never even met her."

"Not in person, no," replied Mendel. "But my Naomi has a friend who saw her at synagogue. She dresses and acts like she's already married to Satan, and she writes forbidden trash for some cheap magazine that glorifies evil."

"Who is this lying troublemaker, anyway? I think you've said quite enough, cousin. I'm normally a peaceful man—"

"She doesn't wear a wig, and I'll bet she's never even seen the inside of a *mikvah*."

"A hank of hair and a dunk in a pool of water don't make a person righteous, Mendel. In His eyes, saying the *Sh'ma* and the *V'ahavta* twice a day—praising and glorifying the Holy One, being a *mensch*, and giving true *tzedakah* are what make a man righteous."

"You're wrong, Izzy. All of it is important to Him. There is never enough."

"You have no idea what you are saying, repeating vicious

45

rumors like they're true." Izzy took hold of Mendel's coat collar with his left hand and pushed him toward the door with his right. "You had better leave my sight before something happens that we will both regret."

"It already has!" shouted Mendel with the door between them. "You'll pay for this, Israel Finestein. I'll see that you do!"

Chapter 7
The Stakes Get Higher
Thursday, January 4th, 2007

The new year, 2007, had just begun and Boris Nabakov was feeling upbeat and optimistic. He just wished his aging body agreed. A few minutes ago, he had signed for a fresh delivery, five wooden crates, at his book restoration shop. Now what? Trying to lift even one corner of the first crate proved heavier than a man of sixty-eight could handle. Frowning, he stroked his wooly reddish-black beard; it joined his thick sideburns and bloomed into an untamed head of same-color hair.

"Hey, Petrovich, gimme a hand with these crates."

Illya Petrovich was a virtual giant of a man, but mentally challenged. His employer, a distant cousin, kept him around for his sheer strength and his unabashed willingness to accomplish any task put before him without so much as a question—definitely a rare brand of loyalty. Best of all, he worked for essentially peanuts.

"Sure, boss, but why you not call me Illya like everybody else? I work for you five years now and you still call me by my last name."

"Never mind that, jus' git your ass over here and bring the pry bar with you." Boris showed him where he wanted to place the pry bar, and Illya did the rest, removing four nailed-down slats with ease. Boris severed the clear plastic wrap with a box knife

47

and cleared away the cedar-smelling padding to reveal twenty-four nineteenth-century books. He immediately recognized them as part of the lot he'd bid on at an estate sale. The other four crates held more of the same. All these books would bring a modest profit once they were cleaned, deodorized, and in some cases re-stitched. But none of them would come near to the kind of profit that Izzy's *sefer* would bring. Word of it had already gotten around. *Why can't I ever come across a gem like that?* he thought. *I'd even settle for an agent's cut if I can get Izzy and his seller to agree. In fact, I can think of just the collector who might be interested. My little address book—I've got her number.*

"Petrovich, finish unpacking those books. Put them on the second shelf in the third stack and then break down the crates and pull all the nails. Leave everything out back for pickup tomorrow." Boris headed for his desk. The smallest key on his key ring fit the lock. The deep right-hand drawer held his address book, a cash box where he kept large bills, checkbooks, and credit card receipts. It also held a revolver and a box of cartridges. He punched the number he sought into the desktop phone. As soon as he recognized the woman's voice on the other end, he began to describe the *Sefer Menorat ha-maor*.

The woman's voice rose with excitement. "Tell me more," she said. They conversed for almost thirty minutes before the topic of legal ownership arose. She was willing to buy regardless of who owned it and whether the final transaction was legal or not. "Boris, I just have to acquire that book. Price is no object."

Illya had stopped pulling crate nails to eavesdrop on his boss's conversation. To Illya, the holy book sounded like the most precious article in the universe.

"How much did you say?" Boris asked her to repeat her price. *I'd do almost anything for that kind of money,* he thought.

"I'll do my best, ma'am. It'll be my pleasure." Exhilarated, he hung up. A list of startling options began reeling through his head.

Illya perceived the mood change in his employer's demeanor. *Maybe I help, too*, he thought. *Maybe he call me Illya then.*

* * * *

Mendel Levinson would have preferred to study the Torah, the Good Book, all day, discussing its merits and arguing the intentions of its authors with his scholarly colleagues. He wanted so much to follow in the footsteps of the Fathers, but unfortunately, there were family needs: a roof over their heads, bread to put on their table, and tuition to be paid out for his two fine sons. So Mendel ran a dry cleaning establishment roughly a dozen blocks from Israel's shop. Thanks to his wife's adept fingers and skill set, Naomi provided extra services as a seamstress—altering hems and cuffs and making the sort of dresses particularly in demand within the Hasidic community. The two worked side by side in the establishment, or rather the full-figured Naomi handled most of the commercial activity while Mendel studied Torah behind the counter. Of course, there were conversations with the customers he knew, and now and then, a short walk to Levi's Delicatessen for a cup of tea and community gossiping.

Today Naomi sat behind the whirring Singer sewing machine, feeding and tugging a heavy brocade fabric through a long seam, still keeping a sharp eye on the front door. Three customers had come and gone in the last half-hour. As she guided the seam to its end, Mendel came through the front door.

Naomi bristled. "You were gone half the morning. How do you expect me to get anything done here if I have to keep shlepping to the counter for everyone that comes in to drop off or pick up? You spend too much time with your cronies down at Levi's."

"So how many times did you really have to get up, Naomi?"

"At least a dozen, including once for my brother." She scratched her forehead under her brown full wig, then readjusted it.

"What did your heathen of a brother want with you this time?"

49

"Keep your shirt on, Mendel. All he did was drop off some cleaning, a pair of slacks and a blue suit. We chatted awhile, too."

"What about?" Mendel sank his bulk into an upholstered chair in front of the shop window.

"What about?" she repeated. "About how unreasonable and scandalous Izzy is, insisting on marrying that horrible person who looks like she's in constant mourning."

"And what business is it of his I'd like to know?"

Naomi ignored his pointed question. "It so happens, dear husband, that he agrees with me. 'That woman isn't for Izzy. They'll never make it to the *chuppah*,' was his exact words."

"So now he's an expert on what people should do? He hasn't set foot in a synagogue since his bar mitzvah twenty-five years ago. Has he found a pretty blonde *shikse* to marry yet or is he still whoring around on East Baltimore Street?"

"That's unfair," she said. "Don't you forget, that's my baby brother you're talking about! At least he's in a respectable position and making good money, more than you'll ever make."

"Aha! When it's your precious policeman brother I can't criticize, but when my cousin Izzy wants to marry a Jew, admittedly a strange one, you have all kinds of criticisms. And every one of them based on rumors and innuendos. Now I'm sorry I had all that *mishegas* with Izzy on Monday. He was working on an important book and I interrupted him. He threw me out of his shop, and it's all your fault."

"My fault?" she retorted. "I didn't go into his shop and insult him. I would have been more diplomatic in getting the scoop on that tramp. As usual, you were the elephant tromping around in the china shop."

"Hah! Diplomacy is an unheard-of word in your family."

"Enough, Mendel. Here comes Bertha Klimple with an armful of cleaning for us."

* * * *

Damon Williams leaned his slouching, thin frame against a

concrete pillar in the downtown Annapolis parking complex. The public garage had many cars on all levels on this mid-afternoon workday, but hardly anyone walking about; an excellent spot for his rendezvous. An acquaintance of a friend had promised to meet him here for the transaction.

At the end of the aisle, a uniformed security guard spotted Damon and tagged him as a potential car thief. Who else hangs around a parking facility? Rolling up on his moped, he asked, "What are you doing here, son?"

"Waiting for my dad to pick me up," Damon lied.

"This isn't a good place. Next time wait outside. Have a nice day." The guard putt-putted off.

As soon as the guard drove out of sight, a teenager in a tank shirt and faded jeans stepped out of the shadows. "You Damon?" He carried a brown paper lunch bag.

"Yeah. You got the heat?"

"Yeah. You got the dough?"

"Let's see the piece first," said Damon. "I don't buy nothin' otherwise."

"Lemme see the dough."

Damon held out a handful of bills.

"Hey, buster, you're two dollars short."

"So sue me. That's all I got."

The sixteen-year-old grabbed the bills and handed over the bag. Inside it, Damon found a .38 caliber revolver. He released the cylinder and examined each of the chambers. "You got any ammo?"

"Ammo's extra," the teen said. "Three dollars a round."

"A fin is all I got, I swear."

"That's what you said before."

"So I lied then," said Damon, as he handed over the five-dollar bill.

The teen took a box out of his pocket, counted out two rounds and handed them to Damon, who inserted them into the chambers and closed the cylinder. When Damon looked up the teen was gone.

* * * *

Anton Gleuck dressed immaculately, stood tall and straight, exuded success, and conveyed a sense of control, for he had two reputations to maintain. As an agent, a go-between for the rich who could afford unique and expensive goods, Anton believed he was noted for his knowledge and integrity. As a dealer, a behind-the-scenes trader in both legal and illegal art objects and rare editions, he was better known for his backstabbing and tough, unscrupulous transactions.

Actually, there was a third reputation, one Anton had to keep in the shadows. If his clients found out about his proclivity for gambling in the high-risk derivative marketplace, his other two reputations would surely crumble. He owed big bucks: $82,000, and the broker was already on his heels, dunning him, threatening to dismantle the rest of his portfolio. No single agent's deal could bring him that kind of money, and the likelihood of multiple deals was indeed slim.

Anton contemplated his financial dilemma while sitting at his glass-topped mahogany desk. A bank loan was out of the question. No reputable bank would touch such a gamble. Strapped, he'd already committed to a short-term loan with a local high-interest shyster to hold off the brokerage wolves. Peter paying Paul, he acknowledged. Anton knew these usurers had severe penalties and significant muscle if he proved delinquent or in default. Yet that was only a matter of time. *Was it time enough?* he asked himself. Elbows on the desk and bald head in his hands, he pondered his options.

The blaring sound of the telephone ripped through the silence of the room, breaking into the gloom and doom of his mood. He picked up the handset. "Fine Works Consulting, Anton Gleuck at your service....Hi, Dan. You and Rivka are ready to commit? That's great. Israel Finestein's a good choice. I'm sure you'll be happy with his work. Buyers? I've got several in mind. Don't worry about that. I'll stay in touch and keep you in the loop. Thank you for your confidence." Anton placed the handset in its cradle and began to mull over the new information. His fee would be high but appropriate, tailored to the total worth. Still, it would amount to a mere down payment on his debt principal.

His shiny face bloomed into a smile with a fresh thought. *Would it be worth the risk? I could save my hide after all.*

> "For a punishment to be most effective,
> the direct relationship between it and the
> deed for which it comes must be clear."
> *Menoras*, p. 103

Chapter 8
Accused!
Monday, January 8th, the Night of Israel's Murder

ll Peggy Fraume remembered was being handcuffed and pushed down into the back seat of a police cruiser. None of this seemed to matter much now that her Izzy was dead. *Murdered in cold blood. Who would want to kill such a good and religious man? My Izzy. What am I going to do without him?* City streets flew by without her seeing them. Stone steps were stumbled up without her feeling them. She followed senselessly through winding aisles of strange yellow lighting, littered desks, and blue uniforms. The hallway around her began to reel, and then, nothing but black.

It seemed like an instant later when something sharp and pungent attacked her olfactories: a woman waving a white pill back and forth under her nose. She shook her head both ways and tried to escape from the pill. There were serious faces, lots of faces, all of them looking down at her as she lay on the hard wooden floor. *I must have passed out*, she realized.

"Where am I?" Peggy asked, trying to sit up. The handcuffs had been removed.

"You're in a police station in the Berea section of east Baltimore," said Detective Sullivan, offering his hand to help her up. "Do you need a cold compress for your neck or maybe a cold drink?

I can get you one, ma'am."

"No thank you. I think I'm okay now." She allowed herself to take his hand and pull her into a standing position. She took stock of her surroundings for the first time. She was in a hallway with many people and many doors, most of them closed. The detective nudged her toward an open one, into a barren room with only a metal table and three wooden chairs. A room where all the many faces had been left behind. It was just the two of them now. She stared at him. "Why am I here?"

"Margaret Fraume, you have been arrested for the murder of one Israel Finestein. You'll be arraigned tomorrow morning at 10:30. By the way, Officer O'Mera told us that he informed you of your Miranda rights. Do you remember that?"

"I think so." Peggy sank into a chair. "Aren't I entitled to one completed telephone call?"

"Yes, ma'am," Detective Sullivan replied, as he took the desktop phone off the shelf behind her and set it on the table, along with a hefty Baltimore phone book. He started for the door. "I'll be right outside. Call me when you're done."

"Thank you."

Peggy dialed the cell phone number of her half-brother, Garry Posner Fraume. It rang, but Garry didn't pick up. Next, she tried his home, a landline number, hoping either Garry or her niece, Phyllis, would pick up. After a dozen rings, she panicked and hung up.

"Detective?" she called through the closed metal door.

"Are you finished?" he asked.

"No, I'm not. I tried my half-brother and my niece, but neither answered. I need to try my sister-in-law next, but it's an Annapolis number, and I haven't memorized it. Can I have my purse?"

"No, ma'am, your purse has been logged in as evidence."

"But my cell phone, my little address book—they're both in my purse. My whole identity is in that purse." Peggy began to sob. Her body trembled. "I can't reach anyone to help me."

"I can get you an Annapolis directory, ma'am." His voice had turned less official. "Why don't you call me Sully like everyone else around here?" He returned with a much thinner phone book and left her to make the most dire phone call of her life.

Peggy flipped through the pages and stopped at the ad for the Double T Diner on West Street. She dialed and a man's voice answered on the second ring with the usual spiel announcing the establishment.

"Is Frieda Fraume there?"

"Frieda Fraume?"

"Frieda Forrester. She's a waitress. Her married name is now Fraume."

"Ah, Frieda Forrester. Just a minute I'll see if she can come to the phone."

"Tell her it's urgent," Peggy shouted to make sure he heard.

The pea-green interrogation room was small, too warm, and damp. Rattled nerves magnified her discomfort while she waited. Finally, Frieda picked up the phone and Peggy poured out all that had happened to her that night. "Where is Garry?" she cried. "He's not answering his phone. I'm going to be arraigned tomorrow morning and I don't have a lawyer. I need a criminal defense-type attorney in a bad way. Oh, God, I need my brother. Where is he when I need him so badly?" Sobs and gasps accompanied her words.

"Garry's down in Southdown Shores on a plumbing job, but he should be coming here soon for his supper. Calm down now, dear. We'll start up there as soon as he shows up. It's only a forty-minute drive. Meanwhile, I'll try to get hold of Joel Wise. He's primarily an estate lawyer, but he should know of a good criminal defense guy. Exactly where are you—which police station?"

"I'm at the Berea station in Baltimore. Wait, I'll look up the address." Peggy flipped through the pages of the Baltimore directory. "It's 1620 Edison Highway between Federal and Lavale. Right near the East Side cemetery."

"Aren't you through with that call yet?" bellowed Sergeant Maury Shap as he barged into the room. "And why hasn't she been booked yet? Damn it, Sully, you know the drill. Or you damn well should by now. Get her to the Central Booking Intake Facility on East Madison Street right now."

"Gotta go now, Frieda," said Peggy. "This is really bad. I think they're taking me to booking."

* * * *

Frieda hauled out her cell phone and punched in the home number of another Double T waitress. After a brief urgent conversation, the other waitress agreed to finish out Frieda's shift. No sooner had Frieda ended that call, she began tapping in Joel Wise's numbers, first at the office and then at home. Answering machines picked up both numbers. Then she remembered. The writers' critique group met on Thursday evenings. She had to skip this one because of work. *Joel will be there*, she thought. The landline phone at The Olde Victorian Bookstore rang six times before Rivka answered.

"Hi, Frieda, we're in the middle of our critique group right now. Joel? Sure, he's here. I'll get him."

But Joel was already on his feet and moving to the phone table. After several minutes, he hung up and grabbed his ski jacket off the coat rack. "Sorry, gang. Duty calls. Gotta go."

"What's Frieda's emergency, Joel?" asked Dan.

"All I know is that Peggy's been arrested, and Frieda needs my help in finding a criminal defense attorney."

"Arrested? Peggy? What for?"

"Murder!" Joel called out over his shoulder from the top of the staircase.

"Who?" Dan yelled down the stairwell.

"Don't know!" Joel shouted back just before the bookstore door shut behind him.

* * * *

The writers' critique group just couldn't continue after

hearing such news. Rivka hauled out the Baltimore phone directory and began flipping through it. Dan placed the telephone within her reach, knowing exactly what she had in mind.

Rivka tried calling Izzy at his home first. With no answer there, she tried the shop and connected with a bully of a voice who wanted to know who she was. Rivka panicked and hung up. As a last resort, Rivka called Frieda's home number. Her daughter, Phyllis, answered.

"It's Rivka Sherman, Phyllis. What's going on?"

"Hi, Mrs. Sherman. Mom just called and told me that Aunt Peggy was arrested for murdering her fiancé, Izzy Finestein. They're on their way up to the police station now. I think Mr. Wise is with them, too."

Israel Finestein's been murdered? As she hung up with barely a goodbye, Rivka's stomach turned into a sickening, churning knot.

* * * *

By 11:15 p.m. Peggy had been officially booked, fed, and placed in a holding cell for the night. Mug shots and fingerprinting were part of the booking process. Her skirt and blouse were replaced with baggy blue jeans and T-shirt. The blood-soaked black skirt and blouse were now in evidence. All interrogation stopped when she told them that her attorney was on the way; however, she had already told the detectives all she really knew.

Frieda, Garry, and Joel arrived shortly and were permitted a thirty-minute visit. Once the emotional exchange settled down, Peggy described her usual visit to bring Izzy his supper, only to discover him dying in the workroom.

"How did you get blood on your skirt?" Joel asked.

"I knelt down next to him when I heard him trying to whisper." Her voice was choked with misery.

"Was he able to tell you anything?" Joel wrote questions and answers on a legal pad in front of him.

"Izzy mumbled some initials, but for the life of me, I don't remember them."

"Keep trying, Peggy. It may be significant," he advised.

"I can't. I'm too upset."

"Did you hear the shot or see anyone leaving the shop as you arrived?" Joel asked.

"No, I didn't hear any shots or see anybody else, except for possibly his landlady leaning out of her upstairs window. My main concern was that the shop was dark. Izzy was supposed to still be there. He was expecting me. I just rushed in."

"Have the police subjected you to any tests yet?" he asked.

"A breathalyzer test and something they called a GSR test on my hands and clothing."

"I'll assume you weren't drinking. The other thing was a gunshot residue test to see if you had recently fired a gun. Did they tell you the result?"

"No, but I did accidentally handle the gun," Peggy admitted.

"Why in hell did you do that? Didn't you realize it might have been the murder weapon?"

"I backed over it when I tried to get up from kneeling on the floor. It hurt—bruised my shin, so I pulled it out and left my prints on it. I tried to wipe them off with the hem of my skirt, and that's what a nasty cop caught me doing when he barged into the shop with his gun out. He yelled at me to put the gun down."

"His exact words?"

"I don't know. I don't remember them exactly." Peggy tried to be angry, but began to cry instead. Black mascara streaked down her pale cheeks. "How could I?"

Frieda put a comforting arm about her shoulders and Garry hugged her just as Sully and Shap entered the room. "None of that stuff!" Shap boomed. "Stay on your side of the table."

"Peggy," Joel said, "I think you've had quite enough questions for now. I'll be here tomorrow morning with Leon Malamud, your criminal defense attorney. He couldn't be here tonight, but he'll be at your arraignment tomorrow. Try to get a good night's sleep and we'll see you in the morning."

"A good night's sleep?" Peggy sobbed. "Are you kidding?"

"Your thirty minutes are up!" groused Shap. "Don't push my good nature, folks. This is a police station and we have rules."

"Aw, don't be such a hard nose, Shap," Sully said when the others had left the room.

"Mind your own damn business and don't interfere."

"Say, Shap, how'd you happen to draw this case, anyway? I thought I was supposed to get paired with Mickey Johnson."

"Like I said before, mind your own business and don't interfere."

"Screw you," Sully mumbled.

"What's that, Detective?"

"Nothing."

"The Torah…emphasizes that justice
demands a diligent search for the truth."
Menoras, p. 125

Chapter 9

Arraignment
Tuesday, January 9th

white van conveyed Peggy and three other female prisoners to the Mitchell Circuit Court building on North
Calvert Street. The courtroom was nearly empty of ob-
servers at 10:30 this morning. The two front rows of polished wood
benches held a dozen or so prisoners and their lawyers. After a few
cases were dispensed with quickly by Judge Luis Rodriguez, the
bailiff called out: "Case Number ACC11207132."

"Good morning, Your Honor. Roland Atwood for the
State." The tall, gaunt assistant district attorney stepped forward
in his $150 suit and checked his Timex watch. The two case detec-
tives sat at the table behind him.

"That's us," declared Peggy's new attorney as he rose to address the judge. Garry, Frieda, and Joel sat behind them in the
second row.

"Good morning, Your Honor. Y. Leon Malamud for the
Defense." He was large and fleshy, in his late fifties, his thinning
hair ending in a brown fringe. The beautifully tailored suit and
Patek Philippe watch spoke of a past filled with success. Despite
his exorbitant fees, his elegant voice and confident manner lifted
Peggy's spirits. He again took his seat, and the judge addressed the
prosecutor.

61

"What are the charges, Mr. Atwood?"

"Murder in the first degree, according to the arresting officer, one James Francis O'Mera, badge number 11355. On the evening of January 8th at approximately 8:15, Officer O'Mera was called to a shop at 59 Beuller Street by a neighbor who said she heard gunfire, two distinct shots. Upon investigating, the officer discovered one Margaret Morris Fraume, aka Peggy Fraume, hovering over the wounded and bloodied victim, later identified as one Israel Finestein. Ms. Fraume was holding the murder weapon and attempting to remove her fingerprints from it. The victim bore no signs of life, so Ms. Fraume was read her rights and taken into custody. Both blood and gunshot residue traces were subsequently detected on her clothing. The apparent motive was deemed a lovers' quarrel. The District Attorney's office requests that Ms. Fraume be bound over for trial and that bail be denied."

"Is the arresting officer present in the court?" asked the judge.

"No, Your Honor, Officer O'Mera had a conflicting court appearance, but the on-the-scene detectives are present," replied Atwood.

"The neighbor witness then?" inquired the judge.

"No, Your Honor, but we have her sworn statement on hand."

Judge Rodriguez nodded and looked to Malamud for his client response.

Malamud rose. "Your Honor, may it please the court. My client regularly brought supper to her fiancé, Israel Finestein, and did so on the evening in question. Discovering a darkened shop, she turned on the lights and found her fiancé dying on the floor of his workroom. The victim was trying to say something to her, so she knelt on the floor beside him to better hear him. She kissed and hugged him as well. Those last few minutes of intimate contact explain the transfer of any blood and gunshot residue to her clothing. Neither was found on her hands. There is absolutely no evidence or even a hearsay basis for a lovers' quarrel motive. They were to be married next month. What the assistant district attorney failed to mention is that the victim, Israel Finestein, restored rare and valuable books. None were found on the premises. We now know that the particular books he had been working on were removed from the shop without the knowledge and permission of the owners, who had engaged the deceased to restore said books. We therefore contend that the actual motive for murder was to cover up the theft of these books. We also point out that these books were not found in either Ms. Fraume's possession or anywhere in the shop where this restoration was taking place. Nor was there any paperwork to demonstrate that any books had been legally removed from the shop. Ergo, she was neither the thief nor the murderer."

Judge Rodriguez nodded and looked to Atwood for any rebuttal.

"Your Honor, this is the first we've heard that there was a dying declaration. I'd like to put the defendant on the witness stand. As for the theft, Ms. Fraume could have had an accomplice. And wearing gloves could have prevented full blood and GSR transfer."

"Did the State's witness, the neighbor, see any persons leaving the shop either before or after my client entered the shop?" rebutted Malamud. "In fact, I'd like to know if she even saw anyone enter the shop. And how would she know it was the defendant? As for gloves—what gloves? Were any found? And lastly, an accomplice? Was anyone else seen leaving the shop?"

"I believe we will save all that for a jury to ponder," replied Judge Rodriguez. "Are there any motions at this time?"

"Yes, Your Honor," said Malamud. "At this time I'd like to raise the question of bail. My client has close ties to the community. She is gainfully employed as a magazine editor. She has a half-brother heading a family of four in Annapolis, and my client fully owns a substantial apartment here in Baltimore."

"All right, I'll set bail at $100,000. A 20 percent bond and pledge to the court cashier is required. That is, providing the defendant surrenders a valid passport." He was about to slam down his gavel when Atwell spoke up.

"Your Honor, may I remind you that this is a first-degree murder case, where Ms. Fraume was caught with the smoking gun in her hands. I object to granting this woman bail."

"Mr. Atwood," said Judge Rodriguez, "I don't need any of your reminders. Your objection is duly noted. However, I don't believe she is a flight risk." This time the gavel slammed home.

"Where am I going to get $20,000?" asked Peggy, her voice trembling. "I spent most of my father's inheritance paying for my new apartment. All the money that's left I need for property taxes and living expenses." Tears started to flow.

"Don't worry, Sis." Garry put a comforting arm around her. "I've still got most of my inheritance. I'll write the check for you, and you can pledge your apartment as security for the rest."

"Garry, you'll need a certified bank check, or postal money order for the court," said Joel. "They don't accept credit cards or personal checks."

Peggy was led out another door.

* * * *

Ivy had just rung up the first sale of the same afternoon and heard the phone ring. "The Olde Victorian Bookstore, Ivy speaking. May I help you?"

The caller identified himself as Detective Sullivan of the Baltimore Police. "Is Mr. or Mrs. Sherman there?"

"Rivka, Rivka! It's the Baltimore Police calling."

"This is Rivka Sherman. What is this about?"

"This is Detective Sullivan of the Baltimore Police. We're investigating the murder of Israel Finestein and possible thefts from his shop and would like to determine if certain books of yours were among the missing items."

"Oh, God, Izzy's death is a terrible thing. We heard about it last night. But our *Sefer Menorat ha-maor* has disappeared? Are you sure?"

"Not entirely," Sully answered. "Would you expect your old books to be in his possession at this time?"

"Yes, of course. Mr. Finestein promised that he would have it ready by next Monday, the fifteenth," replied Rivka. "We brought this Yiddish treasure to him on December nineteenth for restoration. He told us that restoration was an imprecise art and his delicate work would take time and extreme care. There was a second rare book, a partial handbook of plants and animals indigenous to Germany and written in Latin. This second book was to be payment for his work on the *Sefer Menorat ha-maor* Is it missing as well?"

"We're not sure," Detective Sullivan replied. "They're conducting a more complete search as we speak."

"You'll keep us informed, won't you?"

"Yes, of course. But would you mind my dropping in at your bookstore to interview you and your husband for a more complete statement—identifying both books? You know titles, authors, descriptions, and maybe answering a few more ownership questions. I'll be coming with another detective. We'd like to get a better feel for what we're looking for. Would that be possible, Mrs. Sherman?"

"We'll do anything we can to help. The bookstore is open from eight to eight except on weekends. Friday through Sunday nine to six. Of course, we do live on the premises as well. But we're wondering: why are you holding Peggy Fraume for this crime? Those two were planning to be wed next month."

"Sorry, ma'am, I can't discuss that. She's part of an ongoing investigation. Thank you for your cooperation." Sully hung up.

"More news about Peggy's arrest?" asked Ivy, as Dan came down the stairs.

"No," said Rivka. "He wouldn't even talk about that at all. The police are now concerned that our two books might have been stolen during the murder."

"What's that? They've been stolen?"

"Yes, Dan. The police are still searching the premises and promised to keep us informed. They also want to interview us to describe the books."

The phone rang again. "I'm almost afraid to answer it," said Rivka.

"Pick it up anyway," said Dan.

"Bookstore!" announced Rivka. She handed the phone to Ivy. "For you."

"Yes, this is Ivy. Hospital?...Thank you." She hung up slowly, her heart-shaped face clouded with worry.

"Irma?" asked Rivka.

"Yes. The nursing home has called an ambulance to take her to Anne Arundel Medical Center. Irma complained of severe chest pains, so they thought it best to send her. And she'd been doing so well in the nursing home. She was going to be released soon. Do you think it would be okay if I left early and joined her at the hospital?"

Dan looked over at Rivka and saw her nod. "Go ahead, Ivy," he said. "It might make a difference if she sees your face when she wakes up."

Ivy slipped into her wool coat and slid out the door.

Dan turned to Rivka, "Who even knew of the existence of our two rare books, hon?" He scratched his head. "The three of us and Anton on this end, but I suppose Izzy could have told someone up in Baltimore. I can't think of anyone else."

"Me neither," she admitted.

"Wait, Rivvie. There was that lady in the reading room when Anton and I walked in."

"You mean Mrs. Tate-Williams? I can't believe she'd be a thief."

"You never know, hon. You keep saying how she always reads the free papers and magazines and never buys anything. Maybe we should do something about that."

"I haven't the heart to say anything to that sweet old lady," Rivka admitted.

"She's not that old, and how do you know she's sweet? You've never heard anything more than a hello and goodbye from her."

* * * *

Damon Williams sat on the edge of the bathtub with a toy revolver in his hand. It looked real and had some of the same moving parts. It even had a place for wooden bullets. He flipped open the metal cylinder and looked down into each of the chambers. All of them were empty now, just like his real revolver. He squirted several shots of 3-In-One Oil onto a paper towel and rubbed it all over the fake weapon's surfaces, attacking a few rust spots. Then he buffed and dried every surface he could reach. His late father's pipe cleaners served well inside the chambers. When finished, Damon held the toy gun at arm's length, aimed at the bathroom doorknob, and pulled the trigger twice. "Click, click." Smiling, he swung around and pulled twice more, pointing at a perfume bottle on his mother's shelf, "Click, click." *You're dead*, he said to himself. *I wonder what's keeping that guy from calling me back. He said he knew a no-questions-asked fence somewhere in D.C.*

"Righteous people maintain the high spirituality of their souls which live on after their deaths. Sinful people destroy that spirituality even as they live and breathe."

Menoras, p. 104

Chapter 10

Funeral

The Same Day

Leaving the courthouse and police holding cells behind could hardly satisfy Peggy's sense of real freedom. Too much turmoil bumped through her mind like a pinball careening through its chancy, uncharted course. None of it made sense.

Around five Garry phoned for Chinese takeout. Peggy had long ago stopped thinking of him as her half-brother. They were a family now. While they waited on a bench at the little restaurant for their order, he broached the subject of funeral arrangements.

The funeral! Only now, when Garry spoke those words aloud, did Peggy's brain snap to attention. For two days, from the moment she discovered her dying beloved, she had been in a state of despair, then facing terror and helplessness while in police custody. Now she woke up to understand her singular purpose. There was no one else to make the burial arrangements. Mendel, Izzy's only living blood relative, was incapable of doing anything on his own. In the end, the two men weren't even speaking. Slowly, she saw the problems: religious, secular, and even legal. She decided to make a bunch of calls, including one to her lawyer. She required answers, viable solutions that would appease all concerned and not draw adverse attention to her already shaky defense position.

A new deadline loomed in her head. Izzy, a devout Orthodox Jew, had to be interred before Friday at sundown, the next *Shabbat*, and he had to be buried whole with all of his body parts intact. The main problem here existed in the legal requirement for the medical examiner to perform an autopsy on the murder victim.

Because Izzy had essentially alienated himself from the Hasidic community, an Orthodox rabbi, or at least a cantor, had to be found to preside over the funeral. A plain wooden coffin, devoid of nails and metallic hardware, had to be selected. A male member of the *Chevra Kadisha* committee needed to bathe the deceased and shroud him in a plain linen *tachrichim* burial garment. And a *shomer* had to be found to watch over the body until the interment. A burial plot in a cemetery had to be purchased and friends, relatives, and the newspapers had to be notified. Then there was Izzy's apartment and contents to be disposed of. Though she wanted nothing of monetary worth, there might be a memento, a token she'd like to keep. Maybe the chess set. But she had time for that, so she pushed it out of her head for now.

Peggy tried calling Leon's office, but reached an automated after-hours message. It was after ten when the defense lawyer returned her call. She explained the autopsy and funeral time dilemma to him. Leon promised to do what he could to speed the process and meet all of the Orthodox requirements.

* * * *

The next day, a raw, drizzling Wednesday morning, Dan Sherman was working on the bookstore accounts when Peggy called in a state of anxiety and near panic. He listened and listened. "A favor?...Of course. We can try." He replaced the receiver and stared straight ahead.

"Who was that, dear?" asked Rivka. "You have a strange look on your face."

"Peggy Fraume. She's all upset about Izzy's funeral arrangements. That is, the lack of them. The rabbi at his congregation is away this week, and his cantor is booked solid for Thursday and Friday. There's no one answering the phone at his congregation's cemetery office. And he's still being shunned by many of the Hasids, who objected to his liberal behavior. She's been calling all over, but no one seems able to commit to an undetermined date and time—all because everything's dependent on the medical examiner's schedule."

"I heard you say you'd try. What have you gotten us into, Dan?"

"She asked if I would call our rabbi and see if he would preside over the funeral."

"Excellent idea."

"Say," he added, "it wouldn't hurt to find out if there's room in our cemetery."

"Probably is. A phone call is all it'll cost to find out."

"You bet. By the way, Rivvie, maybe you should check on Mrs. Tate-Williams in the reading room. From here it looks like she's bending back the spine of the new *Time* magazine."

* * * *

The corridors at 401 Bosley Avenue in Towson were not unfamiliar to Leon Malamud. Nor were the individual prosecutors' offices in the county State's Attorney system. Still, he'd had little experience with his current opponent, Roland Atwood. Although Leon's mission solely embodied religious compassion for the victim and his grieving client, he couldn't shake the repulsive hat-in-hand feeling.

"I'm surprised to see you, Counselor," said Atwood, rising behind his desk. "Especially on my home turf. It's a little too early for pretrial discovery."

"I'm not here to obtain full discovery, Roland. Nor am I here on a defense matter for my client," said Leon, taking the seat opposite him. "I'm here to help her through a serious personal dilemma. I assume you know that the deceased is an Orthodox Jew in need of special burial considerations."

"Which are?" asked Atwood. "I don't know that much about Judaism, let alone their Orthodox burial customs."

"Essentially, there are only two that concern the prosecutor's office. First, the deceased's remains are to be kept intact, and second, he needs to be buried before the next Sabbath, which is Friday at sundown."

"But today's Wednesday," said Atwood. "The autopsy is to be performed later this afternoon. How can I control that?"

"Easily, Roland, by declaring it unnecessary," said Leon. "I understand that the medical examiner has already pulled the two slugs from the body. At least one was extracted from the heart's right ventricle, giving you a definite cause of death. Are the slugs a match to the weapon found at the crime scene?"

"Yes," said Atwood. "But how did *you* find that out so quickly? I just got the ballistics report a few minutes ago."

"Oh, I have my sources," said Leon. "As you know, an autopsy can't possibly give you any more information than that. So why bother with one?"

"What if I do concede that the autopsy is unnecessary and release the remains?" asked Atwood. "What might I expect in exchange?"

Leon thought for a moment and replied, "I could stipulate to the cause of death and its delivery weapon at the pretrial hearing. That would save the State time and money: no expensive autopsy and shorter trial proceedings as well. Deal?"

Atwood countered: "Would you be willing to stipulate to the prints on the gun as well?"

The prosecutor's question reflected a little more experience than Leon had calculated. "Of course not," Leon replied. "We'll argue that one in court."

"Okay!" said Atwood. "We have a deal. I'll notify the ME, and you should have your remains released first thing tomorrow morning." He extended a hand, and the two men shook on it.

* * * *

The prosecutor kept his word, and all the major obstacles to a Friday morning funeral were eventually surmounted. Dan's call to the head of the cemetery committee bought the purchase of a burial plot and a second call secured Rabbi Barron Abrams to preside over the service. The rabbi, in turn, contacted the funeral home and arranged for the traditional *Chevra Kadisha* and *shomer* to prepare and watch over the body.

Defying the biting temperature of 20 degrees, a minimal group huddled around the open gravesite in caps, gloves, scarves, and heavy overcoats with collars turned up. Two wide-brimmed, black felt fedoras within the gathering indicated the presence of cousin Mendel Levinson, his wife, and at least one male Hasidic friend. Peggy sat in a metal folding chair, flanked by Garry and Frieda. Dan and Rivka nodded to Joel Wise and a cluster of others with familiar faces and unremembered names as they pressed to offer their condolences to Peggy.

As the rabbi began the service, a hush shrouded the winter-brown expanse peppered with headstones. His voice predominated until the call for the final mourners' *Kaddish*. In chorus, they all prayed the Hebrew words of the Great One's glorification. Every-one waited while Israel Finestein's plain wooden coffin slowly de-scended to its permanent resting place.

A workman handed a shovel to the nearest mourner, who took his share of earth from the pile and deposited it over the grave, symbolically carrying out the burial ritual. A second and a third followed before Mendel looked into the face of Boris Nabakov as he handed him the shovel.

"You *gonif!*" Mendel blurted out. "What are you doing here?" He spun around and walked away while his wife deliberately looked in the opposite direction.

"He was a good man, a real *mensch*," Boris called after him. "I don't care what you think of me. He didn't deserve this."

One by one, all who cared to, repeated the shoveling ritual until the last person, Rivka, handed the shovel back to the work-men to complete the task. As she did, Peggy picked up a handful of dirt and sprinkled it over her fiancé's grave, repeating his name softly. She turned, all her pent-up control dissolving, and fell into Rivka's waiting arms, sobbing so hard that Rivka felt Peggy's heaving chest accompanying her wails.

Meanwhile, Dan looked over his shoulder and noticed two men he'd never seen before standing about ten feet away. They were speaking to Naomi Levinson. She was actually laughing. *What could be so funny at a time like this?* he wondered. *Damned strange.*

He itched to find out, but Rivka appeared at his side, tucked her gloved hand in the crook of his arm, and said, "Garry's taking charge of Peggy. Time to leave."

Chapter 11

Strategies

Sunday, January 14th

eggy Fraume had put up her five-room apartment as
bond for her liberty, but troubled nights of sleeplessness
and the whole menu of unknowns ahead placed a strong
lien on any actual sense of freedom. Eight stories up in the mid-
town high-rise gave her a skyline view of the city with a backdrop
of the Inner Harbor. She treasured this place even more after a
whole night in lockup.

Was another nightmare about to start? The lawyers had
given her the much-needed days of rest and contemplation. More
to the point, they allowed her to sit *shiva*, receiving family and
friends during the required seven days of mourning. She knew her
private grief would never end. There was no getting away from the
heartache she felt every time she walked down the hall to the elevator, passing Izzy's apartment right next door to hers. It was all so
unfair—Izzy's life cruelly destroyed. Her marriage to him, and the
joyous prospect of their life together, wrenched away before it had
even begun.

Peggy laid the dish towel down on the granite counter,
picked up her mug of coffee, and walked into the living room. The
door to the second bedroom remained shut, but she could hear her
brother moving about inside. Garry had sent Frieda home to be

with her daughter. He'd done his best to get bail money the night of her arrest, but his bank branch had closed at three, and there was an overnight cooling-off period to withdraw that kind of money elsewhere. He'd been staying with her to offer whatever comfort he could.

This tragedy had brought them closer than ever. *Amazing,* she thought. *A little over a year ago neither of us knew the other existed. Then we discovered we shared the same birth father and his wonderful legacy. I wish we had grown up together. I always wanted a big brother. And now I have one.*

Peggy slid back the glass door and stepped out onto the balcony in the biting cold. Resting her arms on the guard wall, her thoughts went back to Izzy's workshop. She closed her eyes and tried to imagine the front room, his office, the work table, the chairs, the four walls. *What am I missing? What is there that can prove my innocence? Why was he killed, anyway? Couldn't the robber have taken what he wanted and left poor Izzy alive for me? What was he trying to tell me? Who else knew about what he was working on?*

As she drained her mug to the bitter dregs, a clean-shaven Garry appeared behind her and stood tall for a moment in the sliding-door frame. Once she had sensed his presence, Peggy turned to face him. His flannel shirt, jeans, and crew cut gave him a healthy male appearance. He took a few steps and they embraced.

"Good morning, Pegs. Did you sleep at all?"

"Barely," she said. "Garry, dear, I can't stop thinking about this ugly mess. I started out by saying Why me? Then I got to thinking This isn't about me. And it isn't about Izzy either, even though those two thick-headed detectives think it's some kind of bizarre quarrel between us. I know it isn't. No one hated Izzy or even disliked him, for that matter. He was the most agreeable and honest person I've ever known. That leaves robbery as the only motive I can think of."

"Sounds reasonable so far," Garry said. "Do we know what was taken? That would sure help the cause. Say, isn't that your door buzzer I'm hearing or is it a kitchen timer?"

"It's the door all right, probably the two lawyers. Joel said they'd stop by sometime this morning."

Peggy peered through the peephole and opened the door to Joel and Leon. If the purpose of their meeting hadn't been so dire, she might have laughed. They looked like a version of Mutt and Jeff. Leon, six-two and 225 pounds, toted a bulging briefcase; Joel, short and chubby, carried a grocery bag. As they shed their topcoats, she noted that both men wore casual clothes. As it turned out, the bag held three kinds of bagels, a pound of Nova lox, and a tub of cream cheese.

Peggy laid out plates and silverware and also put up a second pot of coffee while the two men seated themselves at the dining room table.

Garry hugged Peggy, and said, "You three have serious business to discuss, and it's time for me to go home to my wife. Peggy, if you need me to spend a few more nights here, I'll be glad to." She hugged him back. "You're a doll, Garry, but I think I'll be okay by myself now."

Peggy joined the men at the table, where Leon laid out a representation agreement for her to sign. He was to be the primary defense counsel, and Joel the referring attorney, who would consult from time to time. The document presented a schedule of specific hourly fees for consult time, court time, and paralegal assistance. Leon patiently explained the legal jargon on each of the pages. She read through them and signed.

"Leon, I know I'm innocent. Murder—any kind of violence—is not in my nature. The police seem to think they have a perfect case against me. Can't you find a way to prove my innocence?"

"My dear, I believe we do have an excellent chance of winning." Leon's jowly face softened as he continued. "We may not have to prove your innocence at all. The burden of proof lies with the prosecution and, with your help, I'm certain I can dismantle most of the so-called evidence currently in their arsenal."

"Leon, you sound so confident I guess I have to trust you.

But to hear that nasty Detective Shap, they have a slam-dunk case against me."

"Peggy, believe me, we're just getting started."

They chatted for half an hour while eating, and then the same loud buzzer heralded someone else at the door. A glance through the peephole produced a smile as she let in Dan and Rivka, who was carrying a rectangular Pyrex dish. "I'm so sorry for your loss, dear," said Dan.

Rivka said, "This is sort of a *shiva* call, so I've brought you a kugel. Noodles, apples, and raisins. It's still warm."

Silent tears of gratitude rolled down Peggy's cheeks as she took the bowl and carried it to the table. Finding her voice, she said, "Take off your jackets and join us. You've come at the perfect time."

Dan and Rivka slipped out of their parkas and laid them across a side chair in the living room. They greeted Joel, who always gave them comfort, not just for his excellent lawyering, but as an even-handed member of their critique group. Peggy introduced Leon to the Shermans and cut the kugel into squares, a succulent dessert for their impromptu brunch.

"Leon," said Peggy, "the missing books belong to Dan and Rivka."

"Excellent," said Leon. "Let's talk about the case now." He turned on a pocket-sized recorder and laid it in the middle of the table. "The most important thing I want to stress is that I don't want any surprises in court, so I expect each of you to be forthcoming with me. The key aspect in this case is the likely motive." He pushed his glasses up his nose.

"Dan and Rivka, I'm glad you're here. I'll need you to explain how you came to be the owners of these books and why they should have been in Israel Finestein's shop. The assistant district attorney is pushing his theory of a lover's quarrel, and I will have to quash that altogether."

The defense attorney took a bite of kugel and munched slowly, savoring it. After a long sip of coffee, he said, "But first,

Peggy, I must establish that no one has ever heard you and Israel arguing or raising your voices in anger."

Peggy straightened up, her posture indignant. "I can't imagine anyone overhearing us arguing at all. We hardly ever disagreed and even then, not in public. Sure, we each had our differences—major differences, but Izzy was such a *mensch*. We were very much in love."

Leon studied her. She looked younger than forty-eight, despite the black turtleneck sweater that gave her delicate oval face a ghostly look. "Was Israel prepared to accept your Goth appearance and your key role as a Goth magazine editor?"

"Oh, yes," Peggy answered quickly. "We had come to an understanding. I would dress Goth and act accordingly for work purposes and I would alter my so-called extremism elsewhere. It was a bit inconvenient for me, but certainly workable. He wasn't adverse to the extra income I would bring in either."

"I see, and his former Hasidic background presented no barrier or irritation for you?"

"Izzy had liberated himself from strict Hasidic tradition years before we met, although that put a major strain on his relations with the rest of his family and friends. I had no problem with what he wanted." She fidgeted in her pocket for a tissue to wipe away fresh tears.

"Don't get me wrong, Izzy was a religious and righteous man. He just didn't go along with their brand of piety. I agreed to attend synagogue with him regularly and keep a strictly kosher home for him. I still believe in a compassionate God. I couldn't promise him much more, but he seemed willing to accept what I had to give. I wasn't about to shave my head and wear wigs and *shmatte* head covers. It took a while, but we found a suitable middle ground we both could live with."

"So at any time during this period of conciliation, no one could possibly have heard you, uh, debating, for lack of a better word?"

"Absolutely not, Leon."

"Then the assistant district attorney has no evidence to support a lovers' quarrel motive." Leon fingered through the multitude of papers in his briefcase and pulled out a single document. "This is a statement I obtained during preliminary discovery. It's an inventory of the police search of the Finestein shop. It states that the shop was sealed off as soon as the Forensics team left. The main issue here is that the steel cabinet where Mr. Finestein kept his unfinished work was not only unlocked, but empty, except for two not very valuable and unrelated manuscripts, plus a virgin papyrus roll."

Leon's gaze met Dan's, then Rivka's. "Mr. and Mrs. Sherman, nowhere else is there any mention of your volumes. To substantiate a robbery motive, we need to establish that a book or books of great value should rightly have been there. At present, all we have is the word of the accused that the deceased was working on one or more rare editions."

"I believe we can help you there," offered Dan.

"I'm sure you can, but first I'd like to ask Peggy if anything else is missing from this list." The lawyer turned to her. "You were a frequent visitor to the shop. Was anything else taken?"

Peggy took a moment to peruse the list, then shook her head. "Not that I can see."

"What about that casserole you told me you carried in for his supper?" reminded Leon. "There's no mention of it on the list." He added this fact to his notes.

"Oh! Of course, the casserole. It was a tuna-noodle dish that Izzy made with cream of mushroom soup. It was in his large yellow crockery bowl with a broad blue stripe around it. Why would they forget that?"

"Indeed, an oversight." Leon ran his large fingers across his clean-shaven chin. "Or perhaps a hidden agenda? But we'll look into that another time. Now, Mr. and Mrs. Sherman, I'd like to learn more about the two books, if you will."

Dan unfolded a clutch of notes that he had stuffed in a pocket before leaving the bookstore. Adjusting his glasses, squaring his broad shoulders, he addressed his audience as if delivering a professional engineering paper. "I compiled a little research from reference books in our store. The more valuable of our two books is a Yiddish translation of the *Sefer Menorat ha-maor. Menorat ha-maor* means *Candlestick of Light. Menorat* is the menorah."

Leon held up his hand. "Is this particular menorah the seven-branch candelabra we use in *Shabbos* worship?"

"Exactly,"

Dan went on to describe the first of the two books in sufficient detail for Leon's understanding. He mentioned the original author, the translator, the publisher, and the printing dates.

Periodically, Leon interrupted him with specific questions, those he might use strategically during the actual trial.

When Dan got around to the handbook, he gave the title in Latin.

At that point Rivka insisted on chiming in with her English equivalent of the pamphlet: "That's Latin for *A Handbook of Plants and Animals of Hamburg and Mienze, Germany in 1567.*"

Dan cast a wary eye toward his wife and continued explaining. "We delivered both books to Mr. Finestein's shop for appraisal about a month ago—Tuesday, December ninth to be exact. He was very enthusiastic about them, but his estimate to restore the *Menorat ha-maor* was out of range for our pocketbook. So he offered us another arrangement. We would give him the second book free and clear. And in return, he would completely restore the *Menorat ha-maor* to maximum saleable condition at no charge to us." He paused long enough for Leon to catch up with his note writing.

"Rivka and I agreed, and we were to pick up the finished restoration on Monday, the 15th of January. That's tomorrow, so we had every expectation that both our volumes would have been in Mr. Finestein's shop last Monday."

Dan scratched his left ear and frowned. "After all my explaining, I've forgotten the most important thing. Israel wrote up our business arrangement, specifying the volumes and the work to be done, all on his letterhead, and gave us a copy before we left.

He was very professional. That piece of paper alone proves that the books exist."

"Excellent!" Leon said. "I'll need a copy of that." He turned to Peggy. "Is there any reason to believe that Israel would have sent their volumes elsewhere for some sort of out-of-shop cleaning or servicing?"

"No way!" replied Peggy. "Izzy was extremely careful and protective of his clients' work. He was known as the best in his field, as well as very respectful of each restoration project. As far as I know, he accomplished every step of the work in-house. He had all the chemicals, oils, bleaches, tools, and driers he needed to do that."

Dan pushed his chair back. "Now that we have made our contribution, it's time for us to get back to the store."

"Before you go," said Leon, "I need to get three more important facts from you. One, how did you come to own these items? Two, who else knew of their existence? Plus, who else knew where and when you were taking them to be restored? And by the way, is your ownership clear of any legal claim by anyone else?"

Dan slowly sat down once more and thought for a few minutes, making sure he was facing the small recorder's microphone.

"First of all, we had an agreement with the former owners, Edythe and Bernard Bender...." Dan spelled out the whole story of how they came to own the bookstore and, in return, provide for Bernie's care as an Alzheimer's patient. "Rivka's a good soul—she often visits him. Just a little over a month ago, in one of his few periods of clarity, he told her where to find the two books and his wish for us to have them. It's really quite amazing. We've owned the store for a year, but had no idea they even existed. Bernie had sealed them up behind a wood panel in one of the poetry stacks."

Dan paused as Leon furiously took notes. "Of course there's our bookstore clerk, Ivy Cohen, but she is certainly above reproach. We did call in an agent of rare books and fine art to appraise the volumes. His name is Anton Gleuck; we assume he's bonded and honest."

"Don't forget Mrs. Tate-Williams," Rivka piped in. "She was sitting at the table in the reading room, but she moved over to a back corner while we were discussing the business with Mr. Gleuck."

"Yeah," added Dan. "We don't really know anything about her, but she couldn't know where we would send our books. Also, there wasn't anyone in the store when we retrieved them from the original cache. We kept them in our safety deposit box at the bank until we delivered them to Israel." Dan stood to leave once more. "Okay if we go now?"

"Yes, thank you, you've been very helpful," said Leon. "Let me know if you can think of anyone else with possible knowledge of your books." He waited until the Shermans had left before continuing. "Now Peggy, who would have had specific knowledge of what Israel was working on?"

"I suppose just about anyone who entered the shop," she replied.

"You mean he allowed prospective customers into his workroom?" asked Joel, who had been silent up to now.

"Oh, no," Peggy said. "Izzy conducted most business in the front room, where he had normal lighting."

"So who did he allow in the workroom?" Leon pressed.

"Owners of the particular books and manuscripts that he was working on, a few of his artisan colleagues for consultations, and sometimes family members when he wanted to show off."

"Had he talked to you about anyone in particular during the past few weeks?"

Peggy sighed. "Izzy did mention dealing with a competitor who has a shop in Towson. Nabakov, Boris Nabakov. That was Wednesday or Thursday a week ago, I'm not sure which."

"Anyone else?"

With one elbow on the table, Peggy rested her chin on her fist while she tried to remember. "Oh, yes," she said, a light bulb going off. "The evening of the very same day the Shermans brought him their two books, he groused about having this big argument—in the afternoon, I think he said—with his cousin Mendel Levinson. It was so bad that he finally threw Mendel out of his shop. He was thrilled about the new, elegant project, and Mendel managed to sour his excitement. I remember the exact day because I went to lunch with the Shermans at the Rusty Scupper after their appointment with Izzy."

"What was the argument about?" asked Joel.

"Mostly about me and our upcoming marriage. Mendel repeated a bunch of slurs from his wife and one of her friends in Annapolis. Izzy was boiling over when I brought him his supper that night. I had to wheedle everything out of him. He didn't want to repeat the slurs to me. I made him. She's a nasty one, that Naomi."

"I see. Would Levinson be someone allowed in the workroom?" asked Leon.

"Yeah, he likes nosing around in everybody's business."

"So I can add Mendel, Naomi, and friend to the list of suspects. I think that's enough for one day." He gathered up the recorder and pad and tucked them in his briefcase. "I have one more matter to discuss with you, Peggy, and please don't think I'm criticizing you."

Peggy's willowy body turned rigid; her dark eyes flickered with suspicion. She figured she was indeed about to get criticized.

Leon wasted no time pussy-footing around. "It's about your appearance when you're in court. Now don't take this personally, but—judge, prosecutor, and if it goes to trial, jurors, they're all human, and first impressions count for a lot. I want you to play down the Goth look. A black suit—skirt, pants, whatever, is fine. Maybe a white blouse. But no dog collar. No black nail polish. No black lipstick. And try to unpunk your hair a little. Soften it if you can. I want you to understand, Peggy, that perception is everything, and a conservative look, a little less outside the mainstream, will help your case."

Peggy's body relaxed, and she actually chuckled. "Got it, Leon, I can do that. Anything that will help prove my innocence."

"Good! Glad to hear it." Leon shook her hand, Joel gave

her a reassuring hug, and the lawyers left.

* * * *　　　•

Two weeks later a closed-door session of the currently em-paneled Grand Jury found sufficient cause to bind Peggy Fraume over for a jury trial.

Chapter 12

Loss and Gain
The Same Day

vy removed her gloves and rubbed her hands together to get the circulation going. The harsh winter day followed her inside the hospital, where the chilly corridors matched her apprehensive mood. She had been making this trip daily to visit Irma Riley, her landlady and dear friend who had survived two near-deadly heart attacks. Ivy entered the dimly lit room and found the patient sitting in a vinyl recliner sipping hot tea from a Styrofoam cup.

"My, my," Ivy said in a lilting tone as she tossed her coat on the end of the bed. "Aren't we the Queen today, sitting up and sipping like Her Majesty at court. You look marvelous." A quick kiss on the patient's sunken cheek and she settled into a chrome-framed side chair.

Irma actually seemed upbeat. "Father Brian was here this morning, and my neighbor came this afternoon. Brought me those flowers, too. The doctor said maybe I could go back to the nursing home soon and even home after a few weeks. How about that?"

"You're here only a few days and you're already talking about leaving? What's wrong? The food isn't any good? They're not serving filet mignon?"

"Oh, dear," Irma chuckled. "With my loose false teeth, I

couldn't chew steak even if they did serve it."

"Kidding aside, Irma, how do you feel?"

"Well enough, except that I'm always sleepy. I think it must be those tiny white pills they keep pushing at me." She clumsily set the weightless cup down on the tray table.

"That's okay, dear, they need you to rest more. I'll pop down to the cafeteria for a cuppa and a sandwich. Maybe you'll be more awake when I get back." Ivy helped her into the bed and plumped up the pillow. Irma's eyes fluttered shut.

After her leisurely bite, Ivy strolled down the corridor to Irma's room. As she approached the door, her breath caught in her throat. The white privacy curtain had been drawn around the bed. Below the curtain she could see the wheels of a blue crash cart and a cluster of legs moving about in an urgent flurry of activity. She heard someone in charge barking short, precise commands and others responding. Monitor alarms continued to beep in periodic cadence. *Maybe,* Ivy thought, *they're fixing her and she'll be okay.* She leaned against the wall opposite the room and waited patiently for the crisis to abate.

The alarming beeps grew faster until they turned into one continuous whine. The hospital room became silent. Minutes later, a harried resident appeared in the doorway, looked across the hall, and discovered Ivy. With a single shake of his head, she knew the battle had been lost. Irma had died.

"We did all we could for her," the doctor said. "She just didn't respond. Are you the next of kin?"

"No, I'm a close friend," replied Ivy, stifling sobs. "I guess I'll have to make some calls."

"We do have a counseling office that can help you with that," offered the resident. "I'm very sorry." He turned and walked down the hall toward the nurses' station.

A distraught Ivy stood frozen for a moment as a nurse and technician returned equipment to the crash cart and rolled it out the door.

Ivy needed to say goodbye. Fearfully, she stepped into the

room. Approaching the bed, she found herself surprised. Irma looked at peace, as if she had merely fallen asleep. Ivy bent over, gently kissed the withered forehead, and backed out of the room. She left the hospital, flagged down one of the usual waiting taxis, and headed for The Olde Victorian Bookstore. Somehow, she didn't want to be alone, and it was early enough in the evening, only ten o'clock; the Shermans should be still awake.

Ivy turned her key in the bookstore lock, entered, and made her way to the bottom of the stairwell. "It's me, may I come up?" she yelled aloft.

"Ivy? My goodness. Of course," Rivka called back. She'd been puttering around the kitchen and quickly closed the door to Dan's snoring in the bedroom. "I thought you were spending the evening at the hospital."

Ivy gave out a single sigh. "Irma died forty-five minutes ago." For the first time tears flooded her cheeks, tears she had been holding back for so long.

Rivka drew Ivy to the shoulder of her robe where she let her grieve. "There, there. You two were so very close."

"She was like a mum to me," murmured Ivy without picking up her head. "Very much like my dear foster mum, Janice, who brought me up like one of her own."

"But you were there for Irma when she needed you most," assured Rivka. "She loved you like a daughter. I suppose there'll have to be funeral and burial arrangements. Are you aware of her last wishes? Is there any family to be notified?"

Ivy dried her cheeks and straightened her long plaid skirt. "One person, in Albany. I suppose I'll have to phone her after I call Joel Wise. Irma told me to contact Joel if anything happened to her."

"All of that can wait until morning," Rivka said. "Get a good night's sleep and everything will be clearer for you. Take a few days off if you wish. Will you be okay tonight, all alone in that big house? I can make up the couch in the living room for you if you like."

"That's so sweet, Rivka, but I'll be fine. It's getting late, and I should be going now. I just needed someone to talk to. I'll let myself out and lock up again. I do plan to come to work as usual tomorrow."

* * * *

At 8:45 the next morning Ivy trudged to the bookstore. Pulling her wool cap down over her ears, she bent her head against the 15-degree chill. Her anxious breath came out in frosty puffs. She'd spent a fitful night, questions playing havoc with her rest. *Will the house be sold? Will I have to look for a new place? How much time before that happens?* It had been too early to make the difficult phone calls from home; she'd make them from the bookstore.

At ten o'clock, when there were only two customers in the aisles, Ivy called Joel Wise's office, but he was in court until noon. Hanging up, she saw no harm in calling Irma's niece in Albany. She had found the phone number in the red leather day book that Irma kept it in the telephone table drawer beside the stairs.

After three rings a throaty voice answered, "Yes?"

"Is this the home of Agnes Winnen?" asked Ivy.

"It was her home," responded the cautious speaker. "She passed away seven months ago. Who's calling, please?"

"My name is Ivy Cohen and I'm a friend of your Aunt Irma and a tenant in her home. Am I speaking to Agnes's stepdaughter?"

"Yes. "I'm Mae Winnen, her daughter. What's this about?"

"I'm so very sorry to inform you that your Aunt Irma passed away last evening from a heart condition. She'd already had two heart attacks."

"Oh, I see," said Mae. "You mentioned that you were a tenant in her home. What kind of house is it?"

Now there's a strange response, thought Ivy. "It's a pretty, three-story Victorian house."

"Thank you!" Mae said, and hung up.

"Rather rude, abrupt with me, like she didn't really care

about her aunt at all," Ivy told Rivka.

But Rivka could only shrug her shoulders. Two men were coming through the front door. "May I help you gentlemen?"

They flashed their badges and the taller, more muscular of the two announced, "I'm Detective Sergeant Maury Shap, and this here is Detective Sullivan." Shap set his leather briefcase down on the checkout counter and undid the straps. Pulling out a small tape recorder, he pushed the RECORD button. "Are you Mrs. Daniel Sherman?"

"I'm Rivka Sherman. We...I already spoke with Detective Sullivan on the phone on Friday. Have you found our missing books yet?"

"No, ma'am, we haven't," replied Sully. "We made a thorough search of the shop, but there were only two older twentieth-century books on the premises—nothing that fit the rare manuscript or book categories. In fact, we'd like a more precise description of your books so we know exactly what we're looking for."

"Excuse me, Officers," said Rivka. "I—"

"Detectives, ma'am," Shap said, as if correcting a first-grade child.

"Oh, yes. I'd like to bring my husband in for this interview. He's downstairs unpacking a shipment of new magazines." Rivka hollered down to him. The heavy thumps on the top stairs announced his arrival. "Dan, this is Detective Sergeant Shap—and Detective Sullivan, the one who called on Friday. They're here about our books. I'm not entirely sure why, but apparently it's part of Israel's murder investigation."

In his Washington Redskins sweatshirt and jeans, Dan strode to the counter and stopped short, large hands on hips. He stared hard from one man to the other and scowled. "Wait a minute. Didn't I see the two of you at the funeral, standing off to the side, talking to Naomi Levinson?"

"Yes, sir," said Shap.

"What were you doing there, Detectives?" Without waiting for an answer, he asked, "Wasn't your appearance at a funeral a tad inappropriate?"

Shap allowed a slight smile to escape. "It's always appropriate, always interesting to see who attends those things and who doesn't. Especially during a homicide investigation. Very revealing. It's all part of our job. Your friend, the so-called bereaved one, is guilty, so butt out, Sherman. I'll decide what's appropriate."

Dan persisted. "How do you know the Levinsons, if I might ask?"

"That's part of our job, too," countered Shap. "But if you must know, he's Finestein's cousin and only living relative."

"Don't mind him, Mr. Sherman," said Detective Sully. "Sometimes my partner gets a little too close to his work." He offered a conciliatory hand to Dan, who shook it, deciding he'd better back off. Out of the corner of his eye he'd seen Rivka's look of near-panic. Her message got through: Don't antagonize the police.

"How can I help you?" he asked.

"As I told your wife, we need a more precise description of your books so we know exactly what we're looking for," said Sully, his demeanor polite and soft-spoken. "Also, we'd like to get a better idea of their value. That way we can determine whether the motive for Mr. Finestein's death was robbery and incidental murder or out-and-out premeditated murder."

Dan took his time before answering. Assessing the situation, his sharp eyes landed on the recorder. For a split second he wondered when they were going to tell him about it. "As for a good description, Mr. Anton Gleuck, our rare book agent, helped us put together an appraisal for our merchandise insurer." Dan pulled open the second drawer of the file cabinet behind the register. He thumbed through a few folders and removed a two-page insurance rider.

Shap stepped forward, nudging his partner out of the way.

"You can keep this," Dan said. "I have another copy." As he was about to hand over the document, his nose wrinkled at an unfamiliar smell, something like diesel fuel. It seemed to be coming from where Shap stood. Dan made a mental note of it as he handed the document to the detective.

Sullivan, looking over Shap's shoulder, whistled at the Estimated Value. "Wow, that much!"

"Certainly enough to kill for," said Shap. "And a tidy amount to scam an insurance company for. Don't you think?"

"Whoa, Detective!" exclaimed Dan. "We resent that. We're not scamming anyone."

"Perhaps you protest too much," returned Shap with a sly grin.

"Bull! There's no way we could possibly collect that kind of insurance."

"And why is that?"

"Read on, Detective. The theft didn't take place from our bookstore. We assumed that Mr. Finestein would have had insurance for his shop, but he'd have been the beneficiary in that case. We'd have to sue his estate to get anything at all. I think that you're the one making false accusations."

"Keep your damn shirt on, Sherman," returned Shap. "All we're trying to do here is establish a viable motive for this murder."

"Easy, Dan," Rivka murmured while she kicked him sharply in his left shin.

"Ow! Isn't robbery a good enough motive for a policeman anymore?" scolded Dan. "According to his fiancé, Finestein was a gentle and religious man without an enemy in the world."

"Consider the source, Sherman," countered Shap. "A fiancé caught with the murder weapon in her hands? A murderer—why wouldn't she say something like that?"

"That's just it," said Rivka. "The books are missing, and you arrested her before she left the Finestein shop. She didn't steal them. Someone else did. And you're trying to say the robbery and murder were coincidental events?"

"Why not? She could have had an accomplice who made off with the books before the officer got there." Shap smirked, pleased with his response.

"You have evidence of this?" Dan asked.

Shap made no response and merely continued his smirk.

There's something malevolent about this guy, thought Dan. *He enjoys needling people far too much.* "If you have no more specific questions for us, I think you had better be on your way. We have a business to run here."

Unaccustomed to being hustled off, Shap gave Dan the evil eye, then he and Sully headed for the street and disappeared from sight. Both the Shermans noted that Detective Sully had looked decidedly uncomfortable throughout the confrontation. Had they just been played in a good cop-bad cop routine? Dan's bushy black eyebrows came together in a frown. *I wonder about Shap. What made the detective so angry? Shouldn't the job require him to be the calm, open-minded, and unbiased type? He's already made up his mind about Peggy. Isn't he even looking elsewhere?*

* * * *

At 1:15 that afternoon Ivy tried the law offices once more and this time the secretary put her through to Joel. News of Irma's death came as no surprise for him. "Irma seemed to think her time was near. As you know, she was eighty-six. So she recently made some significant changes to her will. She told me in no uncertain terms that her sister's death made those changes necessary. Those changes actually made you her chief beneficiary, Ivy."

"Me? Why me? I'm not related to her."

"As Irma put it, you were the best friend she's had since her husband passed away. And you were her devoted caregiver when she needed help most."

"What about her sister's family?" Ivy asked. "I spoke to the stepdaughter earlier today to inform her of Irma's passing."

"That may not have been the wisest thing to do, Ivy, under the circumstances."

"Whatever do you mean, Joel?"

"I think you had better come into the office so we can discuss everything fully. I have an opening at three tomorrow. We'll talk then."

Chapter 13
Will and Will Not
Tuesday Morning, January 16th

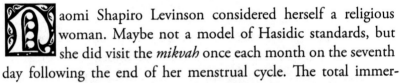aomi Shapiro Levinson considered herself a religious woman. Maybe not a model of Hasidic standards, but she did visit the *mikvah* once each month on the seventh day following the end of her menstrual cycle. The total immersion of her whole body in a pool of circulating tap and rain water was a purifying ritual rather than a cleansing process, for her body had to be physically clean before entry. It was more the spiritual purification, the removal of her less-than-saintly faults that she sought with these visits. But some misdeeds and acts of unkindness proved more resilient than others. Although Naomi valued her role as Mendel's wife and her respected place in the Hasidic female community, she artfully spread gossip, clung to rigid intolerance, and brandished a lashing tongue. But so often one does not see such faults in a mirror.

In a bubbly mood, Naomi climbed the stairs to their third-floor walk-up apartment and let herself inside. She felt the endorphins left over from her early-morning trip to the *mikvah*.

Mendel sat at the kitchen table, tucking his phylacteries, or *tefillin*, into their blue velvet bag. Only moments before, a small black box containing written prayers had been strapped to his forehead; another to his hand by a strap wound about his left arm.

Symbolically, they connect head, hands, and heart, equivalent to thought, deed, and will. Mendel dutifully carried out these daily affirmations to his Maker—perhaps reciting them a little too hurriedly most days. Today his connection with God truly blurred, and his attitude toward fellow beings drifted south.

"Naomi! Where have you been? We open the shop in fifteen minutes."

"Keep your shirt on, Mendel. It's only two blocks away. Plenty of time."

"Naomi, I asked you where you went so early this morning, and you haven't answered me."

Naomi smothered a few of her endorphins and screamed, "Do I have to tell you everywhere that I go? Can't I just surprise you sometimes?"

"I don't like surprises, can't stand 'em. Why can't you just tell me? Are you trying to keep secrets from me?"

"Well, Mr. Busybody, you keep secrets from me."

"What are you talking about, woman? What secrets?"

"Like last week. That night you came home with your briefcase and shoved it all the way back on the top shelf of the closet so I couldn't reach it. You never do that. You leave it in the front hall and I'm always falling over it. If that isn't a secret, I don't know what is. So there, Mr. Levinson! What's in the briefcase that's so important?"

"That's not a secret, my dear wife. That's business. My business."

"But—"

"But nothing. Get your coat and put your *tuchas* in gear. We have a dry cleaning and tailoring establishment to run."

"Mendel, dear. I'll tell you my secret if you tell me yours," she offered in a much sweeter voice.

"No way, Naomi. You started this."

* * * *

Twenty minutes later Mendel sat in his chair by the shop's

front window, studying a volume of Hebrew scriptures. Respect-fully, he brought the book to his lips for a kiss before he laid it down on the little table next to him. Pensively, Mendel began to count on his fingers. Five, six, seven. He slapped his forehead with his left hand. He knew Naomi's secret. Seven days after her cycle. She's now kosher! He smiled to himself for more than one reason.

* * * *

Three o'clock on Wednesday afternoon found an anxious Ivy sitting in Joel Wise's waiting room. Mixed feelings coursed through her mind. The loss of her dear friend, a clouded future, and Joel's veiled scolding on the phone all contributed to her con-fusion.

Another person sat in the waiting room: a graying middle-aged man in a black liveried uniform, holding a cap on his lap. A chauffeur? The receptionist indicated that Mr. Wise was ready to meet with them both.

As they entered, Joel rose from his chair and greeted each of them, a handshake for the man and a quick hug for her. He made introductions. "Ivy Cohen, this is Gino Fachetti. You will each benefit from Irma Riley's will. Mr. Fachetti—"

"Please, calla me Gino."

"All right. Gino, then." Joel seated them in chairs in front of his desk. He held up a sheet of paper. "Gino, Mrs. Riley left you an outright cash grant in the amount of $5,000. As she put it, 'For your wonderful friendship, your valued opinions, and your service in conveying me about town. Getting me where I needed to be.' Congratulations, sir. Sometime in the next six months the probate judge will release the money, and I will cut you a check."

Gino's mustached face lit up, and with watering eyes he said, "Thank you, God. Thank you, Miz Riley, and thank you, Mr. Wise."

"You're most welcome. My secretary will contact you when the check is ready. And now, Gino, my business with Ms. Cohen is little more complex, so if you will excuse us, we can continue in privacy."

Gino bowed and took his leave, popping the cap crookedly on his head and very nearly tripping over himself exiting.

"Our phone conversation left me totally in shock. Why me?" asked Ivy. "Why should Irma leave me anything at all?"

"Ivy, Irma couldn't say enough about you. You came into her life when she needed you most: friend, companion, and nurse. You were like the daughter she never had. Apparently, when she and her late husband were young, he didn't want to be bothered with children, and by the time he changed his mind, it was too late for her. As Irma put it, you became much more of a companion and confidante than her introverted husband ever was."

"How soon will I have to move out of the house?"

"Perhaps never," he replied.

"What do you mean?"

"Irma Riley left her fine old Victorian house and nearly all its contents entirely to you, Ivy, along with her savings and investments. Of course, there'll be taxes, accounting fees, and legal fees, but there will be plenty left over."

"This is all so sudden. I'm having trouble grasping the magnitude of her gift, the inheritance."

"I believe the real estate value is around $200,000. The most recent stockbroker statement estimates the market value of her investment portfolio at $110,000."

He shuffled through a few documents before picking out one in particular. "Ah, here it is. There's a current balance of $3,200 in her savings account. Before I forget, there are a few other beneficiaries. Aside from Mr. Fachetti's check, there are two behests to Irma's favorite charities in the amount of $12,000, and she earmarked a few articles for neighbors and one relative. Aside from those, my dear, you've become an affluent woman overnight."

"I'm overwhelmed. I don't know what to say. My heart is beating so hard, I feel it's coming out of my chest."

"I think I can understand why Irma felt you were so deserving."

"Wait, Joel. You mentioned an article to be inherited by one relative. Might I ask which article and what relative?"

His forefinger scanned a list of items and stopped halfway down. "Item thirty-nine: 'An antique Ming dynasty-era vase is to be given to my stepniece, Mae Winnen, as a token of my affection for my sister Agnes.'"

The lawyer read the attached official appraisal. "Twenty-two inches high. Gold on blue ceramic, circa 1605. Estimated value: $ 6,500." Joel looked up and said, "Item thirty-nine also specifies that 'A single one-dollar bill is to be left to Mae Winnen as well.' It appears to me, Ivy, that this behest carries a hint of a history with it—the remnant of a feud that existed between Irma and Mae."

The door opened and Joel's secretary stepped into the room. "Excuse me for interrupting, but a court messenger has just dropped this off for you, and I believe it may have an important bearing on the Riley estate and your meeting."

Joel tore the seal from the official-looking envelope and slid out the legal document. He unfolded the blue jacket cover, read a few paragraphs into it, and then looked over at Ivy. "Speak of the devil and he shall appear. I generally don't like to speak in clichés, but this is ridiculously coincidental."

"Whatever do you mean, Joel?"

"Mae Winnen has weighed in with a probate court injunction contesting the validity of Irma Riley's Last Will and Testament. It seems that your call to her may have triggered her action. I was afraid this might happen. If I were to guess, Miss Winnen sees an opportunity to benefit, but has no idea who inherits what, and the injunction is simply a ploy until she can find that out for herself."

Ivy's red cowl-neck sweater almost enveloped her, making her petite frame look even smaller than it was. But her firm voice and elegant English accent took over. "I realize now I should have consulted you first, but I just thought it was the right thing to do. In fact, I did call you first, but you were in court. I don't understand this relationship. Mae told me she's Agnes's daughter.

"No," Joel said. "May was Agnes's stepdaughter."

"Oh." Still confused, Ivy asked, "But why was Irma so set against leaving the bulk of her estate to her stepniece?"

Joel cleared his throat. "Irma called her 'horrible' and 'despicable.' Apparently, when Irma went to Albany to visit her sister, Mae Winnen exhibited nothing but disrespect for either one of them. Irma remembered every venomous word. Mae called her stepmother a blood-sucking bitch and said, 'You can go to hell, along with that sister of yours.' Would you believe that?" asked Joel. "How about a drink of water?" He indicated a carafe and spare glasses on a tray before them.

Ivy declined. She watched him pour and down a whole glassful.

"As a result of that traumatic visit, Irma came to me in December and asked me to execute a new will. The original will made no mention of Mae at all, but of course, she would have inherited Irma's estate through her stepmother's will. This is what Irma wanted to avoid."

Ivy flushed. "So you don't think she deserves to inherit through her blood relationship?"

Joel's eyes narrowed. "No, I don't thinks she deserves a red cent. My first duty is to the deceased and Irma Riley's specific wishes. Second, by virtue of having a step-relationship with Agnes, Mae Winnen shares no blood with Irma. She was the only child of Agnes's late husband and his former wife. According to Mrs. Riley, Agnes barely tolerated her stepdaughter, and the two fought constantly."

"How will this piece of paper, this injunction, affect me? Will I have to move out of the house?" Ivy nearly held her breath in anticipation of Joel's response.

"Things might be delayed some," said the attorney, "but I don't think she has any valid grounds to contest this will. It should have strong legal standing in any court of law. I will have to prepare and file a brief in Anne Arundel County probate court. Depending on the preliminary findings, we may have to attend a court hearing to defend our brief. As for your living in Irma's house, even if things did go Winnen's way, she would have to serve you with an eviction notice to remove you. However, I'm sure that's not going to happen. As a delaying action, you might pay forward a few extra months' rent. Don't do anything rash now, as it might affect your own standing. And, above all, avoid any contact with Winnen without me present. Don't worry, my dear. Go back to work and I'll keep you informed."

Chapter 14
Meetings, High and Low
Thursday Morning, January 18th

The Gulfstream jet streaked through the blue European sky above a blanket of marshmallow clouds. The executive class jet possessed every imaginable amenity: personal pilot, plush furniture, and an even-more-personal flight attendant. The lone passenger, a sun-tanned man in a $2,000 Armani suit, relaxed reading the *Wall Street Journal*. Finished with the paper, he adjusted the Corinthian leather recliner to an upright position and pressed the call button. A pretty, eternally smiling face popped around the corner. Without a word, the man tilted his empty Waterford highball glass an inch or two. She took it from him and returned moments later with a fresh Chivas Regal over ice. As she was about to leave, his hand locked about her wrist and pulled her shapely young form down beside him.

The move didn't surprise her. She'd been hired to serve in a variety of ways. They kissed, explored, and fondled for a few minutes—until the phone rang. He waved her away. This would be business calling.

"*Allo? Oui!*" the man said, waiting until he heard the cabin door shut. Then in English to accommodate the caller, "You have connected with the correct number. You may speak freely. You have some art you wish to transact, *n'est-pas? Non?* Two rare books! And

100

you've had them authenticated? How did you come by these books? Why am I asking? Because *le récompense*, your reward, will depend on how honestly you acquired them. If you're implying they're hot, that means fewer buyers for me, *n'est-pas?* I must examine them before we can agree on a price. If you wish to continue this conversation I'll mail you a key to a rental postal box in Cannes. You can safely leave the books there for me. Of course, I must have your contact number and address. Trust is essential among those who deal with acquisitions of nebulous ownership, *n'est-pas?"*

The man ended the conversation in polite agreement. He picked up his glass and drew a long sip of the smooth Scotch. Setting it down, he noticed a lacy black bra draped over one arm of the recliner. He pushed the call button again.

* * * *

Thursday evening usually meant the weekly meeting of the Mystery Writers' Critique Group. They'd had to skip a week because so many of its ten members had been cast into roles in a real-life murder. They met in the third-floor reading room of The Olde Victorian Bookstore at the Shermans' massive dining room table, surrounded by the worldwide books, maps, pamphlets, and posters of the store's Travel Section. Tonight, only Peggy Fraume counted among the missing. Garry had brought along her note thanking her colleagues for their condolences in her time of loss.

Dan, the group's chairman, said, "Supposing you lead off, Rivka. I'm sure everyone's anxious to hear your latest Deputy Glenda Glide story, "Driven Into the Woods." What kind of trouble has she gotten into this time?"

"Oh, I forgot to tell you all," Rivka said, her large hoop earrings dancing as she surveyed the group. "It's no longer a short story. I'm turning it into a novel." She began.

> Entering a sharp curve to the left, a car's taillights shone back at her from the ditch. *Oh-oh*, she thought. *Another driver too drunk, high, or too sleepy to make the curve. Some day they're actually going to put a rail there.*

The county cruiser slowed to a creep, then eased onto a grassy spot at the side of the road. Glenda grabbed the cruiser's radio mike and reported the incident and locale briefly to her dispatcher. She re-hung the mike and pulled a flashlight from the glove box before sliding out onto her feet beside the car. She left her headlights on to illuminate the off-road car ahead. From a few steps away she noted that its front end had mashed into a wide tree trunk. There was no movement inside the wreck. Someone was hunched over the steering wheel. She bent and leaned in to see better. That someone proved to be a male with an execution-style hole in the back of his head. *Shot from a pretty low angle*, she guessed.

The deputy realized that this shot had to have come from the rear seat. She wasn't alone out here with the gunshot victim, yet there didn't appear to be anyone still around. Glenda stepped back and tried to straighten up, but before she could, an eerie sense of someone else's presence barely preceded her sudden blackout.

Glenda awoke minutes later, her upper body butterflied like a shrimp across the cruiser's hood—her attacker leaning heavily on her, struggling to remove her jacket. She reached for her gun. It wasn't there, nor was the utility belt that holstered it. She pushed back against the intruder with all of her strength, trying to dislodge him, but he shoved the nose of his gun deep into her ribs until the pain became too much for her. The deputy cried out and relented.

"I'm in charge now, copper," he announced. "No! Don't turn around. I got no problem with you. Take off your jacket and stay away from that shoulder mike."

"What do you want from me?" Glenda peeled off the jacket. "Take the cruiser and see just how far you'll get."

"Shut up and put both hands back on the hood," he ordered, sidling toward the driver's door, all the while aiming the weapon in her direction.

As the man tossed the jacket across the front seat of the cruiser, she got a glimpse of him: tall, bony face, dark hair, blue and white warm-up jacket, and jeans. She'd remember that. Her utility belt and holster hung from his waist. With the temperature in the mid-thirties, her body chilled quickly, and her nerves jittered alongside her shivers. *What does he want from me? Did he just want my uniform or my transportation or does he have designs on me?*

"Okay, now move!" He pistol-nudged Glenda across the wide ditch and into the edge of the deep woods.

She shuffled forward, stumbling on the uneven ground, bumping against tree branches, then stopped abruptly. "I can't see where I'm going."

He handed her the flashlight. "Here," he said, "and keep on moving if you want to come out of this alive."

She felt they were wandering aimlessly. *Has he some plan, some direction in mind?* Soon the sound of crunching frosted leaves and frozen twigs broke the eternal silence of the deeper woods. They had left the road noises and lights far behind. Only the cruiser's high beams remained a distant glow. She knew that eventually they'd run the car's battery down. Glenda's mind raced through every possible escape scenario.

One idea struck her. She counted on her attacker's attention in following the flashlight's beam on the ground while she gradually steered toward a pliable, low-lying tree branch. Slowly raising her other hand up to the approaching bough, she reached out and grabbed it—bending it back, farther and farther as she moved forward, until her target came into smacking range. She let go of the bent bough, snapped off the flashlight, and ran in a direction she had scouted out moments before.

After a bellowing "Ow" echoed through the woods, Glenda heard a string of furious curses and threats so loud they muffled the darting steps of her getaway. But not for long. A gunshot projectile chipped into a tree next to her. The bark flying off it grazed her left cheek. Though it stung plenty, she shifted direction and the next shot whizzed close by, but thankfully off target. *He must be using the crunching sounds my feet are making to zero in on me.* She zigzagged a few more steps, dropped to the ground, and covered much of her body with prickly leaves mixed with wet snow. Lying still, praying he'd head off in another direction, ...

"Okay, Rivvie. For a minute there I thought you were going to read us the entire novel," said Dan. "Your fifteen minutes are up. Not your fifteen minutes of fame, of course," he added with a sly grin. "Just time to give someone else a chance."

"That was fabulous," said Ivy. "I can't wait to hear more. You stopped at the most exciting part."

"Thanks," Rivka answered, throwing her husband a slightly petulant look, but knowing he was right. "I'm having so much fun I got carried away. Writing fiction is such a great escape from real life."

"I'll read now, if that's okay with the rest of you," said Dan. Without waiting for a protest, he opened up his loose-leaf binder and began to read from the last chapter of his second Kasper Brasse novel, *Shadows of Fear:*

> ....Kasper rolled over onto his stomach and struggled to get up on his knees. He managed to stand on two wobbly feet and straighten up on the third try. The room slowly stopped spinning, and objects around him began taking shape. He recognized his own office. His jaw felt like it had been kicked by a mule. A drop of blood trickled down his cheek from the crack on his forehead. And the lump behind his left ear came close to Ping Pong ball size.
>
> *What happened?* he wondered. Then it all came back to him. He'd been pistol-whipped by Georgio for attempting to save poor Patsy Worth. Georgio had snarled at him. "If I can't have her, no one else can."
>
> Kasper heard voices in his ante room. *They're still here? How long have I been out?* He hobbled toward the barely open door and swung it out of his way. He saw Georgio enter the outer office from the hall. Georgio stopped and stared in horror. Patsy lay in a pool of blood in the middle of the threadbare rug, the gun inches away from her limp right hand.
>
> Suddenly, her hand flipped toward the gun, grappled it into place, and pulled the trigger three times in rapid succession before she dropped back onto the floor. The deafening shots left three holes in the door's frosted glass panel, where her ex-boyfriend had been standing. Georgio Gianetti was now reduced to a crouching heap like a crumpled wad of paper.
>
> Kasper held fingers to each of their necks and found no sign of life in either body. He shook his

head and staggered back to his desk to call 911. *A helluva day. I guess that's one more fee I won't collect....*

"Damn it, that's pretty cynical," said Frieda. "Did you have to kill off both of them?"

Dan splayed out his long legs and crossed his arms over his chest. He loved a good debate. "Well, now, Patsy had to pay for her sins, too, didn't she? She ran off with Georgio, then stole his money and got him fired, practically ruining his life. Don't you think she deserved it?"

"I do not," Frieda said. "That's really sexist, Dan. A woman can pay for her sins without getting killed. A prison term would have sufficed."

Rivka chimed in, "Way to go, Frieda, I agree. It's overkill, darling, if you'll excuse the pun."

Dan didn't answer. His wife was beating him at his own game.

Garry spoke up. "Shouldn't Brasse have picked up the gun when he knelt down to see if Patsy was still alive?"

"Why do you question that?" asked Dan.

Garry shrugged. "I don't know. Maybe because I'm thinking of my poor sister and what she's going through. She handled the gun when she found Izzy lying there. I guess I'm looking for a way to legitimize her doing so."

"That's quite different," said Dan. "Figuring each party was—"

Joel pounded his fist on the table with such force that his coffee cup rattled in its saucer. "Everybody stop! This is a totally inappropriate subject. We have no business talking about a real crime scene in the middle of an investigation."

Dan rolled up the sleeves of his plaid flannel shirt. He couldn't tell whether it was the stuffy room or the conversation that was overheating. "Sorry, Joel, you're right. Let's move on, folks. Who's next?"

"I could read the beginning of my new book, *Ginger's Pride,*" offered Frieda.

"That would be great," said Dan. "By the way, congratulations on publishing your first book, *Ginger's Secret.*"

Everyone clapped. Blushing but happy, Frieda began to read:

....Chapter One, The Birthing. Clara heard her father calling her from the east paddock. She had put Ginger out to feed on the plentiful grass there almost two hours ago. She detected a tremor in his voice, so she dropped the pail of chicken feed on the ground and ran toward the paddock. As Clara came close, she saw her father at the fence and heard Ginger's neigh, a mixture of groan, whine, and scream. Her horse was not standing, but lying on the bed of hay her father had prepared for the mare.

"Papa, what's wrong," she asked. "Is she hurting?"

"Not injured, if that's what you mean. No, my dear, it's just time for Ginger to foal."

"What can we do, Papa? How can I help?"

"Absolutely nothing unless she has a problem," he said.

"Nothing?"

"Yes, we let Mother Nature do her thing."

Suddenly, Ginger's water broke and gushed forth. A minute later, an almost clear sack appeared and, within it, two forelegs. Ginger rocked partway left, then right, and a head popped through atop the forelegs. The rocking continued and more and more of the foal came into view until the entire newborn dropped into the hay. Ginger slowly staggered to her feet to assist the foal's head in breaking through the sack. She licked her newborn here, there, and everywhere. Spent by the huge effort, she lay down to rest while her foal struggled out of the remainder of her sack. which still clung to her hind legs.

That achieved, Ginger licked her youngster vigorously to give encouragement to the intense ordeal of standing for the first time. The foal's repeated attempts consumed the better part of an hour. The forelegs were easier; the hind legs required much more work to lift the weightier part of the body. After minimal rest Ginger, with the afterbirth still attached, continued cleaning her foal.

Throughout the birthing Clara and her dad hung on the fence outside this corner of the paddock, anxiously, reverently watching the miracle unfold.

#

"Oh, my! I've never witnessed the birth of an animal," said Rivka softly. "That was very touching, Frieda."

"Anyone else want to read?" asked Dan. "No? I agree. It's too tough an act to follow."

> "Our early Sages…understood that amiable conversation between men and women is a subtle form of exploratory contact and can easily lead to illicit relationships."
> *Menoras*, p. 145

Chapter 15

Serendipity

Tuesday Afternoon, January 23rd

The southbound train screeched to a stop at the Baltimore-Washington station a few miles from Thurgood Marshall airport. A woman in a black coat and wool cap, with flaming red strands streaking out of it, stood to pull down her bags from the overhead rack. As she struggled to free them, a tall man in a purple Ravens warm-up jacket and jeans leaped up from across the aisle to help her ease the two small bags to the floor.

"Why, thank you, sir. You're a real fine gentleman." Her voice was friendly, but her body language wasn't. She turned sideways and squeezed past him, wheeling the bags, one in front of her, the other behind, down the aisle to the exit steps and platform. She stood for a moment to scout out the environs until she spotted the track's overpass and the stairs leading up to it. *Must be the only way to the station and exit,* she reasoned. The train whistled twice, bumped cars, and moved on its way to the nation's capital. The stop had been only six minutes.

Several dozen steps up, trudging along the overpass, and several dozen down on the other side might have been taxing for most, but she somehow managed—and then discovered, with annoyance, the elevators she could have taken. By now the warmth of many layers of clothing encouraged her to set the bags on the sidewalk and unbutton her coat. The waiting room walkway led to the street, where she searched for a cab stand.

"Hello again," said the Ravens jacket.

"Say, are you following me, young man?"

"Hey, lady, there's only one walkway to the street."

"Sorry. A lady can't be too careful these days."

"I understand," he replied. "But if you're headed into downtown Annapolis, I can save you the cab fare. My pickup's in the parking garage across the street. No strings attached, ma'am."

"I don't know. I don't even know your name."

"It's Cliff, Cliff Mercer," he said, handing her his business card. "I build, remodel, and refurbish houses. All my friends tell me I'm absolutely harmless." He grinned. "I'm not sure whether that's good or bad."

"My name is, uh, Sue," she reciprocated. "And I do have to watch my pennies. So, if you don't mind I'll take you up on your offer."

Having no luggage of his own, Cliff took one of Sue's bags and told her to follow. He paid for the parking stub in the vending machine just outside the complex and ushered her into the elevator. They arrived at his silver Ford 250 on the third level, and he shoved both bags in behind the front seat.

"Visiting someone in town, Sue?" he asked when they had left the station and traveled a mile or two.

"Not really visiting. At least no one in particular," she said. "Just some business I have to attend to."

"What kind of business, if I might ask?"

"Oh, some real estate and some legal stuff. Darned lawyer types. They're gonna be a real pain in the neck, and I'm not looking forward to dealing with them."

"Know what you mean," he agreed. "My sister's married to one, and he sure is a real pain in the butt to deal with, but he's good at what he does. He handles a lot of title work, too, so if you need a lawyer for you real estate stuff, you can get in touch through me. The number's on my card."

"I'll keep that in mind," she said. "Annapolis, what's it like? I've never been there before."

"Well, it's a quaint old town dating from colonial times. Once it was the capital of these whole United States for a short time. Lots of homes and buildings on the National Historic Registry, too. Red-brick sidewalks, brown cedar-shake siding, and plenty of down-to-earth eateries, especially for crab cakes. Then there's Ego Alley at the City Dock, where all the amateur sailors strut their expensive boats for everyone to see and envy. Thousands of tourists, especially in the summer."

"You sure do know a lot about the place, Cliff."

"I ought to. Been brought up in Eastport, just across the bridge from the city, for most of my life—nearly forty-two years of it." He added some years to seem more mature to her.

"I would have thought you to be younger, at least ten years younger," she said. "I wonder why I thought that, Cliff?"

"Clean living, I guess, and I like to work out, too."

"I can see that." She gave him a thorough once-over, eyeing his square, strong face and broad, muscular build.

"Yeah, well, how long will you be in town?" he asked.

"Until the weekend anyway," she said. "Maybe longer if my business takes more time than I planned on."

"Would you be interested in having dinner with me this evening?"

"Thank you. Not tonight," she replied. "I had to get up real early this morning. I've been on two trains, all day, all the way from upstate New York, and I'm completely bushed. I only want to grab a bite in the hotel and crash. Maybe tomorrow night, if that's okay with you. I've got your card. I can call you tomorrow afternoon from the hotel."

"Hotel, hotel!" he exclaimed. "I forgot to ask where you're staying. I need to know where to drop you off."

"I made a reservation at the Maryland Inn on Church Circle. Do you know where that is, by any chance?"

"Sure do," he said.

The pickup left Interstate 97 for U.S. 50, and a few inter-changes later turned south onto Rowe Boulevard. After crossing the two bridges over Weems and College creeks they entered the Maryland state capital. Five minutes later Cliff parked on the hotel side of Duke of Gloucester Street. He set the bags on the red-brick sidewalk and held out his hand for her to shake. She took it, giving it an additional tug and squeeze.

"Tomorrow?" he asked.

"Tomorrow," she confirmed and watched him climb into the truck and drive off.

She wheeled her bags into the triangular-shaped historic building through the King of France tavern, which led upstairs to the hotel reception area. The woman calling herself Sue signed the hotel registry as Mae S. Winnen, 103B Gracie Lane, Albany, New York 12211, and took the elevator to her small, quaint room.

* * * *

On Wednesday morning Rivka reached into the Outgoing basket behind the cashier's desk and gathered up the mail for the daily post office run. At the door she asked, "Anybody feed Lord Byron yet?"

"Anybody meaning me, of course," said Dan. "He must have been really hungry. His royal highness kept winding though my feet until I thought I'd fall over him. He sure is one persistent cat. I cleaned out the box, too, and put in fresh litter."

"You're such a pushover, dear. You shouldn't let him intimi-date you so."

"Look who's talking. Who bought him the Cadillac of scratching posts? And who feeds him gourmet cat food with salm-on and turkey in it? I think our own dinners cost less."

"Not quite, dear, but he's worth it. Remember three years ago? He bit the intruder on the ankle and the blood on the carpet helped the police."

"Yeah, yeah, how can I forget. The burglar turned out to be the killer. It seems like a century ago."

Rivka threw on her parka, wiggled her feet into suede boots, and drew on fleece-lined gloves. "Know what, Dan? I'm always misplacing one glove. Maybe I should sew a string on them like Mom used to do so I wouldn't lose my mittens. Anyway, I'll see you in an hour. I'm going for the mail."

"Taking the car?"

"Nope. Too hard to park. Besides the walk in the fresh air will do me good. I haven't been out of the store since Sunday." She let the door swing shut and briskly walked the twenty-minute trek to the main post office at Church Circle. As Rivka started up the steps, she became aware of a woman standing just outside the entrance.

"Hi, Rivka. The windows won't be open for another seven minutes."

"Katie Silvers, I didn't expect to see you here. How are you?"

"Fine, just picking up some stamps."

"How's your 'Boxcar Bertie' story coming?" asked Rivka. "I think it's a great story line—a woman hobo riding the rails in the 1930s. A lone female in a completely male world during desperate times. Wow!"

"Thanks," Katie said, pulling open the door for the two of them. "I'm really excited about it. Only twelve more chapters to go."

Rivka deposited the bookstore mail in the wall slot. A middle-aged man in a tan trench coat brushed past the two women—so engaged in conversation they hardly noticed him. He picked up some paper slips at the desk, then stepped up to be first in line at the closed service window. He rested a large Priority box on the ledge while he intently filled out his paperwork.

Both lines queued up quickly. "We'd better get in line or we'll be here all day," Rivka said to Katie. They moved into the line on the right.

At precisely nine o'clock the clerks opened for business, and Rivka, a few feet away, heard a verbal exchange at the other window. *I know that voice*, she thought. She leaned forward to catch the speaker's face and immediately recognized the rare book agent Anton Gleuck, pushing his package across the counter to the clerk.

What's he doing mailing a package here in Annapolis? Rivka wondered. *His office is in Baltimore. And that Priority box would fit our rare books exactly.* She watched him push a few bills across to the clerk and accept a receipt in return. Anton Gleuck turned to leave and stood face to face with her. She quickly noted the changes in his expression. *Not just surprise*, she thought. *Sheer alarm. Or guilt maybe?*

"Mrs. Sherman!"

"Anton, what a pleasant surprise. I didn't realize you spent so much time in our fair city."

"It is rather unusual for me, but I have a client a few doors down West Street. In fact, I just mailed a manuscript for him." He moved closer to her in order to talk more softly. "Speaking of manuscripts, I feel terrible about what happened to your books, but who could anticipate robbery and the horrible murder of Israel Finestein?" Anton shuddered visibly. "So tragic. He was the best man for your restoration job. I'm so very sorry."

"You weren't responsible for either of those losses." Then Rivka thought, *Why on earth did I say that? He knew all about the books and just where they'd be and exactly when. He could be the guilty one.* "Perhaps the police will have some news soon," she said.

"Perhaps," he agreed. "I sure hope so. Well, I have to run now—a 10:15 appointment in Baltimore. Nice to have seen you." Anton pocketed his receipt, headed for the door, and was soon out of sight.

Katie finished her postal transactions and whispered to Rivka, "See you at the next meeting."

Rivka concluded her business at the window, retrieved the bookstore's incoming mail, and broke into a trot as she returned to the store. She encountered Dan at the cash register. Breathless, she burst out, "You'll never guess who I ran into at the post office."

"Someone from the critique group?"

"Yes, Katie, but that's not who was important."

"So who already?"

"Anton Gleuck, and he looked suspicious."

"Huh? How does anyone look suspicious?"

"Well, Dan, he was mailing a Priority package that could easily have held our two books. And he was mailing it here in Annapolis, not in Baltimore where his office is."

"Jeez, Rivvie, did you accuse the poor man of robbery and murder right there in front of witnesses?"

"Of course not, silly," she said. "Give me some credit, dear."

"Did he do anything or say anything that made him look suspicious?"

"It was the look on his face when he knew I'd seen him handing the box to the clerk. Like he'd done something wrong and I'd caught him at it."

"Couldn't it have just been a look of surprise?"

"I'm a Jewish mother of two grown children. Don't you think I know guilt when I come across it?"

"You mean he wiggled his nose?"

Rivka chuckled. When the kids were small she had them convinced that if they lied, their noses would wiggle. They were so convinced that they would grab their noses when they attempted a fib.

"Of course he didn't," she replied. "But I just know the man's guilty, and I'm going to prove it."

"Whoa thar, Nervous Nellie. Back down some. You can't go around making accusations. It's called slander or libel. I never know which is which."

"It's slander," said Rivka, sticking out her tongue at him. "It has to be written to be libel."

"Okay, you got me there. But ease up. Don't you go looking for trouble."

"Damn!" said Rivka. She dropped the mail on the counter,

stomped off, and climbed the stairs to their apartment.

"Oh, oh, now you're in for it," said Ivy, approaching the register.

"None of your beeswax, young lady," Dan grumbled.

"Huh? What's that?" The archaic cliché had eluded their English clerk.

"Never mind."

"Jealousy is a despicable emotion and
is rooted in a baseness of the spirit."
Menoras, Prologue, p. 19

Chapter 16
Wake and Take
Wednesday, January 24th

ae Winnen winked opened one eye a little after ten that morning. Feeling rested following yesterday's jarring train rides, she kicked back the covers and lay with her knees up and her fingers locked behind her head. *Not that my daddy wasn't good to me, but he had to go and marry that bitch, Agnes, and move into her tiny one-bedroom cottage, leaving me to sleep on a cot crammed under the staircase for twelve years. She never had a good word for me the whole time I lived there, while I cleaned her pitiful house and did everyone's laundry—her damn slave. The old hag even begrudged me the money Daddy saved for my college education. After Daddy died, she and that sly old sister of hers, Irma Riley, were always plotting against me, so that I wound up with nothing from Daddy's estate and next to nothing from hers. But now it's my turn. I'm going to get something out of this will. Or else. This gal's got a plan: to get exactly what's coming to me. Payment for all my damn suffering.*

Mae straightened her legs and swung them out of bed. She crossed her arms above her shoulders and lifted the nightshirt over her head, tossing it on a nearby chair. For a moment she caught a nude reflection of herself in the bathroom door mirror. She turned sideways and emitted a smile of approval at her five-foot-eight body, quite firm for a woman of forty-six. Her striking looks had always been underestimated. Or rather, she blamed herself for not making the most of them. Until now. Naturally carrot-red hair, almost jarring in its vibrant color, enhanced a pageboy cut, milky skin, and green eyes. A quick shower and shampoo made her feel like a new woman. Ms. Winnen left the room dressed in a prim tan business suit and headed for the Treaty of Paris restaurant downstairs. She fueled her hunger for a slice of Irma's estate with a cappuccino and a waffle smothered in strawberry syrup and whipped cream.

Step One of the Winnen plan had already been accomplished a week earlier from Albany. Mae had succeeded in placing an injunction on the Riley will, preventing it from being executed so that she would have time to examine its intent and content. Step Two required getting in touch with her Aunt Irma's lawyer and arranging to view her Last Will and Testament. Mae searched her purse for the slip of paper containing Mr. Wise's office number, removed her cell phone, and punched in the numbers.

"Legal offices, How may I help you," Joel's secretary answered in a contralto voice.

"I need to make an appointment. Sooner rather than later."

"Can you tell me the nature or purpose of your meeting?"

"No, it's private. I'd rather wait and discuss it with him myself."

"Would two o'clock tomorrow afternoon be suitable? He has an hour available then."

"Isn't there any time open today?" Mae asked.

"I'm afraid he has this afternoon marked for a funeral," replied the secretary.

"Oh? Was it a close relative?"

"No, an elderly client passed away."

"I'd guess that would be the Riley funeral," said Mae, fishing.

"Why, yes. How—" The secretary bit her tongue for accidentally revealing a client's name.

"Then I suppose tomorrow afternoon at two will have to

do. My name is Winnen, Mae S. Winnen."

"Thank you, Ms. Winnen. We'll see you then." The secretary found it difficult to keep a note of surprise out of her voice. She couldn't wait to tell her boss. But when she did, five minutes later, she discovered that Joel had heard her on the phone. She didn't anticipate his anger at her blabbing personal information.

"Let this be a lesson. You don't tell anyone about my schedule, not even that I'm going to a funeral. I expect you to know better."

"Yes, sir, sorry, sir," the secretary murmured, relieved that she wasn't being fired.

In the small Maryland Inn gift shop Mae purchased an Annapolis city map and located Murray Lane on it. Walking distance, she decided. Thirty-five minutes later she stood in front of number 77, a three-story Victorian house on a street arched with mature oaks, elms, and poplars. The tree branches were barren and brown this time of year. Tree roots buckled the sidewalk in roller-coaster fashion. The Riley home bore a two-year-old coat of pearl-gray paint with white trim and all-over wooden curlicue accents. It had a macadam driveway on the left and a small open porch out front. The door was red with a white lace curtain in its tiny window. She noted the nicely trimmed yews out front—green and bushy even in late January. *Oh, yeah, I could get used to this,* she thought as she turned around and started walking back downtown. *Maybe I could even rent out rooms and pay for my keep. I bet it's worth a few hundred thou.*

* * * *

Ivy Cohen took a deep breath before delivering her eulogy. She held her head high, looking dignified in a simple royal blue dress as she looked out over the piddling assembly gathered in the small chapel next to St. Mary's Church. Most were there out of respect for her. Irma Riley had no one else to speak for her life on this earth, and this was her funeral.

Ivy recognized the faces: Rivka and most of the critique group; a cluster of Irma's church friends; and a few neighbors. The arrangements were exactly as Irma had wished. Joel had seen to every aspect: Father Brian, her favorite priest; the chapel, the flowers, and even asking Ivy if she wanted to host a reception at the house. Ivy choked back tears and began.

"It is not a common thing for anyone to have had three mothers. I never knew my birth mother. She was murdered when I was only three months old. I grew up with a loving foster mother, who had to divide her love among her own three children and me. Two years ago, I left happy memories of my foster family in London, England, and emigrated to this country. Amazingly, I found yet another mother in Annapolis on 77 Murray Lane. Irma Riley and I bonded magically. At first I was just a tenant in her home, third floor rear, no meals, no refrigerator or stove privileges. In time, she invited me for tea and chats. We had much to talk about. We were both lonely and needy—even though I was only twenty-three.

"It was a joy that we found each other. We became warm friends and only our age difference brought about the mother-daughter distinction. I wish I could remember all that she told me of her struggling childhood, her unhappy marriage, and her social work for the church. If there truly is a reward in the next life, Irma Riley stands first in line." Ivy paused and continued in a strong, soprano voice.

"Then an accident brought us even closer. She broke her leg falling down the stairs. I can't rightly say how I became her caregiver, it came about so naturally. I genuinely loved Irma and wanted to help her in any way that I could. She appreciated my efforts with hugs, kisses, and kindness at every turn, and that was all I needed. I already miss my third mother deeply."

Approving, sympathetic eyes followed Ivy to her seat in the front row.

Irma had chosen cremation because there would be no family left to visit her grave. Father Brian resumed with the closing prayers, stressing the frailty of human life and the importance of the afterlife. He ended by inviting those in attendance to the reception at the Riley home. Ivy stood at the door with Father Brian, thanking everyone as they filed out.

* * * *

A hand-printed sign hung from a black wreath on the door at 77 Murray Lane: "Welcome, relatives, friends, and neighbors of Irma and Ivy. Come right in."

Well, I'm not exactly an enemy. Yet! thought Mae Winnen as she reached for the knob and stepped into the front hall. She had attended the funeral for only five minutes, seated in the last row, and left unnoticed. She heard someone in the kitchen and decided to tiptoe upstairs before other guests showed up. Mae wanted to have a thorough look-see of the house, the inside, especially. She found a bath and two bedrooms on the second floor. The more spacious one must have been her aunt's. It had a double bed covered with a flowered comforter, a fluffy shag rug, and a lived-in smell. Hearing the front door open as other guests arrived, she scampered up another flight of stairs to escape detection. Now she viewed the two smaller bedrooms and a bath on the third floor. Both bedrooms were neat and stark; neither appeared to be lived in.

By the time Ivy and Rivka reached the Riley home, the dining room table had already been laid out with platters of cold cuts, breads, and pastries. Ivy thanked her two friends who had taken charge, and began circulating among the small group of friends and neighbors. That is, until her new black pumps began to pinch her feet. She trudged up the stairs and headed down the hall to the bedroom next to Irma's. With her landlady's blessing, Ivy had moved downstairs from her third-floor rented room after Irma's first heart attack. "I feel safer with you close by," Irma had convinced her. Afterward, Ivy remained there. It would be her house, her home soon, according to Joel.

Ivy sat down on her bed and pulled off the too-tight pumps, replacing them with her leopard-print fuzzy mules. Wiggling her toes a bit, she sat for a moment to enjoy the relief. In that short moment, the sound of spike heels on the bare third floor struck her senses. *Oh, I'm imagining it,* Ivy thought at first, but then she heard it again. *Who would have the chutzpah to be roaming through the house upstairs?* Ivy stood and moved into the hall, where she heard footsteps padding down the carpeted stairs.

A female figure materialized, a steely-faced woman in a black wool sheath. Ivy realized it was a face she didn't recognize. "Hello, I don't think we've met. Were you at the funeral?" Ivy asked, confused, but still trying to be polite.

"Yes," Mae said. "I sat in the back and left when you began your eulogy."

"Who are you?" challenged Ivy. "And what are you doing up here in my personal living space?"

"We spoke on the phone a few days ago. I'm Mae Winnen. Your sign said relatives were welcome. I think I qualify as a niece. Say, gal, aren't you a little premature in calling this your personal living space? Actually, it will be my home in a couple of weeks. Are you aware that there's a legal injunction against the execution of Irma's phony will? It will never hold water, gal. I'm only surveying what is rightfully mine."

Ivy bristled. "I highly doubt that, Ms. Winnen. Irma's lawyer assures me that her Last Will and Testament will hold up in a Maryland probate court. But even if that will doesn't hold true, I've paid three months' rent to the estate, so this is still my home. And I'm certainly entitled to a measure of privacy here."

"Don't worry, Ms. Ivy, I'll serve you with an eviction notice just as soon as we're through with the damn courts."

"Ms. Whiner, I think you had better leave the premises."

"It's Winnen, you bitch."

"Leave now!" screamed Ivy. "Now, before I call the police."

"Who is considered a wealthy man?
He who is content with what he has."
Menoras, p.111 (The Talmud)

Chapter 17

Maliciously Mine

Thursday, January 25th

Joel Wise appeared in the doorway of his inner office. "Hello, Ms. Winnen. Come in and have a seat. I believe you're a party to your Aunt Irma's will. It's a pleasure to meet and serve you."

That pleasure won't last long, I'm sure, Mae thought, but she said aloud, "That's why I'm here, Mr. Wise. I'd like to have a look at the will and its wording."

"I'm happy to reveal those words that are pertinent to your particular bequest," Joel replied. "However, I must protect the privacy of the other heirs. It's my fiduciary responsibility to them. Especially now, since you have seen fit to order an injunction to stop the execution of Mrs. Riley's will."

"All right. May I now see the wording of my aunt's bequest to me?"

"Of course," Joel replied. "First I'd like to see some picture identification, and then we can proceed."

Mae held out her New York State driver's license.

Joel opened a manila file folder with her name on it and extracted a single sheet, which he handed to her. He examined her expression as she absorbed its contents.

"What?" she cried out. "There must be some mistake. One

lousy dollar and a chunk of old pottery? I'm her only living relative."

"Ms. Winnen, I might point out that this chunk of pottery, as you put it, has been valued at $6,500. Moreover, I believe that the one-dollar bequest is intended as an explicit statement of her displeasure with your behavior toward her. When I confronted her about her wishes in this bequest, she cited a number of occasions where you were rude, boorish, and disrespectful to her."

Mae curled her upper lip, displaying large horsey teeth, as if she were about to whinny. "The old broad had to be off her rocker in the end. Either that or someone has poisoned her against me. It's a conspiracy to cut me out of her will. She always said that I was her favorite niece." Mae leapt to her feet, placed her palms on the desk, and leaned forward, hovering over Joel. He was not intimidated.

"I can assure you that your aunt was of sound mind and sensible attitude right up to the end. There are a number of witnesses who can verify that she remained sane and determined, yet wholly pleasant throughout her illness. There's absolutely no legal basis for you to contest the Riley will."

"I can't believe that," Mae insisted. "I won't believe that and I won't lift the injunction on the will either. I'll fight it."

"Then we will see you two weeks from today, February seventh, in probate court for a hearing. I have already reserved space on the court's calendar. I might suggest that you engage your own legal counsel, Ms. Winnen."

Mae stormed out of the office and made her way back to her hotel room, her temper raging only a few degrees below hyperventilation. She wanted to strike out at someone or something—it didn't matter whom or what. A malevolent scheme struck her. But she couldn't carry it out from her room. She needed a pay phone, or an expendable cell phone—one that couldn't be traced back to her. She remembered that during her morning walk along West Street, she'd seen a convenience store with a public phone booth. She used the telephone book in her room's night table to locate two numbers for her scheme.

Leaving the hotel once more, she hurried back to the store and chose to use the phone booth. Why waste money on a throw-away cell? She dialed. "Hello. Is this the Baltimore Gas and Electric company? My name is Irma Riley and I live at 77 Murray Lane in Annapolis. I'm calling from the hospital and I'd like to turn off the electricity at my home for the duration of my extended stay here. You don't recommend it? Yes, I understand that, but I have to watch my pennies. I'll call back when I'm ready to start service again." Punching in the second number, she ordered the telephone service to the Riley house to be disconnected. Mae hung up, pleased that she could create some serious harassment to alleviate her own distress. But even that relief was only temporary. Frustration edged toward paranoia as she traipsed back to the hotel.

Mae stomped into her room and slammed the door with a vengeance. She threw her coat and purse on the bed, dropped into a recliner, and tossed herself into a way-back position. But a second thought intruded. She brought the chair to the upright position once again and poured herself a quarter-glass of Jack Daniels from the half-filled bottle on the coffee table. She really wanted to gulp the smooth, warm liquor, but resisted the temptation and sipped instead. Her anger subsided and she allowed more rational thoughts to clarify her mind. She had too much to lose to screw up now.

Mae had had several years' experience as a paralegal, yet she realized she was no match for Joel Wise. He had infuriated her, but she had to respect that he knew much more about Irma Riley's affairs and mental state than she did. Also, she was an out-of-stater, unfamiliar with Maryland law. She needed local representation. Her boss in Albany had recommended an old college roommate living in Frederick, Maryland.

Mae set the glass back on the table, reached over to the bed, and retrieved her purse. Finding the slip of paper with the lawyer's name and number inside a zippered pocket, she slid the phone across the night table and dialed.

"Law offices of Thomas and Cassidy. How may I assist you?"

"Is Mr. Thomas available?"

"I'll see if he's free. May I have your name, please?"

"Mae Winnen. I was referred by my employer, Mr. Raymond Brighton of Albany, New York."

"May I tell Mr. Thomas what this is about?"

"Tell him it's about probating my aunt's will."

"One moment, please."

When the line went silent, Mae grabbed her drink for a long pull and had to swallow quickly when she heard him respond before she was ready.

"Ms. Winnen, Elroy Thomas. I'd be glad to assist you in probating your aunt's will if she was a Maryland resident. We can discuss all the details when we meet. I have an hour open just before noon tomorrow. Shall we say 10:45?"

"That will be fine. I'm in Annapolis right now and I believe I can catch a morning bus up to Frederick."

"I don't know of any connection directly from Annapolis to Frederick."

"Then I may have to rent a car. I'll manage somehow."

"Good luck," he said "I'll see you tomorrow."

Mae hung up the phone and returned to her drink and some cautious planning. She had to be careful—her funds were limited. Room and food, enough to last for another two weeks. She had certainly not budgeted for a car rental. Mae's calculating mind tripped over another possibility. Cliff Mercer. *I know he has the hots for me, but why in the world would the poor schmuck want to take me to Frederick and back?* Mae drained her glass, stood up, and walked over to the full-length mirror on the bathroom door. Pirouetting on one foot, she checked out the full package, then opened the top two buttons on her blouse and cupped her hands under each breast to exhibit more of her cleavage. *I've done this kind of thing before*, she thought. *I can do it again. He's not bad looking, and the reward, Aunt Irma's fortune, will be well worth it. Actually, he*

125

might even be fun.

Mae retrieved Cliff Mercer's business card from her purse and punched in his office number.

"Hi, there, Cliff," she said in her sweetest and sexiest rehearsed voice.

"Who is this?"

"Not even one full day and you've already forgotten little ole me?"

"Sue, baby," he drawled. "I was hoping you'd call me. Would you like to have dinner? I can pick you up at the hotel at six-thirty or seven or any time you say."

"You were an absolute sweetheart to drive me here from the airport," Mae oozed. "You deserve a big hug." She blew a kiss and a few deep breaths into the mouthpiece for effect. Did you get that?"

"I sure did, baby. I sure did. Now you've got my full attention. I'm all raring to go."

"Slow down, big man, how does seven sound?"

"I'll be there," he assured her. "What's your room number?"

"Three-oh-nine."

"See you then," he said. "I can hardly wait."

Mae set the receiver down and smiled. Her plan had started to gel. *I've got him panting and we're not even face to face. Time to shower.* She stripped and tossed her clothes onto the bed. The nude temptress in the mirror winked back at her on the way to the bathroom.

* * * *

At five minutes to seven Mae, dressed in the same above-the-knees black sheath she wore to the funeral, answered the knock on the door. She greeted him with a surprise tiptoe kiss on the cheek and a warm breath directed at his right ear. Before he had a chance to react, she grabbed her purse, stepped into the hall, and pulled the door closed behind her.

A pleasurable shudder raced through Cliff's body. *I didn't realize this dame was so hot for me. Lucky me. This is going to be some night.* Cliff's thoughts began entertaining wild visions as they silently rode the elevator and walked out to the truck. He had hardly pulled away from the curb when he sensed her pressing close to him, her left knee touching, then rubbing his right leg. That leg nervously manipulated the accelerator pedal. "Hey, babe, how about we save the good stuff for later. I wanna get us there in one piece," he said, trying to keep his voice light.

"Okay, sweetie pie," she purred.

He chose an expensive seafood restaurant on the South River and ordered a fine Merlot. Going all out as they sipped, he ordered cream of crab soup, shrimp scampi, and a heaping plate of mussels. Each course spawned more conversation until the two comfortably finished off the bottle of wine, chatting and flirting. A string trio, playing hum-along popular music, became an added catalyst. She seemed to be so interested in what he had to say that he rambled on about his business and his basketball aspirations while in high school. He never learned much about the woman he'd been calling Sue.

"I have a confession to make," she said. "Sue is my middle name. Most of my good friends call me Mae."

Not wanting to queer the evening's mood, Cliff simply shrugged and said, "I suppose you had your reasons. It's actually the pretty woman before me that I'm growing so fond of. Her name—Sue or Mae—doesn't matter all that much. I really like you both." He grinned.

When Cliff suggested a second bottle, Mae shook her head. "I've got just the right amount of glow now. I'm ready for anything."

Snuggling close in the truck, they sang some of the familiar songs they'd heard earlier. It didn't matter that most of their singing happily drifted off-key. Periodically, Mae kissed him on the neck and ear, re-stoking the fire she'd already kindled. Her preparation and his response caused a stirring reverberation in her as well. And

127

at 10:30 the evening still looked promising.

Shutting her hotel room door behind her, the two rushed together and grappled with their clothing and with each other—pulling and tearing and tossing and touching and feeling until they finally enjoined in the king-sized bed. Both wound up exhaustively satisfied. Tender cuddling and mindless chatter followed, and somewhere around two in the morning, Mae sprang her plea for a free ride to Frederick on a vulnerable Cliff.

"If we break the will and win the case, I'll be moving to Annapolis," she added. "We can be together as much as we like."

Cliff didn't flinch. He wanted to spend more time with Mae. *She is one hot babe. Being your own boss ain't half bad in a situation like this*, he thought. *I'll take the day off and have another bonus night like this one.* "Sure, Mae, I can handle that. Don't worry, we'll go to Frederick together."

The next morning when the alarm went off at 6:30, Mae found herself captive—a long, hairy arm draped over her hip from the rear. She quickly lifted it off so she could reach out and silence the alarm. She felt Cliff's muscled arm pull her back down and roll her over to face him. And that began a passionate second act. When they finally parted, the two lay motionless, breathing hard for several minutes, until Mae tossed back the blankets and bounded out of bed. Collecting the clothes strewn about on the carpet from the night before, she deposited them on the recliner and carried a fresh set of undies from her suitcase to the bathroom, where she showered and dressed in a gray business suit.

After Cliff finished freshening up, he bought Mae breakfast downstairs in the dining room. Retrieving his truck from the public garage a block away, he drove them out to the highway leading west to Frederick. She sat close and let him rest his free hand high on her thigh for most of the trip. They arrived at the law offices of Thomas and Cassidy a half-hour early, and he chose to wait in the reception room with her.

"Ms. Winnen?" asked the twenty-something brunette behind the desk. "May I get you coffee, tea, or water?"

Mae shook her head and Cliff declined with a thank you as they hung their coats on the tree next to the door.

"Shall I inform Mr. Thomas there will be two of you?"

"No, just myself," Mae answered quickly before Cliff had any nosy ideas.

At 10:45 the inner sanctum opened and a middle-aged couple left the office. When Mae glanced up she saw a tall, distinguished man with glasses and a mustache. The brown tweed suit appeared expensive, yet well worn. She watched him take note of her young man, then turned his attention to her.

"Ms. Winnen, I'm Elroy Thomas. It's a pleasure to meet you," he said. He closed the door and directed her to a chair in front of the desk. "Ms. Winnen, I spoke with your employer, the attorney Ray Brighton, last night, and he brought me up to date on what you're attempting to do. He explained how he executed an injunction against executing your Aunt Irma's Last Will and Testament. In general, there are only so many ways you can challenge the validity of any will. Obviously, your aunt was of legal age. Then there are these questions. Did she have the mental capacity to make a will? Did she have a complete understanding of her net worth and heirs-at-law, that is, whom she wanted to inherit? Or was there some mistake committed in the signing or witnessing of the will? Do you understand what I'm saying?"

"Yes, Mr. Thomas."

"As I understand it, there's a named executor or personal representative, a Mr. Joel Wise. Are you named as an heir-at-law in the will?" Elroy placed both hands on the desk and rolled his armchair backward several inches.

"Yes," she answered. "Aunt Irma left me an antique vase supposedly worth $6,500 and $1 in cash, according to Mr. Wise."

"Did he provide you with a copy of the will, by any chance?"

"No, he only had me read the part pertaining to me," she admitted. "Mr. Wise said he was protecting the other heirs. He also said that the entire will would be available at the probate hearing.

He's planning to get the injunction lifted then."

"Probate hearing?" Elroy Thomas's sandy eyebrows, matching his carefully combed hair, shot north in surprise. "And just when is that?"

"Mr. Wise said it was scheduled for ten o'clock on February 7th. It's the Anne Arundel probate court hearing room."

"I know it well," Mr. Thomas said, making a notation in his date book. "I see. And you're asking me to represent you at this hearing?"

"That's right."

"You've given me very little to go on, Ms. Winnen. I don't have a copy of the will to work with, so I can't promise you any degree of success. What else can you tell me? I understand you have some paralegal training, so you must have some idea on how to attack the validity of this will."

"Well, first of all, I'm Aunt Irma's only living relative. I have a copy of a prior will, where she left everything to my stepmother, Agnes Winnen. I have my stepmother's will, leaving everything to me as her only living relative as well. The woman Aunt Irma left the bulk of the estate to is her tenant—a Ms. Ivy Cohen, someone she's known for less than two years. I think she coerced my aunt into changing her will."

"Do you have proof of this?" Elroy leaned forward, again in surprise.

"No, not really," she confessed. "But how else could it have happened?"

"We'll see. As I said before, Ms. Winnen, I can't promise anything. But I can at least examine the Last Will and Testament at the hearing, where it will become a public document. I warn you now that an appeal in formal probate court may be necessary."

"Then you'll represent me at the hearing?"

"Yes," he replied. "Normally, I'd ask for a retainer of $2,000 in cases like this and billable hours at $140. Double the retainer and fee if we go to formal court. Since you're employed by my colleague in Albany, you can pay as we go at $75 an hour. However, it's full fee and retainer if we go to an appeal. Do you understand?"

"Yes, Mr. Thomas, I do," she replied. "What do I owe for today? I cashed a $500 savings bond, so I'm willing to pay my way."

"That won't be necessary. My first consultation is always free." Elroy stood and held out his hand. "Goodbye for now."

Mae accepted his hand and returned to the waiting room, where she found Cliff with his nose in *Sports Illustrated*.

"The wise person will always take care not
to overindulge his thirst for wine. It will
save him from disgrace and misfortune."
Menoras, p. 144

Chapter 18
Something's Missing
Friday, January 26th

In the silence of early morning, around 5:30, gangly Illya Petrovich awoke and began rattling around in the storeroom behind the Nabakov restoration shop. The fluorescent ceiling light cast a poisonous glow as he fumbled through every barrel, crate, and shelf in his frantic search. Rivulets of sweat caked in his armpits. He was looking for something important. But what? Illya had come home drunk about midnight and fallen asleep on a pile of packing straw. His mind refused to cooperate. He could hardy remember the pub where he'd downed scotch with beer chasers to celebrate what he had done. He couldn't even remember the actual deed that prompted the celebration. He hoped it was something that would make Boris proud of him.

Illya flopped down on a flimsy crate to rest, feeling the gross effects of his worst hangover ever. This simple-minded shipping clerk, willing gofer, and all-around handyman couldn't say which was worse: the knotting nausea or the timpani drums pounding inside his head. Suddenly, he heard a cracking sound, then another as the rickety empty crate collapsed under him, dislodging a tall stack of crates loaded with antiques and supplies. The top crate struck a glancing blow to his temple, knocking him unconscious; the rest of the stack tumbled on top of his helpless body.

Boris Nabakov entered his shop at nine and hung his pea coat and Persian lamb ambassador's hat on the clothes tree. He halted in place, thinking he'd heard a noise coming from the storeroom. Hearing nothing more, he sat down at his desk. Boris removed a key ring from his belt and selected the smallest key for the top right-hand drawer. He heard the sound again, but it still didn't strike a strong enough chord to pay attention.

Boris unlocked the drawer and extracted his day book and checkbook. Normally, he'd pay no attention to the vinyl case he always kept safely hidden in the back of the drawer. But it had slid forward. When he started to push the hinged case back into its place, it felt almost weightless. The case should have held an unloaded Smith and Wesson revolver and a small box of .38 caliber ammunition. He set the case on his desk and snapped it open. It was entirely empty. Dismayed, determined not to panic, Boris stroked his coarse beard and groaned. *How and why would anyone take my gun? I have the only key to the desk. Of course, it is a simple lock, just ripe for picking. But it doesn't appear broken into.*

That same muffled sound again—only this time it sounded more like his own name coming from the storeroom. Leaving the open case on his desk, he strode to the storeroom door and swung it wide. Boris followed the raspy moans and saw his devoted assistant pinned to the floor under a pile of crates. Seeing that Illya couldn't move, the excruciating pain painted across his red face, Boris leaned over and whispered, "Hold on, my friend. I'll get you out of this." His own words stunned him. He had never before acknowledged that this poor creature was actually his friend.

At first Boris couldn't decide what was more important: call for an ambulance or get the crates off. He chose to rescue Illya. Dragging one crate away after another, Boris pulled his trapped assistant to a safer place in the room. Illya passed out from exhaustion and pain.

Boris's quick 911 phone call at his desk set the paramedics in motion. While he waited for them to arrive, he rushed back to Illya and tried unsuccessfully to revive him. Only when the EMTs carried him out on the gurney did his employee wake up.

"Boss, I'm sorry," Illya mumbled weakly. "Please forgive me. I did it for you and messed everything up."

"Did what?" Boris persisted. "What did you do, Illya? Why are you sorry?"

* * * *

Sales at The Olde Victorian Bookstore had kept Ivy busy all morning. She wasn't her usual cheerful self. Rivka noticed her clerk's wan, anxious face. "Maybe you should say something to her, Dan."

"Me?" he asked. "Why me?"

"Aren't you the father figure around here? She listens to you."

"Whatever happened to female camaraderie, sisterhood?" he retorted. "I thought you gals could tell each other anything."

"Ideally, yes." Rivka frowned and adjusted her glasses with their rhinestone frames—a habit when she was formulating a response. "But we're not all cut from the same cloth, obviously. Sometimes it works, sometimes it doesn't. Please, Dan."

"Okay, okay, I'll see what's going on." Dan waited until their clerk had rung up her last sale. "Ivy, you look so unhappy this morning. Is something the matter?"

"Well, yes," she replied. "But I didn't think it showed."

"Something we've done?" Dan asked.

"Oh, no," said Ivy. "You two have been absolutely wonderful to me."

"Care to talk about it?" he questioned.

Ivy sighed with relief. "Yes. I got home from a date with Mark Schwartz last night about 9:30. I waited on the porch until he drove off. I tried to turn on the hall light as soon as I got inside, but it didn't come on. I just assumed the bulb had burned out, but when I tried the parlor lights, they weren't working either. The kitchen either. The fridge was off and the ice cream was melting in the freezer. I looked out the window and saw that the neighbors across the street had lights. The house was cold and seemed to be getting colder by the minute, so I took the flashlight from the hall table and headed up to my bed on the second floor. I piled on extra blankets from the closet and slept in my clothes to keep warm. Not that I slept all that much, I'm not used to that much weight on my body."

Rivka listened close by.

"And in the morning," Ivy continued, "I drank cold coffee from the day before and ate rice cakes and jam instead of toasted muffins. I apologize if I'm not up to snuff this morning."

"Nonsense!" said Rivka. "Why don't you and Dan go back to your house and see if he can find the trouble. Dan's an electrical engineer. He'll figure it out. I'll take over until you guys get back."

"It's not my house yet," declared Ivy. "Irma's niece has put an injunction on the will's execution."

"We know," said Rivka. "But didn't Joel tell you not to worry? He said he'd get the injunction lifted as soon as the probate hearing is finished."

"Yes, but—"

"Well, then, get your *tush* over there and find out what's going on."

"I'll grab my jacket and a couple of tools," said Dan. "Back in a jiff."

A ten-minute walk put them inside the Riley home. The house felt frigid. It struck him that the outside temperature had hovered around the mid-thirties during the night. Luckily. Any lower, the water pipes would have frozen, expanded, and burst, causing no end of damage. Ivy directed him to the basement door off the kitchen. He turned on his flashlight, flipped the wall switch to the ON position, and descended into the basement.

At the bottom of the basement stairs he cast the light beam on each of the four walls until he located a pair of circuit breaker boxes. Even though none of the wiggled breaker switch handles felt soft or loose to the touch, Dan reset every last one of them, including the two master switches at the top. Still no basement light. Next, he unscrewed the front panels of both boxes and applied the double probes of a neon voltage-tester to various points. "This is not good," he said. "There's no electricity entering the boxes at all." He shook his head. *They could save residents a lot of time,* he thought, *if they built neon test lamps into breaker and fuse boxes. A single popped breaker or blown fuse would immediately light up and lead anyone to that box and that particular circuit—even in the dark. No lit neons would mean no electricity entering the house.* Dan was a born problem solver, and with his sense of irony, could never quite understand why the rest of the engineering world wasn't up to his speed.

He secured the front panels to the boxes once more, climbed the stairs, and went outside to search for the electric company's usage meter. His eyes followed the wiring from the utility pole out front to the siding to where the meter should be. There was no meter. A blank plate covered the housing.

Reentering the house, Dan found Ivy dozing on the settee, curled up, small and childlike, wrapped tightly in an afghan. He decided not to disturb her until after he had telephoned the electric company to report the outage. The telephone in the hallway was dead—no dial tone. *Darn, I left my cell phone charging at the store.* He put his hand on Ivy's shoulder and gently shook her. "Ivy, do you have a cell phone?"

Her eyes fluttered open, and this time she heard him. "I don't own one."

"Well, then, there's nothing more we can do here. Let's get back to the store where you can warm up and I can call the electric and phone companies."

Ivy stood up and tossed the afghan onto the couch. They quick-stepped their way back to the bookstore. As soon as they had shed their jackets, Dan sent Ivy upstairs to sleep. He dialed the emergency number for the Baltimore Gas and Electric Company posted on their bulletin board.

"BGE? I want to report a power outage at 77 Murray Lane

in Annapolis."

"I will need your telephone number to pull up your account, sir."

"My telephone number?" Dan slid the store's phone list out of the drawer and ran his finger down to Ivy's number. "410-617-8885," he said.

"I'm sorry, sir. A termination order was posted on January 24th. That service has been disconnected as of January 25th."

"There's a tenant living in that house. You can't turn off the power! Who ordered the power turned off?"

"A Mrs. I. Riley on January 24th," replied the woman in Customer Service. "According to the note here, she was calling from the hospital. We alerted her that she would have to pay a fee to reconnect."

"That's impossible!" cried Dan. "Irma Riley couldn't have authorized this. She passed away twelve days ago, on January 14th. Can I have the power restored before we get a freeze and have all the water pipes in the house burst?"

"You'll have to pay the connection fee and two months minimum, sir."

"Okay, I'll pay for it," Dan said. "How soon will it be restored?" He heard her hitting a keyboard a number of times before he got his answer.

"We can have a truck out there late this afternoon. But first, I'll need your credit card information."

Dan gave her his own Visa card. *I'll get Ivy to reimburse me,* he thought. *Or maybe not.* He thanked the woman and hung up. Then he dialed the second number and went through a similar sequence to get the telephone reconnected. When he had finished he turned to his wife and explained what had transpired. "This is really bad, Rivvie."

"I know. I heard. It's downright scary."

"After the probate hearing," Dan said, "I'll have Ivy call and put everything in her name. I wonder who would want to disconnect those services. A prankster, maybe? Don't they know the damage they could cause?"

"It's more than a prank," Rivka said. "It's downright malicious. Do you think it might be Irma's stepniece?"

"Oh, wow! Could be, babe. We should call Joel. He'll know what to do."

"He who guards his mouth and tongue protects himself from woe."

Menoras, p. 40

Chapter 19
Investigations
The Same Day

Shap, spinning around in the swivel chair at Sully's desk, asked, "Where have you been all morning? I've been trying to get ahold of you."

"What for?" asked Sully. "And what are you doing sitting in my chair? We ain't married and we certainly ain't got any community property," he joked. "Besides, I caught another homicide case. That's where I've been."

"We're not finished with the Finestein case yet," said Shap, "so put a stopper on your sass and don't get too big for your britches, Detective."

"What else is there to do?" questioned Sully. "You're convinced that the Fraume broad did it, and you won't look elsewhere. So what's left?"

"We need to re-interview Finestein's landlady, the frump who said she saw everything from the upstairs window. That fancy defense attorney has asked some screwy questions I need to know the answers to."

"Okay, let's go," grumbled Sully, throwing on his tweed topcoat. "I'm not as convinced as you are that Fraume's all that guilty. You haven't talked to the cousin, the agent, or the competitor yet either."

Shap zipped up his fleece-lined trench coat. His Harley jacket he saved for his days off, when he tooled around town on his new motorcycle, an XL Sportster Nightster.

"Sully? Once in a blue moon you get a perfect smoking gun case, and all you want to do is look a gift horse in the mouth." Arriving at the car, he said, "You drive. I'll ride shotgun." He got in on the passenger side and slammed the door shut.

They rode silently until Sully parked the unmarked cruiser in front of the Finestein restoration shop. On the right, in the same two-story, red-brick building that held the shop, they found a door with the name B. Markus printed below it.

"It's one of those damn doorbells you can't hear, so you never know if it's working or not," Sully said after pushing it three times. He paused, then pressed again.

A second-floor window slid open, and a woman's thick voice grumbled, "Okay, okay, enough already. Who the hell's out there?"

"So the bell's working," Sully admitted with a sheepish grin.

"Police, ma'am," Shap shouted up. "We have a couple of questions to ask you. May we come up?"

"I thought I answered all your questions last time, Offi-cers."

"Detectives, ma'am. Just a few more questions," Shap yelled back.

An entry buzz ended with a loud click as Sully pushed open the door. They climbed up one flight of stairs carpeted in a faded floral pattern. Waiting in the doorway on the right was a sixtyish woman whose girth reflected her culinary skills.

"Mrs. Markus?" asked Shap.

"Call me Bella," she said. "Come in the kitchen. I've got some pots going on the stove, and they needs watching."

"Sure smells good," said Sully. "Cabbage maybe?"

"Right you are, young man. It's stuffed cabbage, tradition-al Hungarian style." She ushered them to the chairs around the

Formica table.

"Thank you, Bella," Sully began." How about you tell us exactly what you saw and heard the night your tenant got himself murdered."

"I was already at the window looking out at the traffic, just passing the time, when I heard two or three shots that appeared to be coming from downstairs."

"Do you remember what time that was?"

"Oh, yes, just before eight, maybe. I was waiting for my favorite show to come on. *Dancing with the Stars.* Wouldn't miss it for anything."

This woman's head is in the stars, Sully thought. "About the shots, Mrs. Markus. Which was it—two or three?"

"Two." Her large bosom heaved under her bibbed apron. "At least I think it was two. Anyway, it took me a minute to get the window open. Can't leave it open in this weather, you know, My heating bills'll go way up and they're too high already."

Sully waited patiently. "And then what, ma'am?"

"I leaned out to see what was happening down there. At first I couldn't see anything or anybody. It was pitch dark, of course, so I started to scream for help. Lucky for me that nice policeman came along."

"And then what?" demanded Shap with more than a touch of impatience in his voice. "Just what did you see, ma'am?"

"Somebody came running out of the shop and headed down the street and around the corner."

"Man or woman?" asked Sully.

"Uh…Woman, I think. Hard to tell."

"Tall or short?" Sully asked.

"Middle. You can't really tell the ups and downs on people from way up here."

"What was she wearing?" Shap asked.

"A dark color coat or something. I couldn't really see. That light pole across the street doesn't put much light on this side."

"Now think carefully, ma'am, before you answer the next

two questions," said Sully. "Did you see this running person between the time you heard the shots and the arrival of the policeman? Or was it afterward?"

"Oh, it was before the officer came all right." Her stocky body gave way to an involuntary twitch. "Now you're making me nervous, sir."

"Sorry, ma'am," said Sully. "Did you see anyone else go in or out of the shop during that same time period?"

"Yes, sir, a woman, and she was carrying something heavy in front of her."

"But that was before you heard those shots," said Shap. "Wasn't it, woman?"

Bella looked slowly at each of the two men before replying in a small intimidated voice, "Uh…I guess so."

"You guess so?" repeated Sully.

Bella's voice refused to cooperate as the taller man with the hawk nose and dark eyes bore into her.

"The woman means Yes," retorted Shap, with an annoyed glance at his partner. "Don't you, Bella?"

"Yeah, I'm sure," she replied in the same small voice.

"Thank you for cooperating, Bella," said Shap. "That wasn't so bad after all, was it?" He took a few steps toward the door and Sully was forced to follow.

As the detectives drove away, Sully asked, "Why did you have to bully the woman so?"

"Now you're questioning my interrogation techniques?"

"Never mind," said Sully, thinking *That good cop-bad cop routine is pretty corny—and useless.* "Forget I said anything. Where to now, chief?"

"What do you say to visiting Finestein's cousin Mendel?"

* * * *

The door jingled at Mendel's Dry Cleaning Emporium. In his traditional black suit and yarmulke, Mendel looked up from his Talmudic studies. His *peyes*, sideburns extending in long ringlets, framed his round face. He immediately recognized his brother-in-law. "Hah! Look what the devil turned up."

"And a good, good afternoon to you, you old fart. How the hell are you?" returned Shap with more than a touch of sarcasm.

"You brought along extra help so you could insult me more?" said Mendel from his chair by the window.

"This here's Detective Sullivan of Baltimore's Finest. I'm not here to hassle you. We're here on official police business, investigating Israel Finestein's death. We need to ask you some questions."

Mendel held out his two fists in front of him in a mocking gesture. "So cuff me already and drag my miserable body down to the station so you can sweat it out of me."

"Sweat what outta you, you nincompoop?"

"See?" said Mendel. "You forgot what you were going to ask me already. Do they teach that on the Force?"

"It'll take a lot more than that to get *my* goat, old man," returned Shap. "By the way, where's that bitchy wife of yours?"

"I suppose you've forgotten it's Friday, you *sheygets*. Naomi went home to cook and clean for *Shabbos*. When's the last time you sat down to a *Shabbos* dinner or went to *shul* for that matter?"

"Now who's hassling who?" asked Shap. "I came here to ask the questions."

"So ask them and stop annoying me," said Mendel.

"Did you have an argument with Izzy the last time you were in his shop?" asked Shap.

"A little disagreement maybe," Mendel replied.

"A disagreement that wound up with him throwing you out of his shop?"

"I suppose so, but not so serious as that might sound. He was always throwing me out, and we'd be friends again the next day. We were second cousins and we didn't always agree. But you I could stay angry with."

"Bullshit," said Shap. "Do you keep a gun in the shop? Or do you even own one?"

"Nope, I'm afraid of the darned things. I wouldn't keep one around. No way would I stop a burglar. Besides, he'd go broke stealing from us."

"Were you aware that Mr. Finestein was working on something of unusual value that last day?" asked Shap.

"Unusual?"

"You know. Costly—old—expensive," Shap explained.

"Sure. Izzy dealt in such things all the time. Why should that day be so unusual?"

"Did you know he was working on a very rare edition of the *Sefer Menorat ha-maor?*" Shap asked.

Mendel's portly body stiffened, alerted to his brother-in-law's proper pronunciation of the sacred book. "I suppose so."

"Did you happen to mention that to anyone else?"

Mendel hesitated. "I might have said something to Naomi in passing."

"Hah! That's as good as telling the whole world, as if you didn't know. My sister could never keep a secret, especially when we were kids over on Eastern Avenue."

"Maury Shapiro, are you accusing us of causing the murder and robbery of my cousin Izzy?"

"I didn't say that—you did." Shap retorted.

"Cut the crap, Shap. Just cut it out," said Sully. "You're bullying the man. You got what you wanted to know. Now leave him be."

Shap scowled but didn't answer. They turned to leave when Mendel remarked, "Next time, gentlemen, bring your dry cleaning. We don't do *your* kind of dirty laundry here."

Shap pivoted, and just as he let go of the door he gave his brother-in-law a middle finger.

Out on the sidewalk, Shap turned to Sully. "I'm the sergeant here, Detective. Do I have to remind you once more that this is my investigation? Besides, I like playing the bully. It's a very effective tool."

"*Yes, sir!*" Sully snapped his heels together and produced a

Boy Scout style of salute, but wondered why Mendel had called his partner Maury Shapiro. "Where to now?"

"Stop being a wise-ass, Sully. We've got an investigation to run. That rival book patcher-upper. Maybe he's got an axe to grind."

"You mean that guy with the Russian name, Boris Nabakov? He's got a shop up in Towson."

"Yeah. Get in the car and drive. As you said, I got what I wanted here."

"What's the beef with the two of you?"

"None of your damn business," snapped Shap as he slid into the passenger seat. "Now drive!"

* * * *

As they neared the address, an ambulance was just pulling away from the curb. Sully commented, "That looks like Nabakov outside. I wonder who's inside the EMT bus?"

"Doesn't matter. It's the shop owner I want to talk to. So pull over."

Sully parked the cruiser at the curb. Shap shouted ahead to the man reentering his place of business. "Hey Nabakov, wait up, police!"

"I am Boris Nabakov. Come inside. What does the Bal'mer Po-leece want with me?" He ushered them into the foyer.

"So who was in the ambulance?" asked Sully.

"My helper. My assistant. My friend, Illya Petrovich," answered Boris thoughtfully. "He came home drunk as a skunk last night and slept in the storeroom too near a pile of crates. When the poor *schlemiel* woke himself up this morning, he disturbed the pile, and the whole shooting-match came tumbling down on top of him. He got a couple broken bones and some cuts and stuff. But there's no way you came here to talk about my Illya's accident."

"A few questions on another subject, if you don't mind."

"Why should I mind? What's this about?"

"You and Israel Finestein were friends, weren't you?" asked

Shap.

"More like associates," replied Boris. "Business associates, I'd say."

"Not friends?"

"Not enemies either. We did a little business now and then. Maybe a few mistrust issues came up here and there, but nothing major."

"Got to fighting, then?" said Shap, trying to dig deeper.

"No, no, nothing like that," said Boris. "Never more than a little shouting. I kind of liked the man, but maybe it wasn't so mutual."

"What kind of business did you conduct with Finestein, anyway?"

"The man was good at his work, a perfectionist, so he was very much in demand. His work would get backed up sometimes and he'd call me. A little bookbinding, a bit of page drying, things like that. He did the same for me when I had too much. The only thing we couldn't agree on all the time was price. He liked to *hondle*, haggle some, but I didn't mind. He was usually fair with me."

"Mr. Nabakov, do you own a gun?" Shap tossed out the question like a hand grenade.

"Uh, yes. Why do you ask? Am I a suspect?" Boris, a large man with a beefy face, demanded.

"Everyone is suspect in this case," said Shap. "Finestein was shot. We would like to eliminate any guns and owners we can. May I see it?"

"I…discovered it was missing just this morning. I usually keep it in the top drawer of my desk—as a precaution against robbery, but I'm not sure I'd have the guts to use it."

"My, how convenient," said Shap. "And just this morning, too. Who had access to this desk drawer?"

Boris shrugged. "Just about anyone could come in off the street and find the gun while I'm in the storeroom or workroom. The drawer is never locked during the day—only at night—and what would be the point, if I needed it in a hurry?"

"I see. When was the last time you saw it?" asked Sully.

"I can't remember, it's been so long," said Boris. "At least a year."

"Why did you look for it today of all days?" asked Sully.

"Atta boy. Good question, Sully," interrupted Shap.

"Nothing unusual or devious, I assure you," replied Boris. "I accessed my office keys and checkbook in the same drawer this morning, like I do every morning. What happened was, when I opened the drawer the gun case slid forward, which was strange, because it's normally too heavy to do that. So I took it out of the drawer to figure out why it was lighter than normal—why it would slide forward the way it did. When I opened the case I was shocked. The gun was gone."

"What's the caliber, make, and model of your gun, Mr. Nabakov," asked Sully.

"It's a typical mail-order .38 caliber revolver. I don't know who made it or any model number. I have a permit under the cash tray in the register if you want to see it."

"Yes, sir, we do want to see it," said Sully.

Boris rang up a no-sale, lifted the tray, and pulled out the gun permit. Sully gave it the once-over, made a few notes in his spiral pad, and handed it back to Boris. "Thank you, sir."

"Anything else I can do for you, gentlemen?"

"Your helper," said Shap. "How did you say he got hurt? Was there a gun involved?"

"He broke a bone or two when some crates fell on him. And no, there was no gun involved."

"Could he have taken the gun?" asked Shap.

"It's possible, but I highly doubt it. He's extremely loyal and not very bright."

Sully handed Boris his business card and said, "If you think of anything that might help us, give me a call."

As they left the shop and returned to their car, Sully said, "A little far-fetched, but he just might be telling the truth."

"Hogwash!" exclaimed Shap. "Everybody lies. Most people

are bothered by what others think of them. Or what they need to believe about themselves. And what they fear others might misconstrue. What *does* matter is precisely what they're trying to cover up. That is, which lies are pertinent to our case."

"What about Anton Gleuck?" asked Sully. "We haven't talked to him yet."

"Haven't you had enough interrogation for one day?" replied Shap. "We'll save him for tomorrow."

> "If one steals even a pennysworth
> from another it is considered as if
> he has stolen that person's soul."
> *Menoras,* p. 115

Chapter 20
Inside and Outside the Mind
Tuesday, January 30th

Rivka bounced down the stairs in her new burgundy pants suit and white turtleneck, ready for her lunch date with Peggy Fraume. Early that morning Peggy had called, a tremor in her voice, needing to "talk." Their meeting was set for 12:30 at a restaurant an hour away, in Towson. She stopped to inform Dan of her plans.

He was studying the Sunday *New York Times* Book Review, getting ideas for their monthly display of bestsellers. He glanced up. "Hey, Rivvie, don't you look smart. Great outfit."

"Thanks," she said, sliding her arms into her quilted down jacket. "I'm taking the rest of the day off, Daniel. I'm having lunch with Peggy at Charlie's Place."

He could almost feel the frost in her tone, especially when she called him Daniel. *What've I done now?* he wondered.

Rivka didn't usually carry a grudge against her husband, certainly not more than a day. But the lunch date somehow revived her annoyance. A week ago, she'd rushed home from the Annapolis post office, bursting to tell Dan that she'd seen Anton Gleuck mailing a Priority box there, and how odd it was, considering that his office was in Towson. *This was about Izzy's murder. The man looked so guilty, he must be guilty of something. And Dan telling me to stay*

149

out of trouble like I'm five years old. Well!

Dan knew better than to argue with her when she behaved like this, so he responded with a cautious smile. "Have a nice time."

"Don't forget to feed Lord Byron."

"As soon as I get a chance," he said. "Oh, and give Peggy my regards. Love you."

She blew him a mechanical kiss and sailed out the door without another word.

* * * *

Charlie's Place was an Italian restaurant noted for its specialties, which Peggy had raved about. Rivka arrived first and chose a quiet corner booth facing the door. Peggy, looking more gaunt than usual in her all-black attire, saw her immediately. When the waitress came to take their order, Peggy selected the filet of sole sandwich, and Rivka, the salmon Florentine. Over an appetizer of bruschetta—grilled bread topped with chopped tomatoes, olive oil, and garlic—they talked about friends and family until the waitress brought their lunch.

Between bites, Rivka said, "I've been having trouble sleeping."

"How come?" asked Peggy.

"Oh, some little spat I had with Daniel over store policy." She was about to explain, but instead took a long sip of Diet Coke. *Stop, girl. Peggy doesn't need to be reminded about her Izzy's robbery and murder. She's still going through all kinds of hell over it, and those two screwy detectives aren't helping much either.* "We'll get over it. Dan and I always do."

"Sleep is the easy part for me," said Peggy. "It's the nightmares I have to contend with. Horrendous, even worse than the ones I used to have about that good-for-nothing ex-husband of mine."

"What are they about, if you don't mind my asking? Not that I'm any kind of shrink. I left my couch back at the store."

"They say there's something therapeutic in talking about

nightmares," Peggy said. "That's actually why I called you for lunch. I have two recurring regulars. The first, I believe I understand. I'm climbing stairs to the gallows. I can see the noose and the rope and the hangman with a black hood over his head. He has cutouts for the eyes. I'm on my way to be punished for a crime I didn't commit. I keep climbing and climbing those stairs, but I never get to the top. It goes on and on until I wake up. I think it must be my frustration over not being able to prove my innocence. I'm forced to sit tight while others control my destiny. That scenario makes some sense to me, but I'm having trouble explaining the other one."

"Your explanation sounds reasonable," said Rivka. "What's with the other one?"

"This one's much harder to talk about. It's a rehash of the night Izzy was murdered. I know I'll never find anyone like him again. I keep seeing him lying there in a pool of blood on the floor, reaching out to me, mumbling the *Shma* over and over. I'm standing over him holding the gun in my hands, and he's looking back at me with angry eyes. I don't know why he's angry with *me*. I didn't shoot him. It's like he wants me to see something or remember something. He finally stops mumbling, and his eyes become ice, seeing nothing. I kneel to kiss his forehead, and his yarmulke comes loose and falls to the floor. I wake up as soon as the cop grabs me."

"Then it's all over for the night? You're okay after that?" asked Rivka.

"Oh, no." Peggy's fingers toyed with her studded dog collar. "It starts all over as soon as I fall asleep again. I think I'm doomed to repeat it until I remember what Izzy expects me to remember." The tears were now streaming down her bony cheeks, leaving trails of mascara. Removing a tissue from her purse, she dabbed away at the wet streaks.

"You poor dear," consoled Rivka, then wished she hadn't said something so trite. "You not only have to deal with the reality of the whole tragedy, you've got to live the terrible nightmare reruns, too." She reached across the table and laid her hand atop

Peggy's. "Did Izzy say anything other than the *Sh'ma* prayer?"

"Some initials, a monogram on a briefcase maybe, I'm not sure. Do you think it's important?"

Rivka's coffee-brown eyes glinted with an urgency. "Yes, it could be. Do keep trying, Peggy. You might come up with something, a detail the police can use." She saw her friend's dejected look. A change of mood was in order. "And you know what else I think?" she asked in a bright voice.

"No, what?"

"I think we should order that famous amaretto cheesecake you've been telling me about." Rivka waved her hand in the direction of their waitress, who hastened over.

"Shall I bring you the dessert menu, ladies?"

"No, ma'am," said Rivka. "We already know what we want: two slices of your signature amaretto cheesecake."

"Oh, I'm so sorry, ladies," said the waitress with a forced, embarrassed smile. "Our pastry chef walked out on us on Saturday. Up and quit, he did, for no good reason. The amaretto cheesecake was *his* specialty. But we have all kinds of cakes and pies and tarts from the bakery down the street."

The two women looked at one another and broke into giggles.

* * * *

Lord Byron opened his amber eyes and lazily stretched his sleek neck and white paws in five different directions. He had no agenda besides eating and sleeping, so he followed his default script: when in doubt, *wash*. He finished his personal hygiene and looked around from his lofty perch above the poetry stacks. In the bookstore's momentary lull, a tour of the aisles seemed in order. He leapt the five feet to the floor in one graceful action and went to his litter box near the back door. Next he sought a snack from his bowl, but found it licked clean. From there he strolled in a zigzag pattern through the aisles and down the stairs until he reached the first-floor reading room. There his pink nose twitched. Sensing something freshly baked, he entered the room, bounded up onto the nearest chair, and from there landed atop the reading table. Startled by the sudden rattling of a newspaper at the far end, he hesitated and settled to a crouch.

At the opposite end of the eight-foot table sat an open tin of chocolate-chip muffins. He barely noticed the wall of newspaper being lowered flat onto the table. Although he could hardly be expected to recognize Marie Tate-Williams, he somehow knew she was a daily fixture in the reading room. She smiled broadly, acknowledging the cat's presence. Lord Byron closely watched the woman's fingers as they dipped into the tin, retrieved a muffin, and carefully broke it into quarters over a small white napkin. She slowly selected one of the quarters, popped it into her mouth, and munched. Her visitor tilted his head questioningly. Marie responded by taking a second quarter and breaking it into smaller morsels, which she laid out in a line, baiting him to come closer to her.

Lord Byron took the bait and was soon nibbling away at the first morsel, a task that took only a minute to accomplish. He eyed the second morsel and advanced to devour his next prize.

"Here kitty, nice kitty," said Marie. "So you like my muffins, do you?" Her hands reached out to him.

Lord Byron backed away a few inches, wary of the outstretched hands. Only when those hands disappeared under the table did he move on the third morsel. When he looked up at her again, one of the hands had returned, hovering over the last morsel. The cat considered his options: a quick retreat or possess another delicious bite while being petted. He chose to stay, seeing the petting as the cost of doing business. He felt her fingers behind his ears caressing gently, then he relaxed to her pleasing rub, even to the point of stretching his neck. When she rewarded him with one last bite, he showed his appreciation by licking the back of her fist with his sandpapery tongue.

Marie refolded the newspaper carefully on the creases and returned it to its rack. To Lord Byron's disappointment, she scooped up the remaining two muffin quarters and pocketed them to eat on the trip home. Purse and tin in hand, she stood to leave. But only a few steps later, her new friend landed on the floor in front of her and began to weave in and out between her feet, impeding each step she attempted. Chuckling, she reached into her pocket, broke off one more muffin morsel, and tossed it behind her. "So that's what you want, kitty," whispered Marie.

The still-hungry feline pounced on it. Marie scooted out of the reading room. She passed the cashier's counter, where Dan was ringing up sales for a line of customers, and headed for the book-store's front door. But before it closed behind Marie, Lord Byron shot outside and stopped defiantly in front of her, as if he had learned the art of hostage-taking in a previous life. She dropped another muffin morsel and chugged off toward home. Two city blocks later, Marie glanced around and noticed that her regal free-loader was still in tow a few yards back. As soon as she opened the front door to her apartment, he squeezed inside.

Setting the muffin tin down on the countertop next to her purse, Marie reached up into the cabinet and lifted out two bowls. One she filled with water and the other with Cheerios. After a few sips and indifferent nibbles, Lord Byron padded back to the door to be let out.

"There, there, kitty," cooed Marie. "You'll be staying with us now." She reached down to pet him, but he wouldn't have any part of it. He wanted out and mewed his message loud and strong.

"Who ya talking to, Ma?" The twangy voice came from another room. "And what's that strange crying sound? Are ya hurt or somethin'? It sounds awful."

"No, I'm just fine, dear. It's a cat you're hearing. She followed me home, and I'm thinking about keeping her."

A slouching form in a torn tank shirt and boxer shorts appeared in the doorway. "What the hell do ya want with a damn cat, Ma?" said Damon Williams. "Ya gotta feed 'em on one end and clean up after 'em on the other. Besides they're smelly creatures."

"That's a lie," she said. "Don't you know that cats are plumb clean? Cats are always washing theirselves. And they're good company for your mom—all day when you're out and about. See how she's taken to you, son?"

"It's a he, Ma."

Lord Byron had already decided to investigate Damon and began nuzzling around the young man's ankles. Damon, in turn, placed a toe under the royal belly, jerking him up to one side and out of his way. That was all the message that Lord Byron needed. This was no place for him. He headed for the apartment door again and scratched at it with a fervor.

Neither Marie nor Damon paid him any attention.

"A person should not let himself be overwhelmed by desires that are inspired by his evil inclination.... The evil inclination is his mortal enemy."

Menoras, p. 101

Chapter 21
At Home and Away
Tuesday, January 30th

Anton Gleuck sat uneasily at his glass-topped desk looking over the latest monthly statement of his depleted investment portfolio. The broker's recommendations had brought him nothing but disappointment. Anton was broke, but he couldn't apply for a new loan; it would only dig him a deeper hole of debt. To make matters worse, the curent usurer's loan came due last Wednesday, and all he could pay was the interest on the loan, leaving him with next to no money to live on.

But the loan usurers were not to be denied. Early this morning, two professional thugs rang the doorbell, forced their way past him into his living room, and worked him over thoroughly and expertly. Though his rib cage felt like tenderized meat, Anton didn't think any bones were broken. Unsure exactly where his kidneys were beforehand, he knew now. They had been the main target. The pain was so excruciating, he couldn't even lean forward, and he dreaded the thought of ever standing up on his two feet again. Just when he thought his life couldn't sink any lower, the doorbell rang a second time.

They've come back for me, Anton thought. *I won't answer it.* But then he considered the consequences of ignoring them. Fighting through the pain, he moaned and groaned and lifted his miserable body out of the chair and shuffled to the front door. A tortured smile emerged when he perceived the two detectives on the front stoop. *Gawd, what do these clowns want with me now? And what if the goons see the cops coming in here?* Anton peered up and down the street. No sign of the thugs. Shap followed his gaze, trying to learn what Anton was searching for.

The junior detective's distaste for the sergeant's interview tactics prompted Shap to allow Sully to take the lead. "I know you're a busy man, Mr. Gleuck. Just a few more questions and we'll be out of your hair."

"Of course," said Anton. "Come in and have a seat." The last thing he wanted was for them to sit down and get comfortable, but he was too sore to stand up much longer.

"Are you all right, Mr. Gleuck?" asked Sully, seeing Anton wince with pain as he lowered himself into an armchair.

"I'll be fine," Anton lied. "I tripped and fell coming down the stairs trying to answer the doorbell. It's just a few bruised ribs." *Damn, these guys are nosy. They don't miss a trick.*

"Sorry," said Sully, taking in the man's half-untucked, rumpled white shirt. "We don't mean to cause you any unnecessary discomfort." His blue eyes and crew cut gave him a youthful, deferential look.

"No, it wasn't you," assured Anton. "It happened maybe fifteen minutes ago. When you rang I was looking up and down the street to see who was coming."

"Okay. We won't take long," said Sully, sitting down on one end of the sofa. "We're still investigating the robbery and murder of Israel Finestein."

"But I thought I answered all your questions two or three weeks ago," Anton protested.

"Ah," said Sully. "But some new information has arisen to put you back in the spotlight."

"What information is that?" Tiny beads of sweat popped out on Anton's pink scalp beneath his thinning hair.

"Our forensic accountants ran a financial scan of your accounts and turned up some rather unexpected results."

"You have no right to invade my private affairs," Anton said. His shirt, unbuttoned at the neck, revealed his Adam's apple throbbing as he swallowed, trying hard to suppress his tension.

"Mr. Gleuck, we have every right to probe the finances of suspects in a murder investigation."

"So now I'm a suspect?"

"Yes," Sully said. "Anyone with knowledge of rare books and manuscripts and their value qualifies as a suspect. And now we've learned that you also had a motive. We subpoenaed your broker and found out the declining state of your investments. Word on the street says that you're into the local loan sharks as well."

"Lots of people need money and get loans," Anton protested. "That doesn't make them thieves and murderers. Besides, I had a good-sized commission riding on this sale, a legitimate one, too."

Shap broke in. He had chosen to remain standing and now loomed over Anton with large hands on his hips. "But you have to admit it's one hell of a motive for robbery and murder. By the way, do you own a gun?"

"Uh…I'm not sure."

"Not sure? Why is that?" Shap replied. "Why did you hesitate in answering such a simple question?"

"I don't have one here in the house or in my office anymore. My ex-wife demanded it as part of our property agreement when she left me. She said living alone she'd have more use for it than I would. I haven't seen it since the divorce three years ago. She took the gun—and the permit along with it. I wanted to answer your question with a simple no, but then I remembered that the gun permit might still be in my name. I haven't spoken with Gracie in over two years."

"Maybe you should contact her," Shap said, "and get the piece properly transferred to her name. And by the way, did you have a buyer or buyers in mind for these books?

"Yes, several, in fact."

"Might we have the names and addresses of those prospective buyers?" asked Shap.

"I'm sorry, gentlemen," replied Anton. "That is protected information. Secrets of the trade, you know. It is essential that we have mutual trust in order to conduct international business. Even though these people purport to be honest, they wish to remain anonymous."

"This is a murder investigation," Shap announced, his baritone voice jagged around the edges. "I can subpoena that information from you—in fact, *all* of your business records."

"If you must, but you'll be putting me totally out of business. There have been no actual transactions, so how can their names and addresses be that important? How can they help you, anyway?"

"We'll see about that, Mr. Gleuck," grumbled Shap. "How do we know there've been no transactions? All we have is your word for it. We've already established motive and means. That simply leaves opportunity and we can tie this up right now. Where were you on the night of the murder: Monday, January 8th?"

"So I'm back to being a suspect again. Let's see," Anton said. He rose slowly, and aching with every step, shuffled into a small room across from the living room that served as his home office. The detectives followed close behind, noting that the blinds were drawn even in the morning sunlight. They saw no amenities here, just a few file cabinets and disorganized bookcases on a threadbare oriental rug. Anton sat down in his high-backed leather chair and flipped through the day book on the desk, stopping on a specific page. "Like most nights, I was here conducting business."

"How does a brief look in your day book tell you all that?" asked Sully.

"Well, Detective, there's this page with a memo documenting the three business calls I made that evening," Anton replied.

"Like I said before, I can subpoena your records and that includes your phone records, too," said Shap."

"So be it, Sergeant, but why are you pushing me so hard?"

"Mr Gleuck, it seems to me that the full going price of these books would be a whole lot more attractive than a mere piddling commission. Don't you think so, Sully?"

"I think we got what we came for," replied his embarrassed partner.

"Almost," said Shap as the detectives headed for the front door. "But we'll be in touch. I still think you're our man, Gleuck. So don't go getting any ideas about leaving town."

Anton controlled his impulse to slam the door behind them and leaned his back against it for several minutes. A new thought crossed his mind. He trudged back into the office and pulled open a file drawer. Flipping through a row of folders, he stopped at one marked "Passport." It wasn't there. He checked the folder in front of it and then the one behind it—the same result. He felt a fresh rush of panic, along with a surge of acid upheaval in his throat and a flash of stomach cramps. He tuned into another brainwave and pulled out the large bottom drawer of his desk. There, tucked haphazardly between his bank statements, lay the misplaced passport. He picked it up and kissed it on the Great Seal. But the acid, the cramps, and the agonizing kidney punches would not go away.

* * * *

As Rivka walked into the bookstore at 4:15 that afternoon, she broke into a huge smile, showing perfect white teeth. Perfect looking, but hiding a history of expensive implants, root canals, and crowns. Dan used to joke that he should have checked her teeth before they married. She came around the counter to where he was seated and nuzzled the back of his scruffy neck with a kiss. "I've decided to forgive you," she said.

"Forgive me? For what? What did I do now?"

"Oh, never mind," she said. "Maybe I'm just grateful for the afternoon off."

"So you had a good time."

"Yeah! Oh, did you remember to feed Lord Byron like I told you?"

"Oops! Nope. I got so busy at the register that I forgot," he confessed.

"And my dear husband, where is his royal highness that he hasn't come calling for his kitty grub before this?"

"How the hell should I know?" replied Dan. "I haven't seen his royal butt all day."

"Where's Ivy, or did you lose her as well?"

"I'm over here," yelled Ivy, "at the end of the English lit aisle."

"Ivy, have you seen Lord Byron lately?" Rivka yelled back.

"Not since noon," she answered. "He was in the first-floor reading room with the Tate-Williams woman. Actually, he was sitting on the table facing her, only a couple feet away. I thought that was kind of strange, though, since he usually keeps clear of our customers."

"I agree," said Rivka.

"I can see his basket from here, and he's not at home," Ivy said. "But he can come and go into the backyard through his swinging cat door. Obviously you know that. Maybe he's out there taunting the neighbor's dog. Give me a minute. I'll take a look."

"Go ahead," said Rivka. "But I don't think so. We'd be hearing that dumb mutt barking his fool head off. Dan, I think we should make an organized search throughout the store. You take the upper two floors and I'll take these two. He may be caught up in something."

"Right." Dan started up the stairs.

The back door slammed and Ivy approached, shaking her head. "No sign of him out there and he's never jumped the fence before. Tell you what, Rivka. I'll take the rear of the store, and you take the front and we'll walk the ends of the aisles till we find him."

When the search on all four levels proved fruitless, the three met on the main floor at the checkout counter. "Let's face it," said Dan. "Lord Byron is out and about. Maybe there's a lady cat involved. You know, *cherchez la femme*, and all that talk about

Byron's lover going a-roving."

"Daniel, you seem to forget, Lord Byron's been neutered."

"Well, Rivvie, that doesn't mean he can't go out a-looking."

"I suppose he could have snuck out the front door with some customer," replied Rivka. "But he's never done that before in all the time we've owned this place. He's an indoor-bookstore cat."

"Hey, you two," Ivy called from the adjacent reading room. "I think I've found something."

"What's that?" asked Dan.

"There are crumbs on the main table and more on the floor," replied Ivy. "Looks like cake or cookies and they smell sort of sweet."

"So someone was eating in here," said Rivka. "It's not the first time a reader smuggled food into the reading room."

Dan reappeared. "Ivy, didn't you say that Lord Byron was visiting the Tate-Williams lady around noon today? I wonder... And crumbs, too. Baiting? No, it's too preposterous."

"That's what I saw," she said, "but he *was* keeping a safe distance from her. I can't imagine him taking off after her."

"I can't either," said Dan. "But the furry guy does like his sweets. How do we go about approaching her? We can't just accuse the woman. It might insult her, and she could sue us."

Rivka couldn't resist. "I think that's a perfect job for you, dear. You're always saying how much more diplomatic you are than I am."

"Now wait one cotton-pickin' minute, my love, you're not foisting this one off on me so easily."

"Of course I am. Now why don't the two of us make a tour of the neighborhood? I'm worried."

* * * *

A few blocks away, the furry one was lying low under one of Mrs. Tate-Williams's beds. His encounter with Damon's right foot hours earlier did more damage to his pride than to his body, but he wasn't willing to risk even that at this point. He was jarred

162

from his current complacency by the sudden sounds of bedsprings stretching. Two stockinged feet momentarily appeared at the side of the bed and disappeared just as quickly. The springs made more noise, the feet walked away, then the light flicked off.

Under cover of darkness, Lord Byron left the safety of the bedroom to explore the rest of the apartment. Escape was foremost in his mind. He padded to the front hall, where he'd originally entered, but the door was closed. A few leaps up at the knob proved hopeless. Next he made the rounds of the living room windows and found those shut tight. The same was true of the bathroom window. But just outside the bathroom he found another door, not quite shut, and squeezed through. Inside, café curtains were fluttering in front of an open window. A double leap from floor-to-chair-to-sill put him next to a fitted nylon wire screen. A pounding paw did little damage, but dragging his claws left longish holes and produced a strange *zezzing* sound.

The lord was so busy at work that he didn't notice an unpleasant visitor approaching. The scraping sounds of the cat's claws had awakened Damon.

Suddenly, Lord Byron felt two strong hands squeeze around his midsection. In one massive squirm he drew his claws the length of Damon's bare arm. Damon let go. The cat jumped to the floor. The same hands followed him around the room. When they came dangerously close, he sank his royal teeth into his captor's right thumb and clamped down on it. Damon screamed. Trying desperately to get free, he flung the cat toward the window with such force that Lord Byron let go of Damon's thumb and broke through the already weakened screening—out into the air, one story above the ground. True to form, Lord Byron landed on all fours and immediately shot out of sight. A block away he stopped and licked his tender paws.

Damon's screams, followed by bellowing curses, pierced the night. Lights came on in neighboring apartments on two floors. He groaned. How was he going to explain that he'd been attacked by a little kitty?

> "…A person of intelligence should look about him and realize that the frenzied pursuits of this world are all emptiness and folly."
> *Menoras*, p. 215

Chapter 22
All the Way Home
Wednesday, January 31st

Sleek, black, and camouflaged in the 3 a.m. darkness, Lord Byron worked his way home. He arrived at the backyard behind the bookstore using his innate global positioning system, then bounded over the rear fence and into the back hall via his trusty cat door. After a short stop for water and a few bites of Kitty-Kool-Kan, he padded to the poetry aisle. Leaping to the top of his personal stack, he climbed into his basket and nestled deep into the tartan plaid cushion. The *laird* quickly fell into an exhausted sleep that would last unnoticed until late that anxious morning.

* * * *

When the Shermans came downstairs after breakfast, they checked the two cat bowls by the rear door and saw no discernable change in content. The assumption was that the Lord High Kitty had *not* returned, so they went about opening up for business.

"I don't think the police would appreciate our trying to file a Missing Cat report," Dan muttered. Ivy entered, toting the bundle of the day's morning papers. She didn't have to ask. A simple shake of Rivka's head told her no. Ivy took the cash register, Dan unpacked a shipment of new books, and Rivka recorded their arrival. They all worked in fretful silence.

Around 10:30 Marie Tate-Williams slipped in the front door, trying to hide herself behind an arriving customer, and headed straight for the main-floor reading room. But she spotted the Shermans during their unpacking. She jerked to a stop, pivoted in her shabby sneakers, and attempted to leave without being seen.

"Mrs. Tate-Williams," Dan called after her. "Wait! May I have a word with you?"

Marie slowly turned back. "I guess so. What about?"

"Please have a seat over here, ma'am." Dan indicated the chair at the end of the table where they had discovered the crumbs. "May I call you Marie?"

"Sure, Mr. Dan, and Hi, Miz Rivka." Marie grabbed the table edge for balance while she settled uneasily into the chair. When she lifted her chapped hands, the left one began to twitch uncontrollably, so she clamped them together on the table and interlocked her fingers.

"There's nothing to be nervous about, Marie," Dan said, hoping to calm her. "Our clerk, Ivy, noticed you in here reading newspapers yesterday. Reading papers is fine with us, Marie, as long as you don't damage their salability."

Rivka couldn't resist. "I know things can be tight at home, but couldn't you just *buy* a paper *once* in awhile?"

"Rivkaaa! Not now!" murmured Dan. He tried to recapture his deferential approach. "However, Marie, we did find some cookie crumbs on the table, and a trail of crumbs across the floor."

She squirmed inside her too-large, second-hand coat. "I'm so sorry, Mr. Dan. You too, Miz. I didn't mean to soil the paper with my muffin crumbs. I'll pay for it. I know I shouldn't bring food into the store and I'll not do it again. I do appreciate your lettin' me read the paper here. I don't have no television and I can't afford no newspaper subscription."

"That's okay, Marie," said Dan. "Forget the ninety-five cents for the paper. That won't be a problem. But the trail of muffin crumbs led out of this room all the way to the street. How do you explain that?"

"Gee, I don't know, Mr. Dan. Maybe I dropped some in my lap an' it spread out when I left. It could've happened that way, couldn't it?"

"Let me remind you that Ivy saw you in here feeding our night-watch cat yesterday. What can you tell us about that?" Dan stretched the truth in telling her that Ivy actually saw him being fed. All Ivy really saw was the two of them in the same room.

Marie laid her head down between her hands. Wisps of grimy gray hair straggled out from her poorly secured bun. Her hefty body began to shake and heave and then she began to sob.

Rivka came close and put her arm around Marie's shoulders. "There, there, Marie. And where is Lord Byron now, my dear?"

"Lord Byron?" asked Marie, her voice quivering.

"The cat, Marie. Our cat," an impatient Dan clarified.

"I don't know," she sniffed. "My son, Damon, told me the cat bit him on the thumb and scratched his arm before jumping out the window. He escaped sometime in the late night."

Dan loomed over her and glared. "What are you saying, Marie? Lord Byron was in *your house*? You took him *home*?"

Barely above a whisper, Marie confessed. "I didn't exactly pick him up or anything, but I did let him follow me in the door and up the stairs, and he just came inside my apartment. I guess he wanted more of my chocolate-chip muffins."

"Is your son okay?" asked Rivka, secretly proud of their pet's courage, but also not looking forward to a hassle at an emergency room. "Did he require medical attention?"

"Oh, no, he's good," Marie replied. "I gave him some antibiotic salve and bandages."

"Did your son mistreat *him* in any way?" pressed Rivka.

"Damon, he don't take no likin' to cats, but he wouldn't harm them none. Just gave it a little kick. Are you gonna put me in jail or sue me? I surely ain't got nuthin' to sue for."

"We haven't made up our minds what to do with you yet," replied Dan, pulling up a chair.

166

Rivka had had enough of this kindness business. She went on the attack. "Marie, you had no right to feed him anything. Apparently you don't know that cats can die from eating chocolate."

The woman visibly flinched.

Rivka enjoyed the reaction. "Yes, Marie, you could have killed him. Besides, you could get your own pet cat from the Humane Society." *Heaven help any pet Marie owns,* she thought.

"I didn't know. I didn't think, Miz Rivka. He's a cute little guy. I jes did it. I'm sorry."

Just then, Lord Byron poked his head into the reading room. He stood inside the door for a moment, then bounded up on the table to announce his presence. When he recognized Marie he snarled, spun away, and leapt down into Dan's lap.

"Kitty, you've come home!" Rivka cried. She rushed over, bent down, and smothered the cat with a kiss on the top of his head.

Marie sat quietly, relieved, but unsure of her current status with the Shermans. Would they prosecute her, banish her from the bookstore, or merely chew her out and let her go? In any case, she found herself in quite a hairy situation. She allowed the Shermans adequate time to relish the return of Lord Byron before she decided to make her move. She got up slowly and sidestepped around the opposite end of the table.

"Whoa, there, Marie," said Dan. "Where do you think you're going? Sit! You've got some explaining to do before you leave here. You're a catnipper, or is that a catnapper? Anyway, you kidnapped our cat, and that's not right." Marie returned to her chair and new tears rolled down her withering cheeks in tiny rivulets. She looked from Dan to Rivka and back again, trying to find the more sympathetic of the two. "I'm so very sorry, Mr. Dan. With Damon gone most days I gets awful lonely, and when the cat took a liking to me, I thought we were a good match. I didn't mean him no harm."

"What about the harm you did to us, Marie?" said Dan. "You stole from us. Worse than that, you stole a living thing, not

167

just a possession—someone we love and who loves us. Isn't that harm? Doesn't that matter? Isn't that worth some jail time?"

"Oh, gawd," she cried, "What are you going to do with me? I said I'm sorry and I'll never do anything like this again. Cross my heart and hope to die if I do."

"I'll tell you what, Marie," said Dan. "You can go home now, and my missus and I will think this over and let you know what we plan to do."

Marie stood up once more, skirted the table, and fled the room as though it were on fire. In the next minute they heard the doorbell jingle and the heavy wood door shut.

"What do you think, Rivvie? Was that enough of a scolding? Think she'll pull a stunt like that again?"

"I doubt it. You had her worried sick, Dan. I think she gave in to a spur-of-the-moment temptation. Lord Byron doesn't look any the worse for his adventure, so we'll say no more about this to Marie if and when she ever comes back to the store. Which I hope she doesn't."

Dan nodded and gently stroked their watch-cat, already deep into his follow-up nap.

* * * *

Mae Winnen answered a knock on her door at the Maryland Inn. She welcomed Cliff with a kiss on his ruddy cheek, another on his neck, and the third on his earlobe. Laying her head on his shoulder, the temptress took him by the arm and led him to the love seat. "Where have you been all day, big boy?"

"Hey, Ms. Leisure, I've got a business to run. As it is, I'm getting to work late every day with this arrangement." He took off his Ravens jacket and threw it on the bed. We've got to make some adjustments here or I'm gonna go broke."

"So am I, Cliff," said Mae. "My hotel bill and meals are eating up all my ready cash. I've got another week to go just to get to the hearing and I'm probably gonna hafta sell my place up in Albany to pay for that lawyer feller over in Frederick. I don't know what to do." She gave him a lingering kiss on the mouth.

Cliff reacted with a shiver and then thought for a moment or two. *She's the best lay I've ever had.* Aloud he said, "We're having a good time together and we seem to be compatible. Maybe I have the solution for both our problems." He took her hand in his. "I've got this three-bedroom house in Davidsonville. It's a community about fifteen miles out of town. Pretty upscale, actually. I built the house there on spec. It still needs work, but I'm living in it myself until it's sold. We could pack you up and move you in with me first thing in the morning. It's not a proposal of marriage, mind you, at least not now, but who knows what the future will bring? It would definitely stop your cash drain, and if I don't have to keep coming here every night, I might actually get to work on time every day. What do you think of that?"

He's one hot lover and he knows how to treat a woman, she thought. "What about my meals?" she asked. "You said it's out in the country."

"We could play house for as long as we both agree. You could cook for us. I'd throw in the groceries and any extras. That way you might want to stick around well after the hearing, at least until the house is ready to sell. How about it?"

"Sure, angel, I'm game."

"Wonderful, baby!" He burrowed his unshaven face into her neck while his fingers flew to the buttons on her blouse.

"Whoa, ease up, Cliff. Let's get a bite to eat first. I'm starving."

He ignored her and managed to open the top button. Pressing his lips against her throat, he moaned.

Her hands captured his prickly face. "*Grrrowl*, tiger, you need to get rid of that roughage."

"Okay, okay, I get the message, sweetie."

Cliff crossed the room to the overnight bag he'd left there over the weekend, pulled out a toiletries kit, and disappeared into the bathroom. She could hear the buzz of the razor through the closed door. When he came out, he found Mae dressed in coat, hat, and gloves ready for the outdoors.

"Yum, you smell good," she said, taking a whiff of his after-shave. "And smooth as a baby's heinie. Why don't we reward you and go down the street to Middleton's. You liked the steak you had there on Sunday."

He shrugged. "Okay, if you insist." He grabbed his jacket and they stepped out into the hall.

Mae turned slightly to hide her triumphant smirk.

> "…someone who withholds the wages he owes to his hireling…is considered a robber…considered by Scripture to have stolen the soul of the robbed."
> *Menoras*, p. 126

Chapter 23
Playing or Keeping House?
The Same Day

The bookstore closing time rapidly approached. Ivy expected Mark Schwartz, her frequent beau, to come through the door any minute. She'd gone up to the Shermans' apartment to change clothes and emerged downstairs wearing a pink blouse, gray skirt, and knee-high suede boots. Small-boned, with large dark eyes and thick black hair framing her face, she moved like an exotic bird, fluttering about to help a teenage customer find *Eye of the Tiger* by Wilbur Smith. When Mark came through the door, he greeted the Shermans, who were at the register cashing out the day's receipts.

"So where are you lovebirds off to tonight?" asked Dan in a jovial mood.

"Dear!" scolded Rivka. "Don't embarrass Mark."

"What did I say?" Dan held his hands out, palms up.

"Your nose is always in someone else's business."

Dan laughed. "So? It's a nice Jewish nose. Besides, Rivvie, who do you think taught me that technique? You've honed it to a fine art."

Rivka pursed her full lips in a pout. "Guilty as charged, but don't remind me."

"Oh, that's okay, Mrs. Sherman," said Mark, with an easy

171

smile showing good white teeth. "My family grills me all the time about my social life. It goes with having lots of cousins." He was too polite to reveal that prying made up a good deal of his parents' conversations.

Rivka couldn't let the subject drop. "But wasn't Dan being a bit presumptuous?"

"Maybe not," said Mark.

"Why? Oh, you sly one," Rivka said. "Have you two actually talked about marriage—already?"

"Just small talk so far," replied Mark. "I'm hoping for more, but I still have to finish my doctorate at Johns Hopkins, and Ivy is still all tied up in those legal matters."

Rivka tried not to stare. She liked Mark's strong, intelligent face, his sincerity and lack of airs. *And he'll make a good living. Ivy could do worse.*

Their clerk had found the novel for their last customer of the day. The moment he was gone, Ivy rushed into her date's embrace.

"Sorry for jumping to conclusions, Mark," said Dan. "So you're not eloping tonight. All I meant to find out is where you were dining."

"I thought we'd try Middleton Tavern."

"Oh, goodie," Ivy said. "I've never been there." Middleton's was an icon at the City Dock in Historic Annapolis. She retrieved her coat from the hook behind the counter, and Mark helped her into it. They said their goodbyes and left. Dan locked the front door. With the day's cash stowed in the safe, the Shermans climbed the stairs to their apartment.

"It looks like those two are serious after all," Dan said. "I hope Ivy likes Middleton's."

"What's not to like?" said Rivka. "All the young people go there."

* * * *

Almost a week had passed since the ambulance had come

for Illya Petrovich. His boss, Boris Nabakov, not only didn't like hospitals, he was deathly afraid of them; everyone he'd ever cared about had died in one.

He found Illya's door barely open. The room was dark and silent except for an occasional monitor bleep. A drawn curtain prevented him from seeing Illya's roommate. Rounding the curtain, Boris at last saw Illya: head bandaged down over half his face and tightly across his jaw. One leg was suspended in a cast from a U-shaped trapeze bar with pulley, rope, and a weight.

Illya's eyes were shut, so Boris nervously sat down in the only chair available, one with a straight back and thinly padded seat. He was here to visit, but certainly didn't want to disturb his resting friend. Consequently, Boris became a victim of his own introspection. *I'm ashamed of how I behave. Illya is so much more than my employee. He's the only loyal friend I have. He's even distant family. I have not been good to him when I treat him like a slave—ordering him here and there. He works so hard to please me. Sure I pay him, but not enough and sometimes I even cheat on his checks. Maybe I'll lose him altogether in the hospital like Momma, beautiful Rosa, and Uncle Tasha. I've always done terrible things and continue to do them.* Boris uttered a deep sigh. *No forgiveness for me. My business colleagues call me unscrupulous. I'm probably too old to change—too much meanness in my already damned soul.*

Boris looked across the bed and noticed that Illya's eyes were now open. Upon seeing his visitor, the corners of his mouth turned up in a pained smile. But he could not speak except for unintelligible grunts because of the tight bandage restricting his jaw.

Boris felt frustrated. He wanted so much to know the meaning of Illya's outburst as the EMTs carried him out on the gurney. *What did he mean "I did it for you"? Did what for me? Sorry for what?* Boris would have to wait until Illya was much improved to find out. Maybe he'd never know.

"Okay, Mr. Petrovich, it's time for your supper," announced a kindly looking nurse, as she hooked up a nutrition bag and feeding tube.

That was Boris's cue to leave.

* * * *

Mae checked out of the hotel and Cliff piled their belongings into the extended cab of his pickup. Half an hour later and several turns off Route 50, the main corridor between the state capital and the nation's capital, Cliff and Mae arrived in the sprawling wooded community of Davidsonville. Cliff turned into a gravel driveway and stopped at a rear stoop with five steps up.

Mae checked out her new surroundings. The large ranch house with masonry trim was new enough to have been primed white, but had not yet received its permanent dress coat. There were no sidewalks, just red clay and sand in piles everywhere. A small combination backhoe and bulldozer sat in the backyard next to a rusted cement mixer lying on its side.

Cliff handed her a key to the door and went to fetch their things from the pickup. The door swung open into a contemporary kitchen with all the amenities. The new stainless-steel sink was filled with dirty dishes, and the granite countertops needed polishing. But Mae's overall impression was favorable. *I've hit a gold mine here. I could live like this. It's twice the house Agnes left me in Albany.*

Cliff followed Mae inside with the bags, kicking the door shut behind him. She tagged along as he headed for the master bedroom. He dropped the bags on the floor and flopped backward on the bed. He sat up and drew her close so he could bury his face in her bosom.

"Hey, sweetie, there's time enough later for that," she said softly. "You were complaining about missing so much work. I can manage here."

"That whole dresser is empty for you. That closet, too."

"You're gonna spoil me altogether. I just have a few of my things with me."

"We could send for the rest."

"Not just yet, lover. I want to see how things work out here first. I don't want to make any promises I can't keep. These legal things are always so tricky, and besides, I have a good job to get back to up in Albany."

Cliff pleaded his case once more. "I don't hafta be anywhere 'til 1:30."

"Good, then we can have lunch together."

"That's not what I had in mind," he muttered.

"I know what you had in mind," she declared, grabbing his privates. "A nooner, but I'm not a machine, Romeo. We did have fun before breakfast."

"Does this mean the honeymoon's over?" he joked. He pulled her down on top of him and stroked her fiery red hair. Sliding his hands down to cup her tight bottom, he wished she'd gotten out of the friggin' sweater and pants.

"Of course not," she whispered as she nuzzled his ear. But Mae wasn't much for prolonged cuddling. She rolled off him onto her right side and propped her head up on one elbow. "What happens when you sell this place?"

"We move to the next one I build and then the next one. That's how I earn my living."

"You said you do remodeling, too?"

"Yeah."

"When I get my house in Annapolis away from that calculating bitch, Ivy, I want to turn it into a bed-and-breakfast, but that's gonna take a lot of remodeling. Two or three extra baths and a modern kitchen, at least. Can you do that sort of stuff?"

"Whatever you say, baby, sure—and at cost, too. Assuming we get the zoning for it, of course. This Ivy person, what right does she have to your aunt's house?"

"That's just it. She doesn't have any right to it. She's not even family." Mae swung herself up to the edge of the bed.

"Then how is this broad making any claim to it?"

"I think she coerced my aunt into changing her will, and I'm going to prove it."

"How are you going to accomplish that?" He sat up next to her.

"Well, this Ivy has lived there as a tenant for not quite two years. Aunt Irma was sick and wasn't herself at the end, so maybe Ivy forced her to make the changes."

"That doesn't sound like proof to me. It sounds more like wishful thinking."

Mae abruptly stood and faced him, her green eyes hard.

"Whose side are you on, lover?"

"Yours, baby, all yours, but what does that lawyer guy from Frederick say?"

"All he said was that he'd represent my interests at the probate hearing. That's when we'll get to see all the provisions of Aunt Irma's will for the first time. We might even have to go to trial. If that's the case, I might have to sell the Albany house to pay for the lawyer and expenses."

A frown creased Cliff's sunburned brow. "That's awful risky, isn't it? What if you out-and-out lose the house? Then what?"

"I'd still have you, lover."

"Sure, but…" A silent alarm went off in his head. It wasn't the first time he'd had these thoughts. *Do I want to spend the rest of my life with this woman? Is she gonna smother me? What the hell have I gotten myself into?*

"But what?" Mae asked. *Is he having second thoughts? Is he on to me? Does he think I'm using him?*

"Nothing. Oh, I see it's almost one. I'd better get to work." Cliff grabbed his jacket and flung it on as he strode out of the house. She heard the truck roar down the driveway.

* * * *

Middleton Tavern, established in 1750, dominated a corner of the Annapolis City Dock. Its original red bricks and large chimneys gave it an authentic colonial charm in Historic Annapolis. Inside, diners sat in crowded but friendly quarters, appreciating the warmth of the two blazing fireplaces.

Mark and Ivy sipped their wine at a cozy table near the back, and fell into comfortable silence as they shared fresh-shucked oysters, Maine lobster, and grilled salmon. They had no reason to notice a couple entering the restaurant.

Mae Winnen and Cliff Mercer had softened their moods toward each other throughout the day. Cliff had come home from work to find his new girlfriend in a slinky velvet pants suit, feeding him prospects of a night full of passion. But first, they planned to fill up on Middleton's signature crab cakes and draft beer.

They were about to be seated, when Cliff had a different idea. He worked his way over to Mark and Ivy's table and boomed, "Well, if it isn't Mark Schwartz! Haven't seen you in a couple of years."

Startled, Mark collected himself. He stood and took the outstretched hand. "Hey, Cliff. Nice to see you again. Ivy, this is Cliff Mercer. I spent one whole summer working for him in construction. The work was tough, but I earned enough for my fall tuition."

Mae stood next to him, her posture as rigid as a sentry's on watch. Ivy's polite smile froze. And then she lost it. She sprang out of her chair so abruptly the glasses of white wine shuddered. "Are you stalking me?" Ivy shouted. "And are you still up to your malicious tricks like cutting off people's electricity and phone service?"

"Nope. Only when it's people who steal my inheritance, you bitch," Mae shot back.

At least fifty forks halted midway to mouths as the surrounding diners gawked to enjoy the impromptu drama.

"You're *insane*," Ivy said, her soprano voice trembling. "Go back to Albany where you belong."

The corners of Mae's lips turned up in a smile, but her green eyes flashed. "If I were you, Ms. Cohen, I wouldn't finish that salmon. The bones will stick in your throat like all your rotten plans to take money that doesn't belong to you."

"You can take your delusional ideas and shove them up your you-know-what," Ivy said. "Irma Riley hated you."

Mae raised her open hand and slapped Ivy hard across the cheek. Ivy lunged for Mae's low-cut shirt and ran her sharp nails down Mae's bare flesh all the way to her cleavage.

Diners gasped. Mark nearly jumped out of his skin. Cliff yanked Mae away.

Middleton's manager came rushing over and bluntly told both couples, "Ladies and gentlemen, you'll have to leave immediately."

Mark hastily paid the bill for their expensive, barely eaten dinners. The four slunk out.

"The jealous person is always trying to take advantage of other people....He nurtures within himself irrational feelings of blind hatred, and he develops a mean and un-savory character. As his character deter-iorates so do his relationships with other people deteriorate."
Menoras, p. 19

Chapter 24
The Critique Group
Thursday, February 1st

he next afternoon Rivka heard a *clang* and a *thud* in the Biography/Memoir aisle. She found Ivy sitting on the floor, head in her hands, and the stepstool turned on its side. "Ivy, are you hurt?"

"No. I was just trying to make some room on the top shelf when the stool flipped out from under me. I wasn't paying enough attention to how my feet were positioned on it. I'm sorry, I'm not myself today."

Rivka's keen intuition took over. "Let's go up to the kitchen for a cup of coffee and you can tell me what's bothering you. Did something happen on your date last night?"

Ivy spilled out every detail. "Mark was humiliated. I doubt he'll ever take me out again. He didn't say a word all the way home, not even goodnight. And you know what? We didn't even get doggy bags."

Throughout the whole story Rivka was pressing her fist to her lips, trying not to laugh, but finally it was all too much. She erupted in a fit of giggles till the tears came. *Darn,* she thought, *I wish I'd been there.*

Ivy paid no attention. She was too obsessed. "What can I do to make it up to him?"

Collecting herself, Rivka said, "A note of apology would be in order, maybe with a fresh batch of brownies. And now, if you'll excuse me, I need to look over the story I'm reading for the critique group tonight."

* * * *

Dan smiled broadly through a hint of five-o'clock shadow and welcomed the writers gathered around the oak dining table. He ran his fingertips over the tabletop like a phrenologist, feeling the ancient nicks and bumps. *What a story they could tell,* he thought. The only no-show that evening was Peggy, who, on the advice of her lawyer, stayed home.

"How's Peggy doing, Garry?" asked Katie Silvers. "Is she still keeping her spirits up? I don't know what I'd do if I were in her shoes."

"She's getting along as well as can be expected," Garry said.

Dan waited for the social chatter to ebb and called the meeting to order. He dispensed with the group's business and chose Rivka to read the ending to her Glenda Glide story, "Driven Into the Woods."

> The same crunching sounds that she had made stepping on frosted leaves and frozen twigs were now working in her favor. She knew exactly where her stalker was with each of his steps. The problem was the sounds were getting louder. Under a bush covered with leaves and snow, she held her breath each time he stopped and reached for the next tree. Louder and louder the crunch, until she realized he was going to pass nearly right over her. He stopped on the other side of her sheltering bush. *Does he see me?* All of a sudden she felt a sneeze coming on. Desperate to stave it off, she grabbed her nose and squeezed hard with thumb and forefinger. *Did he hear me?* Silence. Then, without warning, the crunching continued—loud, steady, then softer, and softer. *I can't stay here,* she decided. *I'll freeze to death.*
>
> Glenda rose to her feet once more in a half-

dozen moves, each separated by hesitations designed for listening. Had the pattern of crunching sounds differed? She kept a broad tree trunk between her and where she thought the crunching sound came from. Shivering, she could still make out the cruiser's headlights, although they were somewhat dimmer now. *Only a fool would head directly toward the police car. He'd see my silhouette against the beams. But if I remember correctly, the terrain falls off, over to the left, toward the city reservoir. There's a path along the edge of the water with a deep embankment next to it. If I can get down this slope to that embankment without being detected, I can make it to my cruiser.*

Glenda crept down the slope, and when she believed she'd put sufficient distance ahead of her stalker, she scurried the rest of the way. As she neared the reservoir's edge, she could hear the wind-driven water lapping the shoreline. But in the dark she sadly misjudged how close the embankment actually was. Exhausted and thoroughly chilled, she slid over the edge and landed six feet below. An involuntary grunt escaped as her backside hit the muddy path. *How loud was I? Did he hear me? How far behind me is he? I've got to keep moving.*

Glenda scrambled to her feet and tried to run. Somehow, her numbing feet could only walk, but they began to warm up and become quicker with each step. Before long, she found herself running down the winding path, her way lit by the starlit sheen of the city's water supply. She was cold, yet sweaty from the running—the moisture freezing on her face and under her hair. She had to keep moving. The path swung way left around a major bend, then headed back toward the road. At last she could see the cruiser once more. Down the ditch, up the other side to the road and twenty yards more to the cruiser. She dropped into the driver's seat and reached for the ignition, but there was no key. She had surrendered it to the killer.

With senses sharpened, she had a flash of another thought, her Plan B, and pulled the trunk release. But as she slid out of the driver's seat, she saw the killer in the dimming headlight beams—with his gun aimed at her from the drainage ditch. A single shot, and the driver's-side windshield shattered into a spider-web of cracked glass. As he climbed out of the ditch onto the road, he fired a second shot. The bullet pinged off the cruiser's roof. She heard him running. Toward her, boots sloshing through wet snow. Glenda ducked down behind the cruiser, raised the trunk lid, and lifted her shotgun off its rack; it was affixed to the inside of the lid for swift removal. Taking precise aim, she turned in his direction, leveled and aimed, anticipating where he would first appear. Releasing the safety, she pulled the trigger. Her calculation proved accurate. At this range, the bullet erupted in the killer's stomach, lifting him off his feet and blowing his body clear across the ditch. Her own gun flew out of his hand. There was no doubt in her mind. The man was dead.

Glenda secured the shotgun back in its rack and wrapped herself tightly in a dark green army blanket stowed in the trunk. Next she retrieved her own purloined handgun from the ground. What she really needed now was the cruiser's ignition key. Remembering that he had shoved it into his left cargo-pants pocket, she had no trouble finding it. He was still wearing her official officer's belt. With a shudder, she unbuckled it and pulled it from his waist, unable to avoid her fingers touching his flannel shirt, shredded and thick with blood.

Back in the driver's seat, Glenda realized the police car wasn't drivable, and she doubted whether it would even start. But there was enough battery power left to get a message off to the county sheriff's office. She locked the cruiser's doors, closed her eyes, and waited for backup.

#

"Wow," said Garry. "I was on the edge of my seat right up to the end and *bam!* Glenda let him have it. My kind of story."

"Thank you," said Rivka. "You don't think the ending is too grisly?"

"Hell, no!" he said.

"About halfway through, I wanted to put my coat on" said

Katie. "The cold was so real. Sitting down in the snow and burying herself with frozen leaves. Brrr."

"I hate to be a spoilsport, Riv, but I do have a comment," said Frieda.

Rivka cocked her head and frowned. She wasn't in the mood, but resolved to get a grip. "Okay, so tell me."

"First of all," said Frieda, drawing herself up officiously. "You overdid the crunches and crunching. Including your reading at our last meeting, I think I counted six. And you repeated 'frozen twigs' and 'frosted leaves.' You need to vary your descriptions, Riv."

"Good point, Frieda," Garry chimed in. "I noticed a couple things, too. It's in the mid-thirties with snow flurries, so the mud wouldn't be soft, and I don't think you want to have him sloshing through the snow. It wouldn't have started to melt yet. But these are fixable. You've got a good plot, Riv, and I'm sure you can work all that stuff out."

Rivka's cheeks reddened. *And I thought I was done.* "Thanks, guys, I'll get on it."

Katie finished the readings by bringing the group up to date on her novel *Boxcar Bertie.*

A near-full moon shone on the tracks a freight car's length away. Bertie Pachet steadied her eyes on the middle-aged guy sitting on a box in the rail yard in front of the dilapidated woodshed. He pulled the cork out of a bottle, tilted his head back, and drew long. *This one's got to be the yard security,* she thought. *The 4:38 is coming through any minute. I need to get to the other side of the tracks without him seeing me.*

Bertie moved silently to her left, stepping carefully so as not to disturb any of the rubble underfoot. Circling around the lone sidelined freight car, she changed direction, crossing the first track and the second, and trotted a hundred yards down the track. Now she was where she needed to be to catch the slow-moving freight train when it pulled away from the loading docks of the New Haven rail yard. But there was one problem with this new spot. It was out in the open; she had nothing to hide behind. Then she spotted a good-sized switching platform and darted behind it, dropping down to her knees.

The yard was quiet at this time in the morning. Looking up at the sky, a few birds flew in awkward patterns in search of food. Bertie's stomach growled, reminding her that she hadn't eaten since the night before. She'd shared a tin can full of watery stew with a nice group sitting around a small fire. Mostly men out of work, forced to beg for scraps, but usually handy and willing to do odd jobs that others couldn't afford to pay for.

Bertie heard the screech of wheels rolling and the bumping of couplings as the train approached her platform. When the engine and the first few cars had passed, she sprang up and began running alongside, looking over her shoulder, searching first for an open door and an unlocked door otherwise. She saw one car open, about four cars farther along. Running faster now to better match the train's speed, she leaped up, grabbed an iron rung, kicked off, and rolled up into the moving car.

Landing hard on her rump, Bertie lay there for a few moments to catch her breath. The boxcar smelled of cattle dung and soiled straw, but she already knew an open door meant that it was being aired out. After a bit, she sat up with her back against the wall. As the train headed northeast she could see the sky begin to lighten, and a tinge of orange marked where the sun would soon be.

Bertie heard a scraping, knocking noise coming from the shadows at the far end of the car. *A stray animal? No, more human-like. A snore?* She was not alone.

#

"Nice job, Katie." Dan interjected. "It's getting late, folks, so we'll save more readings till next time." Rivka served coffee, tea, and pound cake. But her mind was elsewhere. All she could think of was Israel Finestein and the gun that so cruelly took his life.

Chapter 25
Probate and Reprobate
Wednesday, February 7th

Ivy Cohen squirmed in the chair next to Dan's. They were
in an anteroom just outside the chambers of a court-appointed mediator, waiting their turn to be heard. The
probate hearing, testing the validity of Irma's will, was scheduled
for ten o'clock. They had arrived half an hour early. They left their
jackets open and spread wide in the warmish room. Dan had
donned his best blue suit, white shirt, and striped tie. Ivy wore a
gray knee-length business suit with no accessories other than her
wristwatch. She gripped the chair's armrests as though they were
lifelines. Dan placed his hand over one of hers to comfort her. They
sat in total, tense silence.

Dan snapped his head around when the door to the hall
opened and two men and a woman walked in. They settled in
chairs along the opposite wall under a framed print of *George Washington Crossing the Delaware*. Dan gave the woman the once-over.
*Sexy body even in the prim beige suit, but a hard-set jaw. Must be Mae
Winnen. Feels like she's staring right through me.* Dan noted that one
of the men was smartly dressed in a three-piece suit, with a briefcase and serious bearing. But who was the other guy? He turned to
Ivy and saw her pained expression and cringing posture. He didn't
have to guess why. Rivka had told him about the disastrous dinner

date.

"The older man must be her lawyer," Ivy whispered to Dan. "The man in jeans is her boyfriend. He was with her that horrible night at Middleton's."

The outer door opened once more. In walked Joel, his secretary, and Gino Fachetti. Joel greeted Dan and Ivy, then acknowledged the Winnen party with a friendly "Good Morning" and slight nod. Before they had a chance to sit, the inner door opened and a secretary escorted them into a stark office. She gestured for them to be seated.

Behind a steel desk, a sixtyish woman with a confident demeanor and handsome, stoic face stood. "Hello, everybody. I'm Lillian Swanson, your court-appointed mediator in this case. I'm not an official judge, so these preliminary proceedings will be conducted informally as much as possible. However, the great state of Maryland abides by the Uniform Probate Code, and Anne Arundel County hearings follow those rules to a tee. First, would you each please state your name?"

That done, Ms. Swanson continued. "Thank you. I have in my hands what is purported to be the Last Will and Testament of one Irma Anne Fisk Riley, formerly of 77 Murray Lane, the city of Annapolis in Anne Arundel County. Is the executor present?"

"Yes, ma'am. Joel Wise representing the deceased, Irma A. F. Riley. Your document is a certified true and exact copy of the original filed with the Registrar's Office on December 18, 2006."

Ms. Swanson continued. "I also have here an affidavit attesting to the authenticity of this will. I see that it is duly witnessed, notarized, and filed with the county Registrar of Wills. Have the death certificate and all the appropriate notices been mailed and a copy published in the *Annapolis Journal-Gazette?*"

"Yes, ma'am," replied Joel, handing her a file folder. "Here are the proofs of notification and publication. There were no known outstanding debts. Estimated funeral expenses are being held in escrow."

"Have the necessary Federal, state, and local tax documents

been prepared?"

"The estate size is insufficient to warrant a Federal return, ma'am; however, the accounting firm of Maxwell and Sterns is preparing state, county, and local returns. Estimated taxes are also being held in escrow."

"Now then, Mr. Executor, do you believe there is any reason why you should not execute and distribute the Riley estate according to her original intents and wishes as expressed in this Last Will and Testament?"

"No, ma'am, I see no reason not to."

"And yet," added Ms. Swanson, "I hold in hand an injunction disputing such execution and distribution. Is the party initiating that injunction present?"

"Yes, ma'am. Elroy Thomas for the petitioner, Mae Sue Winnen of Albany, New York."

"You're with the firm Thomas and Cassidy. Is that correct, Counselor?"

"Yes, ma'am."

"On what grounds does Ms. Winnen challenge the execution and distribution of the Riley will?"

"Ms. Winnen asserts that she is a rightful niece and sole living relative of the deceased and, as such, is entitled to inherit the majority of the Riley assets, including her house, investments, and savings."

"Counselor Thomas, to what do you attribute this supposed misdirection in the actual will?"

"Ms. Winnen believes that her dear aunt may have been unduly influenced as a result of her advanced years. She might not have been of completely sound mind or she might have been dissuaded from remembering her own family in her latest will. An earlier will left everything to Mrs. Agnes Winnen, Ms. Winnen's stepmother and Irma Riley's diseased sister. I have here Ms. Winnen's birth certificate and the marriage certificate uniting her father, John Edward Winnen, with Agnes Fisk Winnen." Elroy laid these documents out on the mediator's desk. "Agnes Winnen left no official Last Will and Testament, but it can be assumed that her assets would necessarily flow to Mae."

The mediator stared at Elroy behind her granny glasses. "As for your assumption, that is a matter for the state of New York. But are you suggesting criminal persuasion, an act of coercion in this case, Counselor?

Elroy returned her gaze. Despite his fifty years and near-white hair, his face had an unlined, well-cared-for look. "Not exactly, ma'am," he said. "That would require actual evidence not in hand, but certainly worthy of pursuit. We offer conjecture at this time, a possible explanation of how the will could have been misdirected. However, the court should take note that drastic changes were introduced about ninety days before Mrs. Riley's demise. Suspicious, to say the least, especially in light of her eighty-six years."

"Okay, Mr. Wise, you're up," said the mediator. "You may rebut as necessary to defend your client's intents and wishes."

"Before I make my case, may I direct a few pertinent questions to Ms. Winnen?" requested Joel.

"Of course, Counselor."

"Ms. Winnen, what was your exact relationship with Agnes Winnen?"

"She is, I mean, she was, my mother," said Mae.

"Don't you mean stepmother, a nonblood relationship?" Joel asked.

"Yeah," Mae agreed. "Stepmother. But she was a true mother to me."

Elroy stood and addressed Ms. Swanson. "Ma'am, The Uniform Probate Code recognizes steprelationships. So that should not matter in this case."

"Agreed," said the mediator. "Continue, Mr. Wise."

"Ms. Winnen, were you ever formally adopted?"

"No," admitted Mae.

"And was there ever any application to start adoption proceedings?" asked Joel.

"I'm not sure," answered Mae. Her voice remained steady,

but her ramrod-straight back betrayed anxiety, even fear of what was to come.

"Ms. Winnen," said Joel, "I have here a copy of a document from the Albany Family Court attesting to an adoption application by one John Winnen. The application was filed but never recognized due to the lack of Agnes Winnen's signature. How do you explain this?"

"One moment, please," interrupted Elroy. He turned to Mae and they whispered back and forth. "A mere oversight. I might add that Mae Winnen lived in that household for nine years, ate her meals there, slept in one of its beds, and engaged in normal family relations there."

Joel sensed a weakness in his own approach, so he chose a different tack. "Ms. Winnen, what was your relationship with Irma Riley?"

Mae smiled nervously. "Amicable, in general. We had a few differences of opinion like any two related people."

"Were you mentioned at all in her latest will?" asked Joel, sensing that he had struck a chord.

"Yeah," Mae replied. "According to the part you let me read, I was to receive one dollar and some crummy old vase."

"Were you made aware that this crummy old vase, as you put it, is worth in the neighborhood of $6,500?"

"I suppose so, but my Aunt Irma was worth a lot more than that. Why would she want to give so much to a complete stranger? Isn't that an indication she didn't have all her marbles?"

"Your Aunt Irma, as you called her, was quite sane, especially so on the day she dictated her Last Will and Testament," said Joel. "I can attest to that, and so can my secretary here, who acted as the official unbiased witness." He handed two affidavits to the mediator. "I have another question for you, Ms. Winnen. What connotation do you attach to the one-dollar bequest?"

"Connotation?" she asked. "I don't understand."

"What meaning does it hold for you?" pursued Joel.

"I understand the definition of connotation, but I'm not

sure what you're getting at."

"Let me pose it this way. Don't you think your Aunt Irma intended the one dollar bequest as an outright slur to malign *you?* Don't you realize that the expensive vase bequest demonstrates that she has not forgotten you altogether—even though the two of you had an exceedingly strained relationship?"

Mae ignored the first part of Joel's question and plunged straight in to protest the more condemning second part. "That's a bunch of poppycock. I got along fine with Aunt Irma, and no one can dispute it."

"Are you sure you want to perjure yourself that way?" asked Joel.

"Careful, Counselor," cautioned Elroy. "Ms. Winnen is not under oath, and you offer no proof of a less-than-amicable relationship."

"But I do," said Joel. "I offer this tape of my working session with the deceased, Irma Riley." Turning to the mediator, "May I, ma'am?"

The mediator nodded. "I'll allow it."

"The first voice you hear is that of the deceased," explained Joel. "The male voice is mine." He set the tiny digital recorder down on the desk and pressed the PLAY button.

IRMA: I don't have any living relatives since my sister, Agnes Winnen, passed on six months ago. We were close, so she had been my only heir up to now. And I don't want anything of mine to go to that horrible, despicable stepdaughter of hers, Mae Winnen.

JOEL: And just how would you like your estate to be executed then?

IRMA: I would like my home, my savings, and all my possessions to go to Ivy Cohen.

JOEL: I thought she was just renting a room from you, Besides, you've only known her a short time.

IRMA: Sure, Ivy is renting from me, but not for what you call a short time. She's been with me for almost two years, and she means so much more to me than just a tenant. Having her in the house has made a new woman of me. She's become like a daughter to me and the reverse is true, too. She mothered me when I broke my leg. She cooks for me, she's helped me up and down the stairs countless times, and even done my laundry. I couldn't ask for a better companion. We talk for hours on end—she's so literate. I love her and I believe she feels the same way about me.

JOEL: Well, if you are that sure, I'll draw up the necessary papers. Did you have any additional bequests or instructions, Mrs. Riley?

IRMA: Yes, I've written them all out in longhand. One thing I must insist on is that no one know of this will until after my death. Your fee and the funeral and burial costs are also covered in these notes. As for my stepniece, I want it made clear that her inheritance comprises my most prized antique vase and exactly one dollar in cash. Nothing else.

Joel stopped the recorder and said, "There's more, but nothing relevant to this case." As he reached into his briefcase to remove additional documents, Mae burst out. "Anybody can alter a recorder. Besides, I don't think that's even her voice."

Joel offered another document to the mediator, stating: "This is a transcript of the recording you just heard. The signatures at the bottom attest to not only the accuracy of the transcript, but to the recognition of Irma Riley's voice on the specified date."

"Is there any other evidence to be given or disputed at this time?" asked the mediator.

Mae jumped up. "You better believe there's something to dispute. I want to know what this guy's doing here." She pointed savagely at Gino with her index finger. Gino's salt-and-pepper mustache twitched as he fidgeted with embarrassment.

Joel turned to the mediator. "May I respond, ma'am?"

Mediator Swanson nodded.

"Ms. Winnen, Mr. Fachetti here was Irma Riley's trusted cab driver and friend. He happens to be a beneficiary to her will—in the amount of $5,000."

Mae's eyes blazed; her pale cheeks turned blotchy red. "And I get one friggin' buck?"

"Plus the antique vase worth $6,500," replied Joel.

Cliff laid his hand on Mae's arm to calm her. She sank back

in her chair and smoldered in silence.

Ms. Swanson repeated her question. "Is there any other evidence to be brought up?"

"No, ma'am," said Joel.

"No, ma'am," echoed Elroy after a short consultation with Mae.

"Then, thank you, Counselors, and thank you all," said Ms. Swanson. "I will review all the documents and my notes and have my written decision mailed to you within five working days. You have twenty-four hours to submit any additional documents. This has been an informal probate hearing. Both sides have a right to appeal my decision. Of course, any appeal must be filed with the Registrar of Wills and processed by Family Court in what is called an Unsupervised Formal Probate Hearing."

Both attorneys acknowledged her remarks.

Mae, Elroy, and Cliff left the room first. As Joel's group reached the street, they found Mae standing alone at the curb, a look of fury on her contorted face. She stepped forward, grabbed Ivy's arm, and said, "You're going to live to regret this, bitch, I guarantee you."

"…In the end, the jealous person
himself is the one who suffers most…."
Menoras, Prologue, p. 19

Chapter 26
Driven Crazy
Thursday, February 15th

Mae Winnen crouched on the back steps of Cliff's house, arms wrapped around her knees. A whole week had gone by, and she hadn't heard anything from Lillian Swanson. *What the hell's keeping that old woman anyway? Another week cooped up like this and I'll go berserk.* Jarred from her thoughts by the roar of an engine, Mae watched the muddy gray pickup roll up the driveway.

Before the door had even swung open, she shouted, "Where the hell have you been all day?"

Cliff jumped down from the truck. "And a Good Afternoon to you too, dear," he retorted. "At work, damn it. I've got to earn a living, woman."

"I've been trapped all day in this godforsaken house in the middle of the wilderness," she carped.

"There's a TV in the living room and a bookcase full of books. What more do you want?"

"Sure," she said. "A TV with no cable, two broadcast channels of nothing to watch, and a bookcase full of macho male trash—Zane Grey and Louis L'Amour westerns. Then there's the empty fridge, except for beer and catsup and mayo and mustard. Good grief, what's a girl supposed to eat for lunch? There wasn't even a can of soup in the cupboard." She stood to greet him as he started up the steps. "And, of course, I can't go anywhere without wheels."

"So I'll take you out to dinner," Cliff said as he kissed her pouting lips and grabbed a handful of her butt. "And we'll go shopping for groceries afterward."

A somewhat placated Mae followed him inside and sat down on the bed as he peeled off his denim shirt and dust-covered jeans. "But first I've got to take a shower and shed a few layers of working man's dirt."

She couldn't help admiring his hairy, burly physique, glistening with sexy male perspiration as he strode naked to the master bath. As much as he kindled the fire between her legs, she fought off the urge to follow him into the shower, not wanting to spend a minute longer in this house today than necessary. She was already dressed to go out.

"Did you remember to go to the post office and pick up the mail?" she yelled into the bathroom.

Cliff yelled back, "What? I can't hear you. The water's running." He heard her better the second time. "There's a pile on the front seat of the truck. I haven't even looked at what's in it yet."

Mae popped up off the bed and made for the back door. Outside she climbed up into the passenger seat and flipped through the stack until she saw the official-looking envelope with the Maryland seal as part of its return address. She tore open the envelope, removed the tri-folded letter, and read. Moments later, her body shivered with anguish and frustration. Her petition to stop the execution and distribution of Irma's will had been denied. Lines of anger creased the corners of her mouth. Crumbling the letter in her fist, she threw the wad on the floor mat. Not finding a key in the ignition added to her boiling rage.

Mae kicked open the truck door, slid out, and ran up the steps. Once inside, she headed straight for the dresser where Cliff had dropped his truck keys. Just as she reached out to retrieve them a large, hairy hand fell on top of hers. Cliff stood there with a towel wrapped around his waist. As she turned to face him, he discovered a new kind of fierce ire, far from the mere annoyance that had unwelcomed him home.

"What's wrong, baby? Where do you think you're going with my keys? What's happened to you?"

Mae slid her hand out from under his. "The judge denied my petition, and I'm gonna hafta take the whole damn thing to court. That's what."

Cliff rested his hand on her shoulder. "But that's about what we expected. At least, what I expected," he said. "Even Elroy told you your chances were slim to none. And unless you have something new and different to offer, he didn't see any way he could honestly break your aunt's will. So settle down, and we'll go into town and have a nice quiet consolation dinner." *But not at Middleton's, by God*, he told himself.

He pulled her to him, so close she could feel his growing hardness rub against her through the towel. While his hands drifted to her slim waist, the fingers of her left hand wrapped around a corner of his towel. With her right hand, she reached for the keys once more, and before he could react, she yanked the towel off him, threw it on the floor, and raced for the back door. When Mae glanced back at him, he was staring down at where the towel had been, a shocked look on his weathered face. Out the door and into the truck, she started the engine, revved it up, and backed halfway out of the driveway when he appeared at the front door in all his glory.

* * * *

At Irma's house, Ivy slumped on the couch, brooding. Her workday at the bookstore was done; now nothing but painful thoughts filled her head. She feared that her rift with Mark Schwartz was not just serious, but a death knell. She knew he'd been embarrassed and deeply hurt by the way she'd behaved in the restaurant. Going way beyond Rivka's advice of a note and brownies, she'd put together her own version of a peace offering:

two stylish, hand-painted ties and a gold tie clasp to go with them. She gift-wrapped the box in silver and blue foil with a silver ribbon, ready to spring it on him at the *oneg* after the Friday night *Shabbat* service. But he never showed up at the synagogue. She was scared.

Ivy was falling in love with Mark, and even envisioned the possibility of marriage in the not-too-distant future. She couldn't bear the thought of losing him. He hadn't answered the land line phone at his Baltimore apartment. *Perhaps he's in class*, she reasoned. *But what if he has caller ID?* She shuddered at the thought that maybe he'd actually blocked her. Mark had given her his cell phone number with the proviso that she not use it during the week, as he had day and evening classes, as well as labs that ran till all hours. He also needed ample study time so he could come home to Annapolis on weekends. She had a feeling that on Thursday afternoon his classes finished early. So considering this an emergency, Ivy punched in his cell number.

He picked up on the second ring. "Oh, Ivy. Hi."

His voice sounded so cool and indifferent. "Dear," she began, "please excuse me for calling now, but I've been trying to reach you to apologize for the awful way I behaved at Middleton's. You haven't picked up your land line, and I didn't know what else to do. I don't know what got into me. I've never done anything like that before." A lump filled her throat and tears blurred her vision. She began to sob between words. "I know there's no excuse for embarrassing you that way. But Mae came at me so suddenly and so hard, I couldn't just sit there and take her insults."

"Ivy, stop!" Mark ordered. "Don't you know that I can't stay angry with you for very long? Dad told me you called the house. The reason I didn't come home last weekend had nothing to do with you. I had an exam Monday morning, and our little group studied all Saturday and Sunday. Don't worry, I'll be home tomorrow afternoon. I miss you terribly. I'm sorry I didn't call you." What he decided *not* to tell her just yet was that he'd thought things over and actually admired her gutsy physical response.

"Oh, Mark, I'm so glad. I miss you, too. I know I haven't

said it before, but I do love you." Ivy felt agonizing moments of silence pass before Mark confessed, "Ivy, I love you too. I'll pick you up at the house tomorrow night and we'll go to services together."

"I can't wait, darling. I'll let you get back to your studies now." As she was replacing the receiver in its cradle, she heard a car door slam out front. Moving the lace curtain aside, she peered into the darkness and saw the silhouette of a pickup truck on the street. When the doorbell sounded, she turned on the porch light. Someone was there, but facing away. Wishing for a chain and bolt that had never been installed didn't help either. She had to open the door to see who it was.

Turning the deadbolt and then the knob freed the hefty colonial door, but there was no way Ivy expected it to burst inward and nearly bowl her over. A raging Mae Winnen came crashing in, taking Ivy bodily to the rug. Pinning her down by straddling her, Mae pummeled Ivy repeatedly with lefts and rights to the cheeks, shoulders, and chest. Ivy responded by kidney punching Mae on both sides. Although Mae was inches taller and thirty pounds heavier, Ivy had a certain advantage: protection offered by her thick cowl-neck sweater and sturdy corduroy pants. Mae was wearing a silk blouse and miniskirt for an evening out. She winced and straightened up, exposing herself to a second set of kidney punches. She froze. Ivy's right cross to the chin sent Mae onto the rug.

Operating on a jolt of adrenaline, Ivy sprang to her feet, yanked the lamp off the hall table, and let it fall on the floor. She separated the long extension cord from both the short lamp cord and the wall socket. Wrapping several turns of the extension cord around Mae's legs, she joined the two ends in a square knot. Mae reached down and attempted to untie it. Ivy gave her a swift kick in the gut, sending her onto her backside. Ivy flipped Mae over onto her stomach and captured one hand and then the other behind her back with the remaining length of cord. Her attacker was secured for the time being. Ivy's face felt like barbecued chopped meat still afire over the grill, but she couldn't do anything about it just yet.

She wondered what to do with the screaming maniac on

the floor. Mark was too far away. It was the police or the Shermans. Something told her she should call Dan first; he'd know what to do. Ivy sat down in the side chair beside the telephone table, and each time Mae tried to flip herself over, Ivy planted a sneaker in her back, flattening her. She reached for the phone. Dan said he and Rivka would be right over.

Mae quieted down, momentarily resigned to her fate. That is, until the Shermans walked in. She squirmed and shrieked, "Get me out of here! This bitch is holding me prisoner!"

When Ivy explained how she was attacked, both Shermans agreed the police had to be called. Dan dialed 911.

"Your face looks terrible," said Rivka, laying gentle fingers on Ivy's cheek.

"It hurts something awful, Rivka. I made up with Mark and he's coming for me tomorrow. I'll look like a fugitive from a house of correction."

"Let's gets some ice on that swelling. Then we'll see what a little makeup can do. Come on in the kitchen. Dan will keep watch on the nutcase." But there was no time for that.

The police arrived and introduced themselves as Officers Reed and Dalton.

Mae turned her head sideways and spat out, "It's about time! Help me!"

Officer Dalton, fresh-faced and eager to please, knelt down and undid the restraints on Mae's legs and hands, suppressing a smile at the cleverly worked extension cord. He placed one hand under her arm, intending to help her up, but she shrugged it off as if the gesture were an insult. Still eager to be useful, he picked the lamp up off the floor, straightened the cockeyed shade, and set it on the only surface available: the hall table.

These few seconds gave Mae all the ammunition she needed. Pointing to Ivy, she launched into a screeching, nonstop report. "That bitch attacked me without provocation. I came here to apologize for swearing at her in a restaurant. But when I came to the door, she pulled me inside and started beating on me. Then she kicked me in the ribs and in the chest and punched me in my kidneys. They're already really sore. I've got the bruises to prove it."

Mae pulled up her silk blouse and rolled down the elastic waistband of her skirt for all to see. The red welts on her well-toned bare belly were just beginning to turn black and blue. "That's where she kicked me. I'm the victim here."

"Do you want to press charges, ma'am?" asked Officer Reed, the older of the two policemen, with squinting lines of skepticism around his eyes.

"Yeah, I do."

"And what about me?" asked Ivy. "How do you think my face got like this? This is my home. You forced your way in and assaulted me because the court turned down your petition. Yes, I got a letter today, too. By the way, Officers, I'll want to press charges."

Officer Reed turned to Mae. "Any truth to that, ma'am? Was there a letter?"

"No! I mean yes, but it's not like that."

"She's lying," declared Ivy. At the hall table she picked up the envelope that had arrived that morning and handed it to the officer. "Here. See for yourself. Why would I be the instigator of this nasty business?"

The officer slid the letter out of its envelope and read the official document denying the petition. "It has two addressees, Mae Winnen and Ivy Cohen," he said. He looked straight at Ivy. "Are you Ivy Cohen?" He handed the letter and envelope back to her.

"Yes, that's me," she replied. "There's no reason for me to be dissatisfied with that decision. Irma Riley's will is solid and the house will soon be mine."

Officer Reed asked, "Whose truck is that parked outside?"

Dan, Rivka, and Ivy all shook their heads. He turned back to Mae. She reached into her miniskirt pocket and pulled out Cliff's set of keys, holding them up.

"May I see your driver's license and truck registration, please?" asked Officer Reed.

"I forgot my purse with my license in it," she said in an apologetic voice. "But I can have my boyfriend bring them to you. It's his truck."

"Do you have his permission to drive it?" asked Officer Reed.

"Of course I do," she lied. "I drove it here. I didn't steal it now, did I?"

Officer Reed nodded to his partner, who handcuffed Mae's wrists and then intoned her Miranda rights. Turning to the others, he said, "I think you all ought to come down to the precinct with us until we get this business straightened out."

"But I didn't do anything wrong," pleaded Mae. "How can you arrest me?"

"Easily, ma'am. By your own admission, you were driving a vehicle without a license. Perhaps we can add to that later, forced entry and assault. We'll need your statement, too."

"Oh, no!" Mae cried as they took her outside, stumbling down the path to the rear of the awaiting cruiser.

* * * *

Twenty minutes later, the group reconvened at the Taylor Avenue police headquarters to sign statements. The following morning Mae was arraigned on assault charges, driving without a license, and—because Cliff had reported his truck stolen—car theft as well. Both Ivy and Cliff softened and declined to press charges. In front of a judge and a prosecutor, a solution was hammered out. Mae agreed to pay a $250 fine for driving without a license. She also promised not to pursue further legal claims against the Riley estate. And, in accordance with a judicial restraining order, she would have forty-eight hours to leave Maryland. She also had to agree not to return to the state ever again. The alternative would mean up to two years of prison time, as the more serious charges would remain on the books indefinitely. Relieved to get out of town a free woman, Mae returned to Albany and was never heard from again.

A happy Cliff Mercer returned to his house in the woods—

and his perennial bachelor status.

Chapter 27
Pretrial Preparation
Monday, March 19th

The courtroom was fraught with tension during *voir dire*, a French term literally meaning to see, to speak. It's the process of questioning potential jurors to determine their competency and fairness to serve—in this case, for the trial of Peggy Fraume.

Into the second laborious day, Prosecutor Robert Atwood grilled the forty-fifth candidate: a retired Caucasian firefighter from Baltimore. "Is there any reason you couldn't render a just verdict in this case?"

"No, sir. I like to think I'm a pretty fair judge of people."

"Does that mean you judge people by the way they look or how they sound?" Atwood asked.

"Oh, no sir. I need to hear all the evidence first."

"Thank you. Your Honor, prosecution accepts this juror," declared Atwood.

Leon Malamud had been leaning back in his chair listening intently. "One additional question, if I may, sir: Could you be just as fair if you knew that both the victim and the defendant were of the Jewish faith? Would that make a difference to you?"

"I don't think so," the retired firefighter said, after hesitating a moment. "Everything would still depend on the evidence."

"Why the hesitation?"

"The question surprised me. My brother-in-law is Jewish, and I like him a lot."

"Thank you. The defense accepts this juror," said Leon.

He took his place in the jury box. An African-American housewife from Federal Hill was approved as Juror Number Twelve, bringing the tally to seven females and five males. The three alternates, two females and one male, were selected shortly thereafter.

Leon addressed the judge. "Your Honor, I realize that summonses have been sent to all my witnesses, but I've had no response from Anton Gleuck. As a follow-up, I first telephoned the witness and then sent an investigator to the Gleuck home. The investigator found no one home, several days of newspapers, and an overflowing mailbox. He concluded that the witness had taken flight. I'm not quite sure how this might affect my case."

"Are you requesting a delay, Counselor?" asked Judge Rodriguez.

"Not at this time, Your Honor," Leon replied. "But I'd like to reserve that option, if I may."

"Request denied. The court acknowledges your missing witness and will look into the matter further," said Judge Rodriguez. "This court's business is concluded for today. Trial date is set for Wednesday, the twenty-first of March at 8:30 a.m."

* * * *

Naomi Levinson hung up the dish towel and walked by the den that once had been their boys' bedroom. She stuck her head in the doorway. Though the television blared with a boisterous reality show, Mendel snored with even more decibels. Naomi called his name softly, testing to see if he was sleeping lightly or faking. Convinced that his loud orchestrations were genuine, she moved past the door to her intended destination, the front hall closet.

She cautiously opened the door, stepped closer and, on tiptoe, reached for the prize at the rear of the top shelf. She slid her husband's attaché case forward to get a grip on it, grabbed the handle, and brought the case to waist height. With both hands, she tilted it first to one side, then the other. Something inside slid across the bottom. Setting the case down on the coffee table in the living room, she was foiled by a combination latch with four thumbwheel tumblers. She tried several combinations: the dates of his birthday and hers; their two boys' birthdays; their wedding date. None worked. She tinkered with a hairpin and then a metal nail file to no avail. She was too intent on her project to notice that the snores from the den had ceased.

"Have you tried the apartment number?" asked a grinning Mendel, standing in the doorway. "I think it might be a sure bet."

"Oh, dear God, you frightened me," gasped Naomi. "I'm sorry, Mendel dear. I shouldn't be prying into your private stuff."

"Here, let me open it for you," he said. He rolled the tumblers to their correct positions, released the catch, and opened the case to reveal a small gift-wrapped package. "It's for you anyway, although I admit it's two weeks early. You seem too impatient to wait."

Stunned, Naomi ran the upcoming days through her mind until she realized: "*Oy vey!* Our anniversary! And I haven't gotten you anything yet."

* * * *

The following day, Marie Tate-Williams was snoozing in her recliner when she heard a knock on the front door. She shuffled to the door and opened it to the extent of the security chain.

"Who is it?"

"Detective Kelly, Annapolis City Police, ma'am. May I come in?" He showed his credentials through the narrow opening. Marie pushed the door back and unhooked the chain. "What's this all about?"

"Is your son at home?"

"Yes, at least I think so." She turned away. "Damon! Damon!" No answer. "Last I seen him he was in his bedroom. Second door down the hall on the left. What do you want with my boy?"

Officer Mitch Kelly was already on his way down the hall when she asked the question. Damon wasn't in his room, nor in any other room in the small apartment where Mitch searched. He did notice the bedroom window open, and when he looked out, a torn window screen lay on the grass one story below.

"Detective, you didn't answer my question. What do you want with my boy? He's not in trouble, is he?"

"We've arrested a young man named Harley Farrel on a stolen-guns charge. He claims he sold Damon one of the guns. Ma'am, all I want to do is question your son. He's not in any trouble yet. But do you think he may have gone out the window to avoid me?"

"Of course not. Damon's a good boy," she pleaded, hugging her threadbare sweater. "He wouldn't get mixed up in anything like that."

Kelly handed Marie his card. "Have Damon get in touch with me when he returns. Good day, ma'am." *Another stone wall,* he thought. *To a mother, the son is always a good boy.*

Chapter 28
Atwood for the Prosecution
Wednesday, March 21st

he bailiff called out, "All rise for the Honorable Luis Rodriguez," in a courtroom full of interested parties and
polished dark-grained woods.

The small-framed, sixty-four-year-old judge took his place
on the bench and motioned for everyone to be seated once more.
Court was in session. A hush fell over the assembly. He nodded to
the bailiff, who read off the case's administrative particulars, followed by the second-degree murder charge levied against the defendant, Margaret ("Peggy") Morris Fraume.

"If there are no new motions, the court will now hear opening arguments from the prosecution," ordered Judge Rodriguez.

Prosecutor Roland Atwood walked briskly to the jury box.
"Ladies and gentlemen of the jury. Second-degree murder, as it ap-
plies in this case, constitutes the taking of a life impulsively without
premeditation. That is, void of planning, yet carried out with mal-
ice, an intent to do harm. In order to prove a case of second-degree
murder, I need to ascertain three things: motive, means, and opportunity."

"First," he said, "I plan to establish motive by showing that
the defendant and the deceased came from extremely differing
cultures and argued regularly over resolving those difficulties. The

prosecution believes that this murder took place during the heat of one of those arguments, one that spiraled out of control. Second, I plan to establish opportunity by having a reliable witness testify that the shots fired were heard while the defendant was with Israel Finestein in his book restoration workshop at 59 Beuller Street. Third, I plan to establish means by having an officer of the law testify that he apprehended the defendant while she was in the process of wiping her prints from the murder weapon. In addition, it should be noted that the defendant's hands and clothing have tested positive for both gunshot residue and the victim's blood." During his thoroughly rehearsed argument, Atwood strode from one end of the jury box to the other and back again, only occasionally glancing at the individuals seated there.

"You will hear testimony from the Medical Examiner's office stating that two .38 caliber bullets were removed from the deceased's chest. The second bullet, believed by the Medical Examiner's office to be the ultimate cause of death, was removed from the left ventricle chamber of the heart. A ballistics expert will show that both bullets were discharged from a Saturday Night Special, a .38 caliber gun, the very same gun taken from the defendant's own hands. The defense has already stipulated to the cause of death and identified that gun as the weapon that caused the murder of Israel Finestein.

"It is my belief that you, ladies and gentlemen of the jury, will have no trouble finding the defendant guilty. Thank you." Atwood turned away from the jury and confidently walked back to his seat at the prosecution's table.

"Now the court will hear opening remarks by the defense," ordered the judge.

Leon Malamud stood and took his place in front of the jury. Before starting, he made deliberate eye contact with each juror to command their attention and demonstrate his respect for them. His voice came across as friendlier and lower in pitch than the prosecutor's. Leon also noted Atwood's habit of using the terms "victim" and "defendant." He, on the other hand, chose to use their names, to make them real people in the minds of the jurors. And especially, to make Peggy a sympathetic, falsely accused victim in her own right.

"Ladies and gentlemen of the jury, our esteemed prosecutor would have you believe that he has taken on an open-and-shut case, a slam-dunk, to put it in the sports vernacular. What he really has is an accumulation of grossly misinterpreted circumstantial evidence. I will introduce witnesses to demonstrate that the deceased, Israel Finestein, and the defendant, Peggy Fraume, were very much in love and eager to get married. In fact, they had just sent out save- the-date announcements to their families and friends. Both Israel and Peggy had already made major compromises to resolve their religious and secular differences. Witnesses will tell you that Israel had begun these secularizing steps long before he met Peggy. And Peggy had already made life-changing concessions to accommodate Israel's religious beliefs and housekeeping agendas. She was so deeply committed to Israel that she had agreed to establish a kosher home. I will also introduce testimony to demonstrate that robbery, by an as-yet unidentified third party, was the real motive for this murder, not any sort of acrimony between Peggy and her betrothed. Additional witnesses will testify that two rare and valuable books were missing from Israel's restoration shop and should have been there at the time of his murder."

As the keen defense attorney made his points, he continued to make eye contact for several moments with each juror so they would feel that he was addressing them personally.

"Ask yourselves this, friends: If you found a loved one lying on the floor uttering barely perceptible words—maybe even his or her last words, what would you do?" He hesitated for several seconds, looking up and down the two rows of faces while giving the jurors time to think about this. Then he continued.

"I know I'd want to come closer, close enough to hear and maybe exchange a final hug or a kiss—maybe thinking these are the last acts of affection between us. Or maybe it's a rare opportunity to listen and learn who was responsible for this terrible act."

Another dramatic pause.

"How easy is it to transfer gunshot residue and body fluids between people reacting in such a manner? Well, we'll leave that testimony to the experts. And yes, there was a gun left behind, a gun unnoticed by the defendant until she found it stuck under her shin and ankle, irritating her enough to pull it out. Again, what would you do if you suddenly realized you'd handled a likely murder weapon accidentally? And who should walk in at precisely that moment, but a policeman." Leon paused again and took a deep breath, allowing the jurors to mull over his logic.

"There is a prosecution witness who believes she saw the defendant enter the Finestein shop before she heard the shots and saw someone leaving the shop after she heard the shots. Someone else? Maybe a woman? Description useless. So you see, ladies and gentlemen, there is a plausible explanation for each of the prosecution's loosely strung premises. Once you hear all the testimony and view all the evidence, I'm confident that you will return a verdict of not guilty. Thank you."

As Leon took his seat behind the defense table, the judge asked the prosecution to call its first witness. Dr. Janice Yuan of the Medical Examiner's office took the stand and detailed the exact cause and approximate time of death. Next, Sergeant Michael Bailey from Ballistics confirmed that the bullets removed from the victim were fired from Exhibit A, a .38 caliber gun, now encased in a plastic evidence bag. When asked whether the defense wanted to cross-examine these witnesses, Leon responded, "No. The defense has already stipulated to these facts." Next, Patrolman James Francis O'Mera was called to the stand and sworn in.

"Officer O'Mera," began Atwood, "would you explain what you encountered on the evening of January 8th?"

"Yes, sir," replied O'Mera. He took out a small spiral notebook and flipped a few pages to where he wanted to be. "At 8:09 on the night of January 8th I was on foot patrol on Beuller Street in Baltimore when I heard a female frantically shouting "Help! Help!" from a second-story window of Number 59 Beuller. She was leaning out and waving to get my attention and pointing to the shop entrance immediately below her window."

"What was she shouting about, Officer?" asked Atwood.

"She was screaming 'Gunshots!' I entered the shop and saw a woman standing over a body lying on the floor in the next room. This woman had blood smeared all over her chest and she had a gun in her right hand and a piece of her skirt in her left hand. She appeared to be wiping her prints from the gun with the skirt."

"Officer O'Mera, is that woman in this courtroom?"

"Yes. That's her at the defense table." He pointed to Peggy Fraume.

"What did you do then, Officer?"

"I ordered her to place the gun on the floor, and she obeyed immediately. I told her she was under arrest. Then I cuffed her wrists behind her back and sat her down in a nearby chair while I read the Miranda rights to her. Next, I rechecked the victim to see if there were any signs of life. After I determined that he was already beyond any assistance, I called in my collar to my supervisors and secured the crime scene. While we waited in the front room, I positively identified my prisoner as a Ms. Margaret Fraume. That wait ended at 8:26 p.m. when Sergeant Shap and Detective Sullivan took charge of both the crime scene and the prisoner."

"Thank you, Officer," said Atwood with a smug, proud look on his young face as he turned to Leon. "Your witness."

"Your Honor, I'd like to reserve my cross-examination of this witness for a little later in the proceedings."

"So noted," said the judge. He looked back at Atwood.

"Call your next witness."

Sherie Bonner, the Forensics team leader, was called to the stand and sworn in. She described the scene, the body position, the apparent wounds, the blood pooling, the evidence collection, and the lab results. The two isolated fingerprints on the gun matched the prisoner's right index and thumb prints. Bonner also stated that she subjected the prisoner to a gunshot residue (GSR) test and obtained a trace result. Further testing of the prisoner's clothing not only turned up more GSR but blood of the victim's blood type. Later tests positively matched the DNA between the victim and the prisoner's clothing stains."

"Ms. Bonner, was there any evidence that the body had been moved or tampered with in any way?"

"No, sir," she replied. "The only things out of the ordinary were a forced separation of the blood pool on the left side of the body and a partial smearing of the blood in the chest area."

"Did you attach any particular significance to these anomalies?" Atwood asked.

"Just that it was highly likely that someone had knelt in that blood pool."

"I see. Thank you, Ms. Bonner," said Atwood. "No further questions."

"Ms. Bonner," said Leon as he approached the stand. "Could the smearing of blood on the victim's chest and the blood on the defendant's clothing be consistent with a hug of desperate affection?"

"I would have to say yes," she answered, "considering that there is a likely knee print there as well."

"You did say that the fingerprint match was to the defendant's right-hand digits. And the GSR trace—where was that found?"

"Also on the right hand," Ms. Bonner replied.

"Was there a mere trace of GSR on the victim as well?"

"No, sir. The lack of GSR found there indicated that the shooter stood at least six to eight feet from the victim when the weapon was fired."

"I see," said Leon. "And yet the only GSR trace found on the defendant was on the right hand."

"That's correct," said Ms. Bonner.

"Then is it likely that the defendant actually fired the gun?" asked Leon.

"That's difficult to say. She could have worn gloves or made an attempt to wipe her hands clean."

"Were any gloves found or, for that matter, anything she could have wiped her hands with?"

"No, sir, except for another patch of GSR found at the defendant's skirt hem."

"Couldn't that have come from the gun itself?" asked Leon.

"Yes. That's also possible."

"Where on the gun were the prints found?"

"On either side of the grips," she replied.

"One way to pick up a gun, perhaps—not to fire one. Was there a print on the trigger mechanism?"

"No, sir. It was wiped clean."

Leon turned from the stand to face the jury. "May I point out to the court that the defendant is left-handed, which is borne out by Officer O'Mera's testimony. I believe he said he interrupted the woman holding the gun in the right hand and wiping with the left."

After the court stenographer read back a more exacting version of the same facts, Leon said he had no more questions for the witness and would reserve the right to finish cross-examining her at a later time. The judge nodded his assent.

Atwood chose not to re-cross. Instead, he called Bella Rosen Markus, the landlady, to the stand, where she swore to give truthful testimony.

"Mrs. Markus—" started Atwood.

"Bella, please."

"Right. Bella, what prompted you to shout out the window for help on January 8th?"

"I heard some gunshots downstairs in Mr. Finestein's workshop."

"Tell me, Bella, how could you be so sure they were gunshots? Couldn't it have been a car backfiring?"

"I hear gunshots all the time in this neighborhood. I think I know gunshots when I hear 'em."

"Ma'am, where were you when you heard this gunfire?"

"I was standing at the window in my front room."

"At the time of the gunfire, was the window open or closed?"

"It was closed, but it only took a minute or two to get it open—undo the latch and all."

"Bella, what did you see outside while you were standing there?"

"I saw that lady carry a covered bowl or something like it into the shop downstairs." She pointed at Peggy.

"But didn't you tell the detectives you saw her before you heard the shots?"

"I...uh, yes, sir."

"Did you see anyone else?"

"Yes, sir," said Bella. "There was another person leaving the shop just as I got the window open."

"Could you identify or even describe that person?"

"Not really," Bella admitted. "Dark coat. Maybe a woman. It was dark, away from the streetlight."

"And what direction was this person going?"

"To the left," she answered. "South, I think. Toward the Inner Harbor, anyway."

"At what point did you call the police, ma'am?"

"I didn't have to call 'em. I was going to, but there was a policeman coming down the street. On his beat, I guess. When I saw him I waved and shouted at him from my window."

"Thank you, Bella," said Atwood. He turned to Leon. "Your witness."

"Hi, Bella," said Leon as he approached. "Thank you for testifying today. Please tell the court how far you were from the closed window when you heard the shots."

"Oh, maybe two feet or three," she replied. "I was looking out and up at the stars. They were clear that night. I remember."

"Very good," said Leon. "Prior to hearing the shots, were you any closer to the window?"

"Nope, I wouldn't have any reason to be closer. Besides, I

would have had to move the chair away from in front of the window."

"Let me make sure I understand," said Leon. "Now you're saying there was a chair in front of the window. What kind of chair, Bella?"

"Oh, it's a nice side chair. A needlepoint seat. Looked like new when I got it at a yard sale in Arbutus."

Leon felt a mini-surge of adrenaline. "Is this nice chair always in front of the window?"

"Yeah."

"But you said you were standing at the window looking out at the stars. Were you actually sitting in the chair?"

Bella lowered her head to avoid Leon's gaze. Looking down, her chins doubled and chubby fingers clutched her purse, as if seeking strength from the worn leather.

"Bella? Please answer the question."

She raised her head. "I was standing behind the chair."

"Thank you. How did you open the window if the chair was in front of it?"

"It wasn't that hard, Mr. whatever-your-name-is. If you must know, I knelt on the chair, just with one knee, to open the window. It wasn't a big deal. Don't treat me like an old lady. I'm only sixty-three."

"I apologize. So, Bella, you were standing behind the chair looking out at the stars. From that distance, two or three feet from the window, would you say?"

A slightly sullen tone entered her response. "I guess so."

"Could you see any part of the near sidewalk? The sidewalk that goes past your home?"

"Of course not. All I could see was the street and the sidewalk on the other side."

Leon eyed Bella closely. "May I remind you, Bella, that you are under oath. My client's guilt or innocence might rest on your testimony. Now perhaps you would like to tell the court how you could have seen the defendant enter the shop before the shots were fired."

"I couldn't have," Bella admitted, shoulders slumping inside her cardigan sweater. "I'm so sorry. I made a mistake. I think that detective confused me some."

A rumble of voices echoed through the courtroom, ending only after the judge called "Order!" Having made his point that Peggy did not arrive until after the shots were fired, Leon decided that the witness was no longer needed.

"Would you like to re-cross the witness?" Judge Rodriguez asked Atwood. "No? Then we will recess for lunch. Court will reconvene at two o'clock." He slammed down the gavel.

* * * *

At 2:10 p.m. Detective Sergeant Shap was sworn in. He described the crime scene as he perceived it and his interrogation and processing of the prisoner. He testified that he took a complete inventory of the restoration shop and found no work-in-progress, nor any items awaiting attention other than a few early twentieth-century pamphlets.

"Sergeant," said Atwood, "other than the victim, defendant, and arresting officer, did you come across anyone or anything else of interest to the court?"

"Yes," replied Shap. "On the counter in the front room, I noticed a yellow crockery bowl roughly a quarter-full of tuna casserole. It had messy sides and was covered with a smeared plastic wrap."

"And what did you conclude from this casserole, Sergeant?"

"It was obvious to me that most of it had already been eaten. Surely not by the defendant, after hauling it from her apartment, so it must have been eaten by the deceased. This indicates to me that the deceased was still alive and well for some time after the defendant arrived with it."

"Couldn't someone else have eaten from the casserole?" asked Atwood.

"Who?" asked Shap. "The defendant or the accomplice? There wasn't anyone else."

"Accomplice?" asked Atwood.

"Yeah! The other person seen leaving the shop."

"Thank you, Sergeant, for re-establishing the defendant's presence at the time of the shooting," He turned toward Leon. "Defense's witness."

"No questions at this time, Your Honor, but I'd like to re-call this witness at a later time."

"So noted," said the judge. "Prosecution?"

Atwood called Rebbi Joshua Solomon, a Hasidic rabbi, to the stand. The heavily bearded man in his seventies was dressed in black from brimmed hat to shoes. He took the oath and related to the court the essential requirements and expectations of being a Hasidic Jew.

"Rabbi, why do Hasidic Jews dress in the way that they do?" asked Atwood.

"We try to dress alike to demonstrate that each person is equal—that the scholarly are no different than the unlettered, and no different than the common man. We dress in our black attire every day to remind us that each day must be dedicated to the Holy One, praised be He. We trace our simple history to the Baal Shem Tov, the Master of the Good Name, who lived in the eighteenth century."

"Do all Hasidic women shave their heads?" Atwood asked.

"Not all, but yes, married women do. It is a sign of respect and dedication to their husbands and to the Holy One as well."

"Would a Hasidic man accept a woman who refused to shave her head, keep a strictly kosher home, or dress as you have described?"

Rabbi Solomon shook his head vigorously. "No! No respectable man would."

"Would he accept someone like the defendant?"

Again the rabbi said, "No! Of course not. She also doesn't have a *get*, permission from her first husband, to make a kosher

216

divorce."

"Thank you," said Atwood before turning him over to Leon.

"Rabbi Solomon," addressed Leon, "was Israel Finestein a member of your flock?"

"He was brought up and schooled in the strict Hasidic traditions, yes."

"What I meant, Rabbi Solomon, was he currently a member of your *shul,* your congregation?"

"Oh, no. Several years ago Israel, of blessed memory, left our congregation for a more secular life, as he put it. That is, he wanted to learn and live the so-called freer ways of his non-Jewish neighbors. To do this he neglected his daily study of Torah and Talmud and altered his mode of dress. He even cut off his beard and *peyes,* his long sideburns. I was sorry to hear that he chose to attend a modern Orthodox *shul* in another neighborhood. Israel was never a bad man, a little misguided maybe."

"Thank you. However, I seriously question your statement that Israel neglected his daily study of Torah and Talmud after he left the Hasidic community. How could you possibly know that?" The rabbi shifted slightly in the witness chair, but chose not to respond. Noting the body language, Leon decided not to pursue it.

"Rabbi, your testimony demonstrates that the deceased had previously separated himself from the strict Hasidic culture and was on the road to compromising his Hasidic practices before he even met his betrothed."

"Those are not the words I would have chosen, but your meaning is essentially correct," the rabbi responded.

Leon smiled and walked away from the stand.

With no further questions for the rabbi, Atwood called his next witness, Teri Rooke. The courtroom hushed as a young woman swathed in a sea of Gothic black walked through the courtroom doors and down the aisle to take the stand. To be sworn in, she removed a black net veil to reveal an angelic too-white face and a rhinestone-studded dog collar about her neck.

217

"Ms. Rooke," started Atwood, "what is your profession?"

"I'm editor-in-chief of *Completely Dark* magazine."

"And Ms. Rooke, what is the nature of *Completely Dark* magazine?"

"Our magazine is designed to serve the greater Goth community: events, news, fashion, advertising, and articles of interest to our subscribers, much in the way any other magazine might," she replied.

"Perhaps," said Atwood, "you should enlighten the court as to what Goth means to you."

Rooke thought for a moment. "I'd have to say that Goth is a statement of dissatisfaction with one's beginnings, poor treatment, or lack of self-esteem. The Goth community has been called a subculture or counterculture. But I like to think of it more as a refuge for the 'Under-Generation'—a viable option for the under-appreciated, the under-respected, and the under-loved individual. Yes, we share a historical mode of dress, makeup, and behavior that sets us apart from the mainstream of the population. Yet it's that same rebel appearance that identifies where the 'under' individual might turn for camaraderie. It makes us visible."

"What about demonism and violence," pressed Atwood. "Are they a necessary part of the Goth culture."

"Necessary? My God, no!" said Rooke. "Absolutely not! But the period from which our mode of dress is derived reeks of demonism, vampires, cruelty, and violence. Some deviants, under the umbrella of Goth, have explored and adopted these evil rituals, but the vast majority of Goths abhor and want nothing to do with them."

"Thank you for your enlightenment," said Atwood. "On another subject: Do you know the defendant?"

"Oh, yes," she replied. "Peggy is one of my editors."

"How long have you known her?"

"I'd say about three months."

"How dedicated to Goth would you say she is?" asked Atwood.

"Objection!" Leon called out. "Witness has defined Goth too broadly to answer that question fairly."

"Sustained," replied Judge Rodriguez.

"How dedicated to mainstream Goth would you say she is?" rephrased Atwood.

"From her writings thus far, I'd have to say very dedicated. But I certainly couldn't say as much about her personal life."

"Thank you," said Atwood before turning the floor over to Leon.

"Ms. Rooke," began Leon. "Your comment about the defendant's personal life—what did you mean by that?"

"I came across Peggy and Israel at a kosher restaurant downtown one evening, and she had on a blue chiffon spaghetti-strap dress. That's hardly Goth-wear."

"So you believe the defendant kept her work and private life separate?"

"Apparently so," said Rooke. "But I never confronted her about it. Actually, it was none of my business."

"Have you ever known the defendant to explore or engage in the demonic or violent aspects of Goth?" he asked.

"Never!" she replied. "The Peggy I know is a kind and respectful person. She's also an intelligent and efficient worker, mindful of her coworkers."

Leon declined to re-cross.

"The prosecution rests," said Atwood.

"In that case," said Judge Rodriguez, "the court will reconvene tomorrow morning at nine a.m.."

Peggy Fraume sat like a pillar of stone in her wooden armchair at the defense table. The testimony had brought her a glimmer of hope. But not enough. She still worried that the path to acquittal would be like cutting through the Amazon jungle with a manicure scissors.

> "Look at yourselves! Look at your
> actions and your deeds. Let each
> one of you abandon his sinful
> ways and attitudes which bear no
> good. Let him return to God."
> *Menoras*, p. 42 ("The Days of Awe")

Chapter 29
Malamud for the Defense
Thursday, March 22nd

Once again the bailiff called out, "All rise for the Honorable Luis Rodriguez." The judge motioned for everyone to be seated.

"Good morning. The defense will call its first witness," said the judge.

"The defense calls Daniel Sherman to the stand."

"What is your profession, Mr. Sherman?" asked Leon Malamud.

"My wife and I own The Olde Victorian Bookstore in Annapolis. We're booksellers."

"And tell us, what's your connection to the deceased, Israel Finestein?"

"On December 19th we brought Israel Finestein two very old, very rare books to be restored. We delivered them in person to his shop on Beuller Street in Baltimore. He agreed to restore the more valuable book, the *Menorat ha-maor*, for us in return for ownership of the second book, which was incomplete. The work was to be picked up one month later on the 15th of January."

"Mr. Sherman, please describe for us, as succinctly as you can, what these two books are about."

"*Menorat ha-maor* means *Candlestick of Light*. It was written in the fourteenth century as a moral and religious household guide for Jews in the Middle Ages—one of the most important books of its time. It's filled with biblical topics and rabbinical interpretations on righteous living. It was originally in Hebrew, then translated into Spanish, Ladino, Yiddish, and German. The other book, *A Handbook of Flowers and Animals of Germany,* is from the sixteenth century. But apparently a third of it is missing."

"Mr. Sherman, do you read any of those languages?"

"No, sir."

"Then how do you know what's in these two volumes?"

"We had a rare-book dealer, a Mr. Anton Gleuck, come to our bookstore to explain them to us and appraise them."

Leon asked, "Just how valuable are they?"

"Mr. Gleuck appraised them both for insurance and resale purposes. I'm sorry, I didn't bring a copy of his document, but I did give a copy to Sergeant Shap on January 14th. Maybe he brought it with him."

"Detective?" inquired the judge.

"Yes, sir." Shap was sitting in the third row of the gallery behind the attorneys' tables. He picked up his tan vertical briefcase, and edged his way to the aisle. Approaching the end of the evidence table, he asked Leon, "May I set it here?"

"Please do, Sergeant."

Shap stood the briefcase upright on the table, undid the buckles on the two straps, released the lock under the straps, and opened it. Rummaging through some papers, he withdrew a two-page document, handed it to Leon, and remained standing next to the open briefcase while Leon read through it.

In the witness chair, just a few feet away, Dan's sensitive nostrils twitched as an odor wafted from the document and the open briefcase itself. *Whew. That smell,* he thought. *I recognize it. Ah! I know what it is, and now I know who stole our books, but I can't just blurt it out here.*

Leon finished reading. "Thank you, Sergeant." Shap closed the briefcase and carried it back to his seat.

"Mr. Sherman, is this the document you referred to?" asked

221

Leon as he handed it to Dan.

"Yes." Dan pointed to a list on the first page. Here's the appraisal: $49,000 for the *Menorat ha-maor* and $9,800 for the Latin book. That's $58,800 worth of rare books that should have been in the shop at the time of Israel Finestein's murder."

"Would you read the descriptions of these two books to the court, as they appear on this document, Mr. Sherman?"

"Of course," said Dan. He read not only the titles, but also the dates, authors, illustrators, publishers, and page counts, as well as Anton's list of flaws needing repair.

Leon turned to Atwood. "Your witness."

"Your Honor, shouldn't the appraiser himself have presented this evidence?" asked Atwood.

While the judge pondered his response, Leon said, "Your Honor, this is the witness who did not respond to his subpoena."

"What is the name of this individual?" asked Judge Rodriguez.

"Anton M. Gleuck," answered Dan. "He's a bonded agent in the field of rare books."

"Is the document signed and certified by him?" the judge asked.

"Yes, Your Honor."

The judge motioned for Leon to approach with the document. The judge perused it, handed it back, and said, "I'll allow it as evidence."

"No further questions for this witness," declared Atwood.

"The defense calls Rivka Sherman to the stand."

Rivka took the oath and settled in for a series of questions dealing with how she knew Peggy and her opinion of Peggy's character and behavior. Leon asked Rivka to explain the measures Peggy had already taken to accommodate Israel. Atwood objected, calling it hearsay and unsubstantiated personal opinion. Leon suspected that the prosecutor wanted Peggy herself on the stand to give this explanation, so he changed strategies.

"Mrs. Sherman," said Leon, "can you tell the court how

you and your husband came to acquire these books? We would like to establish ownership for the court."

Rivka drew herself up, poised in her navy-blue suit and white blouse. "First, I need to explain how we came to own The Olde Victorian Bookstore."

Atwood leaped up. "Objection, Your Honor. Goes to relevance."

Judge Rodriguez leaned toward Rivka. "I'll allow it, Mrs. Sherman, but make it brief."

"Thank you, Your Honor, I will," she replied. "Dan and I bought the bookstore from Bernard and Edythe Bender. Bernie has Alzheimer's. Edythe, may she rest in peace, was dying of cancer. She turned the bookstore over to us with the understanding that we would pay fully for Bernie's nursing home care and upkeep. Which we gladly do. He's a dear man, and I visit him when I can." Rivka's delivery was strong but sincere. "And here's where the books come in. On my visit to him in December, he had one of his infrequent lucid moments. He told me there were two books he wanted Dan and me to have, and he recited a poem to reveal where he had hidden them. The poem was difficult, a real puzzle, and took us days to figure it out, but we finally found the books. They were hidden behind a secret panel in the poetry stacks. We'll be forever grateful to Bernie. And that's when we called Anton Gleuck. We had no idea what the books were about or what they were worth."

Rivka described Anton's recommendation that they have the books restored before attempting to sell them. Their valuations were based on satisfactory restoration.

"And did he indeed have a ready buyer for you?" asked Leon.

"According to Anton, he had several in mind," she replied.

"Mrs. Sherman, your husband testified that he left both books with Israel Finestein at his restoration shop. Were you also present when he placed them in his guardianship?"

"Yes," she answered. "We were together when we dropped them off."

"And do you confirm the agreed-upon pickup date of the 15th of January?"

"Yes, that was our agreement."

"Thank you, Mrs. Sherman," said Leon.

Atwood declined to cross-examine Rivka. But before Leon could call his next defense witness, Judge Rodriguez recessed the court until two that afternoon. During the lunch break, Leon conferred with Dan and learned the significance of the strange odor that Dan had sniffed.

* * * *

When the court reconvened, Leon called his next witness. "Detective Edward Sullivan, I understand you helped to prepare the inventory list for the restoration shop on the night of the murder. That is, the list that Sergeant Shap introduced in his testimony."

"That's correct," said Sully.

"Is this the list in question, and do you believe it to be complete and correct?" Leon asked, holding it up in its plastic evidence bag.

"Yes, sir, I do to both questions."

"Is there any entry on this list that describes the Sherman books?"

"No, sir."

"Earlier testimony puts the books in the shop before the murder. What would you conclude from that, Detective?"

"The books were missing on or before that night and possibly stolen," he replied.

"Stolen," repeated Leon. "Then could robbery be a viable motive for the murder?"

"Possibly, sir, although I couldn't say for sure. Over a one-month span of time, robbery or removal and murder might be separate actions or even separate crimes."

"If the books had been stolen before that night, isn't it reasonable to believe that Mr. Finestein would have reported the crime to the police?"

"Yes, especially if the books were valuable," said Sully.

"Then let me ask you again: Could robbery be a viable motive for the murder?"

"I suppose so," mumbled Sully.

"Should the court interpret that as a yes response?" pressed Leon.

"Yes!"

"By the way, Detective, how did you happen to be assigned to this case?"

"Captain Eliot Tanner called me into his office. I guess I was next in rotation."

"Was Sergeant Shap your partner in this case?"

"No, sir. Captain Tanner told me I was to be paired with Detective Johnson on this case. Mickey Johnson and I work together a lot on homicide cases."

"Then what happened to change that?" asked Leon.

"Sergeant Shap showed up at the crime scene and took over. He never explained why. He just sent Mickey back to the station."

"Your witness, Counselor," said Leon.

"No cross, Your Honor," replied Atwood.

"Defense recalls Officer James O'Mera to the stand."

O'Mera approached with a quizzical look on his jowly red face. The judge reminded him that he was still under oath.

Leon began. "Officer O'Mera, you were the first officer on the scene. During the period of time you were in Mr. Finestein's shop, when did you first notice the yellow crockery bowl left on the display case?"

A pitiful expression spread over O'Mera's face. He knew where this inquiry was going. "I saw it first just inside the door when I entered the shop and chose to neglect it. I had more pressing business, sir."

"And when you had secured both your prisoner and the crime scene, did you examine its contents?"

"No, sir," said O'Mera. "Not until the detectives took over. I lifted up the cover and took a peek."

"What did you find in the bowl?"

"Tuna casserole, sir, covered with Saran wrap."

"How full was this bowl when you first examined it?"

"Almost full," O'Mera mumbled.

"Speak up, please. How full?"

"Almost full," O'Mera admitted, much louder.

"Was the Saran wrap seal disturbed in any way at that time?"

"No, sir," he confessed.

"Then how do you suppose Sergeant Shap was able to testify that he found this casserole three-quarters eaten?"

"I was alone with it in the front room while they were interrogating the prisoner in the workshop. I hadn't had but a muffin all day and I was hungry. So I thought it wouldn't matter if I sampled a little bit from it. Just a scoop with two fingers. Then one bite led to another. Man, it was delicious. I wish my wife had the recipe."

Giggles rippled through the gallery. The judge frowned.

O'Mera's usual police voice melted into a whine. "Honest to God, sir, I'm sorry. I had no idea it would become evidence."

"You better believe it became evidence," said Leon. "Sergeant Shap assumed that the deceased had eaten from the casserole and therefore concluded that Mr. Finestein was shot after the defendant arrived. Apparently, this was not true. Do you realize that your actions could have helped to wrongly convict the defendant?"

O'Mera looked stricken. "'I realize it now and I'm extremely sorry. I will probably have to face charges for this mistake."

"Nothing further," said Leon.

"Your Honor," started Atwood, "may it please the court to note that Officer O'Mera's earlier testimony has now been negated. It no longer has any bearing on whether the deceased was alive, dying, or dead when the defendant arrived."

"So noted," said Judge Rodriguez. "The jury will disregard prior testimony related to the state of Mr. Finestein's well-being upon the arrival of the defendant. The defense will call its next witness."

"The defense calls Mr. Boris Nabakov to the stand."

When Boris had been seated and sworn in, Leon asked, "Mr. Nabakov, what was your relationship to the deceased?"

"Izzy and I were colleagues in the same business, sometimes friends and sometimes competitors," offered Boris.

"Exactly what is that business?" asked Leon.

"We're professional book and manuscript restorers—they're sometimes rare, sometimes old, and sometimes both."

"Mr. Nabakov, were you aware of the restoration that Mr. Finestein was working on just prior to his death?"

"Oh, yes. I stopped in his shop the day before his death and saw the beautiful job he was doing on the *Menorat ha-maor*. Exquisite!"

"Did you ever work with Mr. Finestein?"

"Sometimes," Boris said. "Occasionally, one of us had more work than we could handle. Then we would work together. He was more of an artist while I'm more of a craftsman. But we were very good together at what we did."

"Do your restorations ever involve the treatment of leather bindings, stitching, and covers?"

"Absolutely. It's quite common with the rare old books. Leather covers can dry out and become brittle."

Leon turned to the bench. "Your Honor, I beg the court's indulgence at this time. I would like to perform a little experiment concerning leather."

"Does it have a direct bearing on this case?"

"Absolutely, Your Honor. It will become quite clear."

"Very well, I'll allow it."

Leon turned around to face the courtroom spectators. "First, I'd like to borrow someone's leather briefcase. Anyone? I promise I won't harm it in the least. Sergeant Shap, might I borrow yours?"

"Uh...yeah, sure." Taken by surprise, Shap half-stumbled getting out of the third row before he brought the case forward and handed it to Leon. "Should I empty it?"

"That won't be necessary," said Leon as he set the closed briefcase on the evidence table in front of the witness stand. He waited until Shap had returned to his seat.

"Now then, Mr. Nabakov, I'm assuming you're accustomed to working with the chemicals and treatments used in your profession. But are you also an expert at detecting their odors? Would that be true?"

"You better believe it," Boris said, with a burst of unintended laughter. "Some of the smells are so strong they stink up my whole shop." He squeezed his nostrils together to make his point. Chuckles echoed throughout the courtroom. Jurors suppressed smiles.

"Mr. Nabakov, take a few deep breaths to clear your lungs. It'll be like clearing the palate before sampling a new bottle of wine." As Leon spoke, he undid the buckles and straps of the top-loading briefcase and held it unopened beneath Boris's nose. With a flourish, he peeled the flap back and spread the case wide open. "What do you smell on the inside of this case?"

Boris's response was immediate and unwavering. "Neatsfoot oil, sir. Without question, neatsfoot oil."

"And would you please tell the court what neatsfoot oil is?"

"It's used to revitalize leather—soften, moisturize, and sometimes darken leather. I believe it's manufactured from the ankle bones of cattle. That's the main ingredient. I'm sorry, I don't know what's added or the actual process involved."

"Would you say it has a distinctive smell?"

"Very! Some say it smells like diesel fuel, but I'd say the stink is stronger, more acrid. There's no mistaking it."

"Why would such a smell be coming from an ordinary briefcase?" asked Leon.

"It is strange," said Boris. "Most likely, the briefcase was used to transport manuscripts or books whose leather covers had been freshly treated with neatsfoot oil."

"Your witness, Counselor."

Roland Atwood stepped forward. "Mr. Nabakov, how can

you be so sure that book-binding leather was involved in producing that smell? Couldn't it have come from the leather briefcase itself?"

"No," said Boris in a firm bass voice. "I didn't start to smell the neatsfoot until Mr. Malamud opened the case. The smell definitely came from inside. And I can see, even from this chair, that the cloth liner inside is unevenly stained. Have a look."

Atwood peered inside and turned away quickly from the repugnant odor. The prosecutor's next move was to glance at the jury to assess the damage done. He didn't find even a hint of skepticism. "No further questions for this witness."

"The defense calls Naomi Levinson to the stand."

Naomi took the court's oath. Her anxious gray eyes darted from side to side. She had no idea what to expect.

"Mrs. Levinson, tell me, what is your relationship to Israel Finestein?"

"He is—was—my husband's second cousin on his father's side."

Leon heard a disturbance from the gallery. He spun about to see Shap sidling along in the third row. "Your Honor, I will need Sergeant Shap's further testimony. Would you ask him not to leave the courtroom just yet?"

"Your Honor, I'm only going out to pee," said Shap.

A snicker rippled through the courtroom.

"Then we'll have the sergeant-at-arms accompany you," said the judge. The two men left together.

"Now, then, Mrs. Levinson," said Leon, "suppose you tell the court what you and your husband do for a living."

"We run a dry cleaning establishment, and I do some tailoring and dressmaking."

"What exactly does your husband do?"

"Mostly, he studies the Torah and Talmud, but he likes to discuss these things with his friends down at the deli. Occasionally, he minds the shop when I'm busy sewing."

"Did he spend much time with his cousin Israel?"

"Oh, he would drop in at Izzy's shop several times a week," she replied. "They were friends, too."

The courtroom again stirred as Shap took his seat once more.

"Did your husband and Israel get along?" asked Leon.

"Here and there," Naomi said. "They liked to argue a bit, and sometimes Izzy would ask him to leave the shop, but they always made up and were at it again the next day."

"So certainly your husband would be well aware of what Israel Finestein was working on at any given time. Isn't that true?"

"I should think so."

"Did your husband happen to tell you about the *Menorat ha-maor* that Israel had in the shop and what it was worth?"

"He may have mentioned it," Naomi said, barely above a whisper.

"May have?" asked Leon in a surprised voice.

"Yes, he told me all about it." Her fingers, knobby with arthritis, plucked frantically at the full skirt of her dress.

"Did you happen to tell anyone else?"

She hesitated and finally said, "Not that I can think of."

It became apparent to Leon that the last question had unnerved her. He pressed on. "What is your maiden name, Mrs. Levinson?"

"Shapiro," she responded. "Naomi Shapiro, but I don't see what that has to do with anything."

"Do you have a brother, Mrs. Levinson?"

Naomi began to cry, and between sobs murmured, "Yes. My baby brother."

"I'll ask you once more. Did you happen to tell anyone else about the *Menorat ha-maor?*"

"Yes, my baby brother." She pulled a handkerchief from her purse and wiped her eyes.

"Is your baby brother in this courtroom?"

"Yes," she nodded.

"No further questions," said Leon.

"Mr. Atwood?" asked the judge.

Atwood saw his case falling apart, but he couldn't for the life of him think of a line of questioning for this witness. He reluctantly replied, "No questions, Your Honor."

"The defense calls Sergeant Maury Shap to the stand."

Shap came forward in long strides and took his seat. Clean-shaven, jaw square and determined, he gave the impression of clenched teeth ready to do battle. As soon as he was sworn in, Leon asked him if the name he'd stated to the court clerk was correct.

"Yes, Shap is the name I go by."

"But it's not the name on your birth certificate, is it, Sergeant?"

"The name on my birth certificate is Shapiro, Maurice Shapiro. So I shortened my name. That's not a crime."

"Of course not, Sergeant, but is Naomi Shapiro Levinson related to you?"

"Yes. She's my older sister."

"Did she convey any information to you about Israel's rare books and their purported value?"

"She may have, but I don't recall," Shap answered. His dark eyes glinted. "I don't pay much attention to a lot of things my sister tells me, especially when it has to do with that lazy husband of hers."

"How often do you see and speak with your sister?"

"I don't come to the house anymore because of Mendel, but we speak on the phone a couple times a week."

"So you actually communicate with each other on a regular basis."

"Yes."

"Now, Sergeant, how did you happen to get assigned to this case?"

"By Captain Tanner, my superior, of course."

"But according to Detective Sullivan's testimony, you weren't the captain's first choice," reminded Leon.

"Sullivan doesn't know what he's talking about," Shap stammered.

"If you wish, we can subpoena the captain," threatened Leon.

"All right, all right," Shap admitted. "So I volunteered for the assignment. So what?"

"So you must have had a good reason to do so. What was that reason, Sergeant? So you could steer the investigation away from the guilty party? Yourself, perhaps?"

Atwood sprang up from his seat at the prosecutor's table. "Objection, Your Honor. Leading the witness."

"Sustained. The jury will disregard the last question."

"I'll rephrase," Leon said. "Sergeant, why did you volunteer for this case?"

"I had a helluva good reason. In fact, more than one," said Shap, belligerence sneaking into his voice. "I recognized the address when it was radioed in. First, I was only a few blocks away and could respond quickly. And second, it involved my wife's family. I wanted to find the killer for them."

"Very gallant of you, Sergeant, but shouldn't you have recused yourself when you found out the case involved your family? Isn't that standard police policy?"

"Sure, but this is distant family, sir—not direct family," corrected Shap. "What are you trying to do here? Railroad me?"

"No, Sergeant," returned Leon. "You're doing a pretty good job of that yourself. Do you know what Israel Finestein's last words were?"

"I think the defendant claimed he recited the *Sh'ma*, a Hebrew prayer."

"Wasn't there something else?"

Shap reached into his jacket pocket and pulled out his small notepad. He flipped through the pages, then stopped abruptly and looked up and out over the courtroom.

"What's wrong, Sergeant?"

Shap let out a deep sigh and looked down again at his own handwriting.

Leon didn't wait for an answer. He pounced. "Shocking, Sergeant. Foiled by your own hand. When you were questioning the defendant, who was handcuffed, she told you she had heard Israel's last words: three initials and the word 'briefcase.' In that notebook you're holding, you wrote down what she said. Shall I tell you what the three initials were?"

"M-P-S," recited Shap in a slow, defeatist monotone.

"What does the P stand for?" Leon asked.

"Paul. Maurice Paul Shapiro."

At the evidence table Leon lifted up Shap's briefcase. He carried it to the jury box, holding it so the gold-embossed monogram, MPS, was clearly visible. Walking the length of the box, he paused before each juror in the first row, then held the briefcase high for the benefit of the six in the second row. At last he turned back to his witness. The large, confident detective sergeant now sat with his head in his hands.

"Your Honor, may we approach the bench?" asked Atwood.

"Approach!"

Prosecutor and defense attorney stood shoulder to shoulder as Atwood leaned forward to address the judge. "Your Honor, I believe that counsel for the defense has successfully executed an alternative-party defense. He dismantled, or put in question, most of my prosecution's assertions. Therefore, I feel I can no longer pursue a *prima facie* case against the defendant. I had convinced myself that the defendant's guilt was self-evident. But I was wrong. I recommend that the case against Margaret Fraume be dismissed with the State's apologies. I further recommend that the current witness, Detective Sergeant Shap, be bound over for trial for the crimes of murder and grand larceny."

"I agree," nodded Judge Rodriguez. "And you, Mr. Malamud?"

"I most certainly agree," said Leon. "Thank you, Your Honor."

The judge addressed the jury. "I have concluded—in agreement with both the prosecution and the defense—that a *prima facie* case can no longer be pursued against the defendant. I order that the case be dismissed with the State's apologies. Ms. Margaret Fraume, you are free to go. I further order that the current witness, Detective Sergeant Maurice Shap, be bound over for trial for the crimes of first-degree murder and grand larceny. The jury is hereby dismissed with the court's thanks." He slammed down the gavel.

A much-shaken Shap was taken into custody, while a jubilant crowd of well-wishers converged on Peggy and Leon.

"There are three things necessary for the preservation of civilization: justice, truth, and peace."
Menoras, p. 251 (The Talmud)

Chapter 30
And Judgment for All
Thursday, March 29th

It had been a whole week since Peggy Fraume's murder trial. It had lasted only two days, but for Peggy, every second of those hours had been terrifying. She'd been forced to sit silently at the defense table, allowing Leon Malamud and witnesses to completely control her destiny. She thanked God that justice had prevailed, allowing her to escape from her own worst nightmares.

Now a free Peggy was more than eager to attend this evening's meeting of the writers' critique group at The Olde Victorian Bookstore. She had missed nearly three months because she simply couldn't think about writing for pleasure. It had been hard enough concentrating on her writing and editing at *Completely Dark*. Besides, Leon had told her at one point to stay home.

Once Peggy had climbed the stairs to the second-floor reading room she saw that Garry had saved her a seat next to him. Her happiness at being there, among her friends, dissolved in tears— tears of freedom's joy and tears of grief. Izzy's violent death would haunt her forever.

A fired-up Garry couldn't resist talking about the trial. "I thought it was pretty clever, the way Malamud used that Russian shopkeeper to trip up Sergeant Shap."

"The business about the neatsfoot oil, that was brilliant," said Dan, silently patting himself on the back for his own contribution.

"I have more news," Peggy said. "I wrote to that nice Boris Nabakov to thank him for his testimony. But you know what?"

"No. Tell us already," said Garry.

"Boris called me on Tuesday. He said the police had also considered him a suspect because he knew about the books before the murder and theft. They became especially interested in him when he told them his ex-wife's gun was missing. He did not tell them that he thought his simple-minded friend, Illya, had taken it. Just two days ago, Illya confessed to Boris. He did take the gun from Boris's desk drawer. He thought he was being helpful. He planned to go to Israel's shop and steal the precious books at gunpoint. But that very night he went out for a few beers, got drunk, and dropped the gun in a sewer. He was so confused when he returned home that he thought he'd dropped it among the crates in Boris's storage room. That's when the poor fellow had an accident and got a bad concussion. He's out of the hospital now after a long stay. But Boris feels terrible about the way he had treated his pathetic cousin in the past, so he's taken Illya into his own home to live with him on a permanent basis."

"Sounds to me like a man doing serious penance," offered Frieda.

Dan had a burning question. "Peggy, now that Detective Shap's crimes have been uncovered, what's going to happen to him?"

Joel broke in. "I can answer that. I spoke with Leon this morning. The state of Maryland still has capital punishment. Shap's attorney advised him that any repeal of capital punishment was years away and not likely to contain retroactive provisions. So Maury Shap pled out to save his own life. He agreed to life in prison without the possibility of parole in return for a full confession to murder and grand larceny. He confessed to a few other, lesser, crimes as well."

"Won't he be exposed to prisoners he helped put away?" asked Rivka.

"He would be, but he'll serve his time at a prison out of state under another name," answered Joel. "It was made an integral part of his plea agreement."

"Joel, did the courts ever find out what his real motive was?" asked Garry.

"Apparently, it had to do with those lesser crimes," replied Joel. "Shap had been taking dirty money from street drugs and prostitution for years and living way above his police salary. A recent crime sweep shut down his main cash flow. He knew he was going to be exposed by Internal Affairs. As a result, he claimed he needed quick cash from the sale of the two books for potential legal fees. Go figure."

"Dan, whatever happened to the witness who didn't show up? Wasn't he your rare book agent?" asked Peggy.

"Yeah, Anton Gleuck," replied Dan. "I read in the *Baltimore Sun* that he was shot in a parking lot by some thug associated with a usury loan ring. Seems Gleuck will survive with a pair of blown-out knees. I don't know what kind of punishment the court will impose on him for ignoring his subpoena. But at least the shooter was apprehended and he, in turn, ratted out his bosses."

From a relaxed slouch, Rivka bounced upright in her chair. "Guys, there's something I forgot to tell Dan. I guess I shouldn't be talking about it in front of all of you, but I'm afraid if I don't I'll forget it; my head is in too many places at once. So if you'll all bear with me for a moment. There's a bedraggled woman who comes in to read our papers every day. Maybe you've seen her. Marie Tate-Williams, and once she actually kidnapped our cat, would you believe? Anyway, Dan, this morning she called. She wants permission to use the reading room again. She promises not to bother Lord Byron anymore. In fact, she adopted a calico cat called Sneakers from the Humane Society. And...this is the best part. Her son, Damon, was arrested for sticking up a local pharmacy. He fired two shots into the ceiling and got away with a 500-count box of oxycodone pills, plus cash. Then he sold the pills. He's slated to do three years for armed robbery and drug distribution."

Dan broke into a broad smile. "Man, that's good news. I always thought he was a lazy, undisciplined ruffian. But I kind of feel sorry for Marie. She's all alone now. I hope you're going to say yes."

"I hope you don't mind, but I already said yes," admitted Rivka with a sheepish grin. "Thanks for listening, everyone."

Garry burst in. "Are you kidding? That's a great story. Thank you for sharing."

Dan rolled the sleeves of his sport shirt halfway up his forearms, pushed his chair back, and stood. "Good grief, guys," he said. "Isn't anyone going to ask me what happened to the books?"

"What did happen to them?" asked Peggy.

"Once Shap had been taken into custody, Detective Sullivan and his regular partner went to search the sergeant's home for evidence. There was no trace of our books until they went through his incoming mail. One piece was a notice to pick up a package at the main post office. The notice arrived on the second day of the trial, so Shap hadn't had a chance to pick it up."

Dan's five-o'clock shadow gave him a rugged, deeply serious look as he continued. "When the two detectives arrived at the post office, they were met by the FBI. They learned that the book covers—still damp from Israel's neatsfoot oil treatments—had leeched through and stained the outer brown paper wrapping of the package, and emanated a foul odor that couldn't be explained. Since it's illegal to ship chemicals, the postal authorities called in the Feds. They opened the package and found our books! Shap had mailed them to himself. Recognizing what they had uncovered, the FBI placed them in the custody of the Maryland Museum of Fine Arts for caretaking until ownership could be established. Detective Sullivan cleared that problem up in a hurry."

"Thank God for that," said Peggy. "I'm so glad you have your beautiful books back."

"Not exactly," Rivka said. "The museum turned them over

to Boris Nabakov to finish the extensive drying process. And even when that's finished, they'll be going on two separate journeys. The flora and fauna handbook will be returned to the art museum. An acquisition director said they'd like to buy it for a nominal fee, even though it's incomplete, for their permanent display combining the histories of bookbinding and early literature."

Ivy couldn't stand the suspense. "What about the *Menorat ha-maor?* With that appraisal you should be able to get big bucks for it."

Rivka smiled and paused, as if she were harboring a momentous secret.

Dan noticed, for the first time, small creased lines around his wife's generous mouth. Lines of wisdom, he decided.

Rivka adjusted the collar of her cashmere sweater and crossed her arms over her chest. "Actually, Dan and I are much more than commercial dealers. We're book lovers, and, above all, we're the protectors of this holy book. So we have big news. We are not selling it. It will be our honor to donate it to the Klau Library of the Hebrew Union College-Jewish Institute of Religion in Cincinnati, Ohio."

The group burst into spontaneous applause.

But Rivka wasn't quite finished. Her cheeks flushed and her eyes lit up. "Dan, and dear friends. Before we begin our critique meeting, let us take a moment to remember Peggy's beloved, a fine man who brought light into her life."

They all joined hands and bowed their heads. Rivka prayed. "May Israel Finestein rest in peace. His memory will continue to shine brightly and be a blessing. Amen."

"Amen."

The End

Also by Rosemary and Larry

The Paco and Molly
Mystery Series

Locks and Cream Cheese—In scandal-ridden Black Rain Corners, a Chesapeake Bay mansion harbors locked rooms and deadly secrets. A wily detective and a gourmet cook tackle the case.

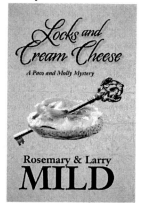

Hot Grudge Sunday—Bank robbers and conspirators derail the sleuths' blissful honeymoon at the Grand Canyon. Can they nail the suspects after they themselves become targets?

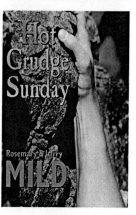

Boston Scream Pie—A teenage girl's nightmare triggers a sinister tale of twins, two warring families, and a blonde bombshell who hates being called "Mom."

Available on Amazon.com and as E-Books

Also by Rosemary and Larry

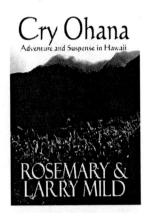

Cry Ohana, Adventure and Suspense in Hawaii—A car accident and murder tear apart a Hawaiian *ohana* (family). Danger erupts at a Filipino wedding, a Maui resort, and amid the Big Island's volcanic steam vents. Can the family re-unite and bring down the killer?

The Dan and Rivka Sherman Mystery Series

Death Goes Postal—Rare 15th century typesetting artifacts journey through time, leaving a horrifying imprint in their wake. Dan and Rivka risk life and limb to locate the treasures and unmask the murderer. Not quite what they expected when they bought The Olde Victorian Bookstore.

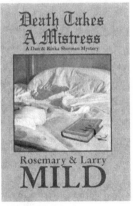

Death Takes A Mistress— After 23 years, Ivy Cohen seeks revenge on the lover who killed her mother. She follows the clues from London to Maryland, where she makes a shocking discovery.

Available on Amazon.com and as E-Books

Also by Rosemary and Larry

8 Short Stories

The Misadventures of Slim O. Wittz, Soft-Boiled Detective—If you're looking for a truly soft-boiled gumshoe, you want me, Slim. I'm rarely in charge, frequently behind the eight ball and seldom paid; but in spite of all that, my case record is remarkably shaky.

Also by Rosemary

Miriam's World—and Mine—Miriam Luby Wolfe, a junior at Syracuse U., spent her fall semester in London exploring her talents: singing, dancing, acting, and writing. But she never made it home. A terrorist bomb destroyed her plane over Lockerbie, Scotland. Learn about Miriam, the Pan Am families, the bombers, and the political fallout.

Love! Laugh! Panic! Life with My Mother—Rosemary's hilarious and heartwarming story of her super-achieving mother. Luby Pollack was a journalist, popular book author, and psychiatrist's wife. Always the Heroine, and sometimes the Villain, from the viewpoint of her loving but ornery daughter.

Available on Amazon.com and as E-Books

Also by Rosemary and Larry

18 Short Stories

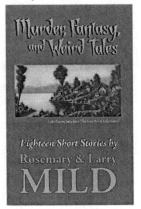

Murder, Fantasy, and Weird Tales—Join us as we tell tales of the brave, the foolhardy, and the wicked on their journeys to the unknown in Hawaii, Japan, Cambodia, Italy, and elsewhere. Art lovers, hitwomen, a vampire, a lively hologram, and others reveal their secret compulsions.

Rosemary and Larry Mild, cheerful partners in crime, coauthor mysteries and thrillers. Their short stories appear in two anthologies: *Mystery in Paradise: 13 Tales of Suspense* and *Chesapeake Crimes: Homicidal Holidays.* In 2013 the Milds waved goodbye to Severna Park, Maryland, and moved to Honolulu, Hawaii, where they cherish time with their children and grandchildren. The Milds are members of Mystery Writers of America, Sisters in Crime, and Hawaii Fiction Writers.

E-mail the Milds at: roselarry@magicile.com

Visit them at: www.magicile.com

CPSIA information can be obtained
at www.ICGtesting.com
Printed in the USA
FFOW02n0223260816
27097FF